THE AUTHORS

RVK / Rainer von Kürten, born 1966 in Düsseldorf, Germany has been working in the hospitality industry for more than 30 years until he changed his career goals, from top hotel manager to bestseller author. At his last GM position, he had the idea to have a TV series to be filmed in his hotel, which would have been supporting his marketing strategy. For this he searched for someone who could assist him with the script. He found Maxmilian Nemec, alias Omar Zahid, see below, and they wrote 7 episodes of Egeria together, though online, as one worked in Karlovy Vary, Czech Republic and the other in Barcelona, Spain.

Unfortunately no producer was ready to step into this endeavour and the script went into the book shelves. Thinking about the time and money spent, it was obvious, that there should be another strategy to get things done successfully. So the author decided to take the script and transform it to a novel, which is a bit trickier, as usually a novel is transformed into a script.

The COVID-19 crisis supported his decision, as hotel businesses were closed for months and time for writing available.

Just to make it clear, the authors do not want to win the noble price in literature, they want the readers to enjoy the stories. Should the book be accepted and positively rated by a lot of people, the second book and the TV serial will be the next step.

OMAR ZAHID / Maxmilian Nemec, born 1973 in Havířov, Czech Republic is our Earth global citizen who travels from place to place. He has a searching personality, looking for answers and discovering, how he relates to different parts of the world. Above all, moving around keeps him young. Max studied film and scriptwriting in Belfast, Northern Ireland.

He assisted Rainer von Kürten in writing 7 episodes for the TV series Egeria.

Under his pseudonym Omar Zahid he works on film screenplays, music and commercial videos.

Zero Justice is his first novel.

Besides writing stories for newspapers, he also directs and produces audiovisual projects. His short films The Man From Hankow Road and The Territory of Dust were screened at the festivals. His feature debut was a guerrilla made espionage thriller.

Thanks to my lovely wife Andrea, who supported me writing this book, never rushing me to finish.

Thanks to Gabriela as she inspired me to name the novel "Egeria".

Thanks to Max, who was helpful in writing the script as well as providing his input for the novel.

Thanks to Salima and Ryan, who were assisting Max with the script.

Thanks to all the guests and co-workers encountered during my hospitality career on which the characters of the novel are based.

Thanks to more than 30 years in the hospitality industry, it might not be the easiest way to make a dime, but for sure the most vivid and fun one.

EGERIA

THE LAUNCH

by

RVK & OMAR ZAHID

"BY MONEY OR BY BLOOD"

The weather is rainy and the heavy clouds fly low through the dark sky, but it is hot here in Bogota, especially when you are in the favelas, where possessing an air-condition is a luxury and otherwise the humidity kills you. Nevertheless some kids are on the street doing some freestyle rapping and the sound multiplies between the narrow buildings made from mud, plastic and all other stuff the people could find on the big garbage hill just across the valley.

The sharp music comes from the powerful bass speaker around the neck of one of the boys and they convey their messages through the microphone.

A man shoots them onto his smart phone and the starts smiling when the young boys are getting to the end of their song. He has a pistol stuck visible in his jeans.

An old American ship on four wheels passes them, it's a 1965 Electra, which has some trouble to sail through the poverty messy, muddy, narrow streets of the favelas.

In the car sits a bunch of gangster lookalikes smoking marijuana, which already had effect on them as they are staring out of the windows with big open eyes, greeting the rappers with a short "Olá".

The Electra stops in front of a food store and the gangsters get off to enter the shop.

There – a loud conversation is already going on.

Pepe El Guella, who is leading a "lending office", which lends to everyone, but with crazy interest rates and for sure one gets a visit of strongs guys, if the rates are not paid in time. This loan shark is talking in a creepy violent, sharp voice.

"Hey Juan, let me tell you a tragic story from my childhood. It was at my friend's twelfth birthday party. His mom had hired a clown. He made balloon animals, told jokes, he even did magic tricks. When he was about to leave I went up to him while he was packing his stuff and the other kids were outside eating. He was wearing one of those gag flowers - the kind that squirt you. I asked if I could take a closer look. Then he squirted me, but not with water. I don't know what it was but I couldn't move and he dragged me down to the basement. You can imagine the rest…but," with a laughter in his voice, "…no one is ever going to fuck me over again…Do you understand me Juan?"

Juan is scared, but he is also ready to fight.

"I will have that money for you, I swear! The business just slowed down…It takes some time…"

"I am coming tomorrow, Juan! Tomorrow, you give me my money… otherwise…."

He makes a treating gesture as he was slitting his throat.

"Yes…"

Pepe points his walking stick against Juan's belly.

"Don't fuck with me - Juan! If you want to play, you have to pay - either in cash or in blood."

Turning around for leaving the room Pepe adds, "See you tomorrow at 5 p.m.! …and don't expect your mama to help you this time! My guys are prepared for beating the money out of you!"

With a smile on his face he is turning to the gang just coming in. "Is that right guys? You will take care, if this bastard is not paying until tomorrow at 5 p.m.!"

"Yes Pepe, we are ready and be sure you will get the money, even if we need to beat up also his whole family" says the driver of the Electra, who seems to be the small boss of the Team and the only one who looks sauber.

"BACK TO THE SCENE"

If you think of New Orleans, there is one thing which comes to your mind immediately, yes – Jazz music and the French Quarter with the colourful buildings of the South.

But there are also other great buildings which are icons and which have stories to tell. One of them is the "Royal Hotel".

To the chill out music of Vangelis a young waitress cleans the restaurant before the closing. She looks up at the sky just to catch a departing plane disappearing in the night haze, which embraces permanently this hilly city. She cleans the plates and empty glasses off the last table at the terrace with a view on New Orleans glittering downtown.

All of a sudden an elderly gentleman emerges at the terrace - leaning against the banisters starting to talk to the waitress. It is Peter Willington, "Can I have a look?"

"Sure you can!" answers the waitress.

He stares at the shiny glass buildings shimmering in the neon lights and whispers, "I see you, Ellis! I see the palm of your hand with the pink rose…You will be with me, everywhere I go, I know…But…how can I cross this abyss…the eternal sea of darkness, that God had placed between us?"

The waitress approaches Peter Willington and joins him to stare at the buildings with myriads of tiny yellow light squares, saying, "It is a nice view, huh?!"

"Yeah. I used to work here, a long time ago…Like you…" says the gentleman.

"Oh, really? That is awesome!" the waitress shows her interest.

"In the 80's…of the last century" continues the gentleman.

"Wow, that was a hell of a time!" comments the young servant.

"You remind me of my colleague and my…Connie. Yeah. The history - the myth." The gentleman adds with a sigh.

To get her guest in a better mood she adds, "You were young…"

"I have never changed…" and he leaves in the direction of the hotel main entrance heading into the late night abandoned streets down to the concrete labyrinth lit by the colours of life.

Peter Willington strolls the town and disappears somewhere in the vapour swirling up from the canals.

"BLOODY PAPERWORK"

Bogota's international airport is nearly empty and only a handful of people waiting for check-in and departure gates shown on the monitors.

Juan is running towards the airport terminal turnstile door and asking breathless at the counter for the soonest flight to Europe.

It is the one to Prague in the Czech Republic...

Juan turns around as he has the feeling, that someone follows him...

He runs to hide in the airport toilet, washes his face nervously, there is no-one else.

All of a sudden, someone enters it.

In the mirror - Juan sees the face of one of Pepe's gang members, Leo, the one of whom everybody knows, that he has killed for Pepe several times! It is obvious to him, why he is here.

Juan faces himself in the crystal clear mirror above the sink. He stares into his own eyes - the reflection of the room distorts, he bites his tongue and makes a firm decision.

Juan turns around to Leo behind him with a "friendly" smile - and as the tough guy approaches him showing his sharp teeth - he pulls up the pen from the chest pocket.

Leo with a compressed shouting, so nobody will hear them outside the lavatory,

"Where the fuck you think you are going?"

He pulls up the knife and hastily approaches Juan.

Juan calmly, "I wasn't thinking of going anywhere. On the contrary, I was waiting for my partner to show up with your bosses money. How 'bout I give you the money now? The deadline was 5 p.m., but you can have it right now - if you want."

Leo suspiciously, "Alright, show me the money!"

"OK", while putting his leather suitcase on the sink. Juan opens it up - and pulls out the check book and pen...

"Hey, wait a minute!!" Leo approaches Juan with the knife - real close - examining the piece of paper.

Leo shouts: "Juan, we need cash! Pepe won't accept fucking checks."

"Yes Sir, understand..."

He rises the check book close to the gangster's face, "Let me write the check on your name, then you can either give the money to Pepe or keep it saying that you were not able to find me at the airport!"

Juan writes a sum onto it - and as the gangster looks closer to see the figures - Juan rims swiftly the pen into the left eye of Leo!

Leo screams full of pain and tries to stab Juan with his knife, but Juan disarms the gangster, takes the knife and stabs him right into his heart, again and again.

Then - as the victim falls down on the floor - Juan blocks the door of the toilet. He drags the gangster into one of the cubicles, locks the door from inside, climbs the wall of the cubicle and crawls over it. He washes his hands full of blood, only a small spot on the sleeves will identify that he was in a fight, but hopefully nobody will ask any questions.

He leaves the lavatory and checks if, he does not see anyone he knows from Pepe's guys. There is no one so he can go calmly to the gate. At boarding he is still nervous, but when he is sitting in his seat, he knows in a couple of minutes he takes off to a new life in Europe.

What Juan does not know that a security guard finds Leo's body and alarms the police. Immediately the police starts to investigate the footage on many screens in the security room. They quickly identify Juan and know the destination, where he is going to fly to. A team arrives hastily at the gate, but the plane has already left the parking position and is on the runway, ready to disappear in the darkness of the night sky, welcomed by glittering stars just the sound of the engines last.

Fortunate for Juan that communication between Columbian police and Czech authorities is not established and therefore Juan enters Europe without any problems.

"CHILL-OUT PEOPLE"

It is a bright sunny day close to Zhanjiang City in South East China, which is close to the Vietnamese border, some name it the paradise.

The white MB 62 sails the dusty reddish road between the palms that copy the coastline.

A black man drives it wearing red leather gloves and red sun glasses. He has a pistol with silencer right on the seat besides him and safely navigates this luxury "ship of the streets" through the tropical jungle.

The driver Bony Eins comes from Barbados and one of his neighbours - back there - was also Rihanna, when she was younger. He is the bodyguard of that Chinese couple, indulging in the matters of body chemistry, passion and love – right behind his back.

Bony Eins is the master of loyalty and he would not hesitate to kill for his boss – the Chinese multi-millionaire Jonathan Lee and his wife Jennifer.

Jonathan knows this and considers Bony not much being one of his hundreds of employees, but rather Bony being his older brother. Besides, Bony comes from the decent middle-class family himself, wealthy enough - not to be way too humble.

The couple is making love in the rhythm of soft music which crawls out of the highend speakers at the same time a music video is playing on the big LCD screen.

The sighing of the lovers in the back turns gradually into a scream and the driver presses the volume way up on the driving wheel not to hear the sounds of the two.

Bony is in his mid 50's, but sometimes he could unconsciously force an assumption onto the others, that he is a decade younger.

The car keeps moving through the forrest along the coastline. The ocean waves are nearly not visible, the sea is so calm.

The limo arrives at the small harbour and the couple and their bodyguard climb onboard Lee's speedboat. When Bony starts the engines, everyone in the harbour turns towards them. The Ferrari engines' sound is so loud, that motorboat lovers need to identify the yacht where it comes from.

Outside the safe harbour walls, the boat gets to a high speed quickly and seems to fly above the water surface.

Capitan of the yacht is Bony Eins - this time his outfit changed into the appropriate one adhering to the vision of the "old wolf" sailor. The hat, blue striped T-shirt… but his red gloves and red sunglasses did stay on his hands and eyes. He navigates the boat safely between rocks, sand banks and sharks.

The Chinese couple just continues what they did in the limousine.

Bony has the instruction to drive the boat to the beautiful beach about 10 miles away, where the Chinese couple seeks to relax.

Relay means to slowly walk through the white sand dunes of the narrow stripe of the beach having glasses with colourful cocktails in their hands. Behind them Bony Eins in a colourful shirt and straw hat, but of course… with his red gloves and glasses on. He holds a coconut and sips the nectar via the straw. Behind his pants, the gun with its silencer.

There is nobody else.

Jonathan decides to change the location and says to Bony, "Bony, lets get back to the boat and drive to the Marriott Resort beach, they have a good pier for the boat and great drinks at the bar."

"Sure Sir Jonathan, you will be there very quickly once we are back to our rocket," answers Bony smiling at the beautiful boat on the beach - he really enjoys driving fast…

Arriving to the pier of the resort, the sun starts to slowly hit the horizon and the guests start to leave the white shiny beach, heading to their accommodation facilities or the beach bar to get the final drink before getting ready for dinner.

Jonathan, Jennifer and Bony walk straight to the beach bar, where the two lovers get their favourite drink, freshly made Pina Colada and the guard the virgin version.

The DJ mixes the music behind his instruments and people dance and enjoy the great night outdoor. The Chinese couple dances under the surveillance of Bony's eyes sitting at the bar not too far from them…

Some young girls try to flirt with Bony and he talks with them, as his impressive body, his dark skin and big smile in his face attracts not only Chinese girls. But he is very attentive by keeping one hand on his pistol, whereas the other one is busy with the girls.

There is a big thick glass of pure water with plenty of crushed ice and limes on the bar in front of Bony as he already had enough of the sweet cocktail. A big bottle of "Egeria" mineral water stands right next to his glass.

"THE BEGINNING"

Peter Willington is in his mid 70's and observing the countryside below the plane that is about to land at the Karlovy Vary airport. He wears a cowboy hat and white long shirt from good quality material, in the chests pocket of it - the yellow flower. In his hand he holds a leaflet with the pictures of hotel Egeria. On his neck he has a medallion with the photo of a beautiful woman. There are tears in his eyes.

He sips from the coffee cup. Then he destroys the cup with rage, he has deep wrinkles in his face and puts his sun glasses on to hide his expression of long-term mourning.

The beautiful stewardess comes with the bag collecting money for orphans from the Syrian war. Without twinkle of an eye he pulls out some banknotes and drops them in.

The flight attendants usually do not comment, but besides "Thank you so much Sir! The children will have good food and medical support from this money. Are you sure?"

Peter Willington with a smile, "No worries…"

The voice from the speakers announces: "Please fasten your seatbelt, the toilets are no longer in use, we are about to land in 5 minutes, the weather in Karlovy Vary is rather cold and one more thing, please take good care of your belongings while your stay in Karlovy Vary, because there is an infamous gang of street robbers raging - they are called Phantoms. Apart of this, it is a beautiful and safe place and the captain and crew wish you a wonderful time in Bohemia!"

It is January and Karlovy Vary city is covered in white glittering snow it looks like it starts snowing again any minute.

Peter Willington catches the first taxi outside the small airport and asks the driver to bring him to the hotel Egeria. It is a relatively short drive through the forrest, but enough time for Peter to read the ID of the taxi driver, the name sounds Russian, Igor Kirkorov. From the mirror hangs a rosary and a picture of the Orthodox saint.

The GPS displays the map and Peter can see clearly their move towards the hotel Egeria. At the way down on Old Prague Road Peter asks to stop the car.

He wants to examine the countryside above the city of Karlovy Vary. He can see already the hotel.

The driver stands behind him next to the car and smokes a cigarette. Igor looks bored or rather emotionally detached and sighs when Peter finally gets back into the car and they can continue their transfer to the hotel.

The taxi disappears in falling snow and haze and leaves Peter and his suitcase in front of the massive hotel property.

Peter walks towards the main gate where there a man in his mid 30's awaits him next to a black S-class in the white snow. He is the real estate agent, Pavel Novotny, who was structuring the sales of the property and who did all the communication between the owners and Peter. He holds a big bunch of keys in one hand and a black business suitcase in the other. He waves at Peter. Peter waves at him as well and approaches slowly. Pavel is wearing a long black coat and a hat, which is obviously the best in this miserable weather.

Pavel welcomes Peter shaking his hands, "Hello Peter, how are you?"

"Morning, Pavel. Good! How are you?"

"I'm well, aside from the unfortunate weather. We'd better go inside!"

Peter is happy about this offer, as he is not used to the temperature yet,"Good idea!"

Entering the hallway Pavel offers, "Peter, let me walk you through the property…"

Peter just wishing to be alone to get the feeling for the hotel, "Pavel, thank you, but no need. Just give me the keys and I will find my way to learn everything about the property myself."

"As you wish. Here are the keys", handing a big havy bunch of keys to Peter with a soft smile."There is also a keycard system installed, but you would need to reboot it and check all the locks. The masterkeys are in the safe."

"We'll stay in touch…" Peter is taking the keys, happy that they got tags with some description on them. Though in Czech, but that will not be a problem, when he employs his secretary.

"Definitely, if you need anything, you know where my office is, but here," he pulls a business card out of a silver case and hands it over to Peter. "Don't hesitate to call."

"Don't worry I will do, if I need you."

Pavel leaves the hotel thinking, 'what a brave man, being in this hughe property all on his own.'

Being alone, Peter takes a big breath and says loud to himself, "What the hack did bring me to buy this place?"

Peter walks through the empty abandoned hotel with the heavy set of keys. He enters the rooms, halls, corridors, kitchen, restaurants. As he passes the restaurant he got scarred suddenly as he has seen some ghost… Then he realises it was his reflection in the mirror. The walls are covered by a variety of mirrors… He laughs and comes closer.

Peter stares into his own eyes. He touches his face and sees the many wrinkles and sighs.

Leaving the lower floors, he comes to the accommodation areas.

Peter enters one of the rooms. Apparently it is the King Suite. It is in a desolate state. Some item on the table near the wall strikes his eye. He comes closer to examine the thing. It is an old radio. He takes it into his hands and plays with the buttons. It works!

He strolls through the channels frequencies and finally he finds one with the clear sound. Music plays, but Peter does not understand a word. The song somehow adheres to his momentarily feelings and therefore he sits slowly down in both desperation and atonement. He stares through the big window at the falling snow flakes. He takes his cowboy hat down and puts it on the table next to the radio. There, from his eye, a perfectly shaped tear finally runs down his cheek.

The snow flakes gradually merge into a massive white silent haze - only the song continues to play in the far distant reverberations.

Peter is getting a flashback, to the days in Louisiana, when he went to the cemetery to be with his wife. Where Peter sits on the grave with his cowboy hat in his hands. There are fresh yellow daffodils in the vase and new lit candles besides the gravestone. The writing on it says:

Ellis Willington
1939 - 2019
The Lord is my God!

"She passed through glory's morning gate and walked in paradise. Time takes even the simple and smallest memories we hold of those we love and silently turns them into gold. She will always be with us...in our hearts, in our memories, in our lives."

Back to reality, Peter looks at the radio and smashes it against the wall, stands slowly up and walks away from the room.

It is already night over the time he spends to get the feeling for the hotel and Peter's stomach starts to give signs of hunger. So he strolls through the vast spaces of the hotel's main kitchen and looks for something to eat, but the only edible things he finds, is some left over coffee powder and old biscuits. After hesitating a bit, he decides to be happy with it for tonight as he does not want to go out to dine in some of the restaurants in the city nearby, additionally the weather is harsh and he is tired after the busy travel day. He boils the water for his coffee and puts the biscuits on a plate.

With coffee in the right and the plate with the biscuits in the other hand he treads through the endless hallways to the small boardroom, where he eats the biscuits and drinks the hot coffee with unexpected delight.

He starts laughing suddenly and shakes his head. Suddenly the door squeaks! Peter looks at that direction, realising to his surprise, that a small cat enters the room, curious as cats are!

They stare at each other for a moment.

Peter, " Hello my friend!"

The Cat replies with a "meow".
"So you're the owner of the hotel?!"
The Cat comes close…
"Maybe you're hungry?"
The Cat comes even closer…

Peter takes some biscuit pieces and puts them on the floor. The cat comes to them, sniffs at them but leaves them untouched and looks up to Peter. "Ah, you prefer meat… Sorry pal! No meat tonight… Look at me…" and he bites in a biscuit with a smile.

The cat turns and runs away, disappearing in the darkness of the hallway.

Peter decides to reside in Room 404, which has a beautiful view to the forrest and a balcony to step out and take a breath of fresh air from time to time.

The first night, he is not able to sleep very well and wakes up several times, due to jetleg and the continious thoughts about what is going to happen in the next days.

Being half awake and half asleep he hears steps on the wooden creaking planks and sees the door slowly open with grating.

A voice whispers in his ear "AL - ABU - ABLU - DUBLAG…AL – ABU - ABLU…"

A ghost in a long coat and hood - leans over Peter. Peter sees his own distorted face in the place, where should be the face of the ghost! Peter sees his own face mutilated without one eye. He realises, it is his own reflection in the baroque style framed mirror!

Peter screams and wakes up in his clothes and shoes having his cowboy hat covering his face like the cowboys in the films on the Wilde Wide West…

The old man touches his neck in an attempt to monitor his pulse. The heart beats soft but fast. His look falls immediately on the cat from yesterday, which sits on the bed right besides him with a mouse in front of it. Peter glances at the mouse and then at the cat. He smiles. "Oh good God! It's you, cat!" With a look on the mouse "Oh boy! Now that's what I call room service! Yeah!"

Peter checks the time and realizes, that he slept nearly the whole day and it is already afternoon. So he gets up and goes to the GM office on the first floor.

He finds a yellow sticker on the screen of the secretary computer, advertising "PIZZA DELIVERY"! His bored old wrinkled face switches gradually into a lustful grin… He looks around the desk and pulls the nearby standing phone closer to him. But nothing happens, no signal, no beep, nothing. So he takes out his mobile and dials the number.

Within 30 minutes he receives the ordered "quattro stagioni" and is happy with the first hot food in 24 hours. He can not even wait and eat it in the restaurant, no, he has the first bite & slice between the door and the hall, walking towards the reception.

After finishing the delicious food, even though at this time anything would have been delicious to Peter, he does some reception desk surveillance with curiosity. Then opens randomly chosen drawers and examines what's inside. Papers, office tools, old staplers, some photo of a woman in uniform…it is an Asiatic young woman in hotel uniform…then there is a set of chess figures and the board.

He opens the box, sits on the chair and lays the figures on the board, both black and white. He starts to make moves…

Then he stops and contemplates his situation and the state the hotel is in. After few more chess moves he decides and pulls out his mobile.

He makes a call to his son back in Los Angeles.

As he dials…he spots the cat who followed Peter to the reception area with a fat slice of pizza in his cute mouth. There he stops, sits and eats it with delight making the cat's noise of pleasure feelings.

Peter grins and one can hear him shouting into the phone as the connection seems to be bad.

"Hi son, this is dad! … Yeah. … Cold! Damn Cold! … But interesting, lovely place…

Yeah…. Hey, James, I need your help! … What kind of help?"

Peter plays with the white Queen figure in between his fingers.

"Listen, why don't you come here with Jane…and…"

On the other end, in Los Angeles, the sun rises only above the horizon and James is ready to take his morning swim in the rooftop pool on the skyscraper where the young Willington lives. James looks like being in the 50's but in reality he is only 48. His excessive lifestyle during his Youth and University paid its tribute.

James, takes a sip from the coffee mug he brought up to the pool area, as nothing is better than to wake-up with a hot coffee having a beautiful view from the roof.

"Dad, remember when I asked you for help when we were buying our apartment, did you help us? No… You see! … Oh…oh…you wanted us to stand on our own two legs…oh… And now you're on your knees begging me. Nevertheless, my wife would never ever agree to go to Europe! … Hmm… Yeah… Yes, the same wife you called a whore…do you remember?! … Ah..really…you don't drink anymore…good! … Good for you! … Good for the rest of the world too!"

Whereas Peter standing in the lobby, "Son, I'm sorry, really I am! … I'm a different man now! … I quit drinking, I would always help you, if you asked me again! … Sure thing … You know, I'm in this Hotel I bought in the Czech Republic, in Karlovy Vary … Karlovy Vary! … K A R L O V Y V A R Y, damn! …

It is…not far from the border with Germany… No, not Russia … And no, not Czechoslovakia. That country doesn't exist anymore. It's two countries: the Czech Republic and Slovakia now. And I am in the Czech part … Are you kidding me?

… It's a wonderful country, beautiful Hotel …well it's totally empty…only me here… yeah, only me…"

Peter glances at the cat, who observes him with a silent accusation…

" ..and one cat!"

In L.A. a blonde tall slim woman in a white bikini and bathrobe approaches the swimming pool area with breakfast on a tray. James looks up to her and smiles. He covers the speaker of the mobile to make sure his dad cannot hear anything.

James whispering, "It's dad… He want's me and my wife to come to Europe to help him to launch and manage the hotel for a while…"

"I won't let you go!" She puts the tray down in front of James and jumps into the swimming pool. Then she hugs him from the back and kisses his ear. "I will never ever let you go!"

"Don't worry honey, my wife will never agree to go to Europe." He puts his finger to his lips, "Psst…"

He uncovers the speaker of the mobile phone, "Dad, I'm sorry! You have to fight it out on your own and stand on your own two legs…! Anyway, are you aware of the fact, that you're turning 80 in a couple of years…?! I really don't know, why'd you take on such a big risk…? Gotta go… Talk soon."

James drops the mobile on the tray between the scrambled eggs, croissants and orange juice. He turns back towards his secret lover and both start kissing as the red sun rises above their heads.

Peter drops the Queen on the chess board and sits back deep into the chair with empty look. He looks out of the main entrance turnstile door glass to see that it is getting slowly dark outside and the snow keeps falling down as it would be designed to never ever finish.

"NIGHTLIFE"

A black strech limousine rides the narrow, curvy streets of Karlovy Vary. There is a small group of people sitting inside. Some men, some women - all wear fancy dresses and expensive shoes. Between them a younger Chinese man with very neat hair in a red suit, it is Jonathan Lee, who plays chess with some other sleak guy in his 40's. His names is Juan Alexandro Polpo, he comes from Bogota, Columbia, he has coloured white hair and wears black glasses with a thick frame.

Just to explain how Juan got to know Jonathan. Only a few days after arriving at the airport in Prague, Juan was looking for a counterfeiter, who would help him to get a new passport and identity. The gentleman he found is working for Jonathan Lee as well and the day Juan received his documents, Jonathan was by chance also there. They started to speak about gambling and chess and Jonathan liked Juan from the first moment. That he had plans with him, nobody knew at that time.

All, other than the chess players, drink champagne and talk loud in the excitement of wild adventurous night expectations. The music is on, the bass beats let the windows vibrate. The chess players focus on their game.

Jonathan with a smile,"3 moves and you're done!"

Juan conters,"Check!"

The Chinese guy keeps his poker face and makes a thorough surveillance of the chess board. Then, he suddenly glances out of the window just to meet the eyes of a random passer by. They are Peter Willington's. His eyes look at him from below the cowboy hat from his face partly covered by his silver mustache.

At the very same moment, the limo stops at the red lights. Peter shifts his sight away and keeps walking across the street. Jonathan smiles as he sees his own Casino on the other side.

"Oh, we're getting close to my Casino! Look, Juan!"

"Wow!"

"Let's call it draw?"

"As you wish…but…you would've won as usual."

"Who knows?! You're a perilous player!"

"You flatter me, Jonathan…But you're a very tough opponent!"

Jonathan satisfied,"Let's play other games tonight too! Here we are, let's go! Ladies…and gents…welcome to my casino…and please spend all the money you got on you…don't be shy!!."

Everybody is laughing as they exit the limo.

On the other side of the road Peter enters the Italian restaurant called "Ristorante PALERMO", one hears pleasant Italian music from the outside speakers, which work all year round – in Summer for the people on the terrace, in Winter to attract people to enter.

It is a more classy dining place than Peter expected, where you have to book the table prior coming. The porter at the door is a guy in his mid 50's, he has a very neat appearance, his hair perfectly fixed by gel, he looks bit like Bela Lugosi and have distinctive "Count Dracula" like facial features. He looks younger and more kind hearted than he actually is. His eyes send certain warning signals to those who pay attention… The porter welcomes Peter, "Good evening Sir. Do you have a reservation?"

Peter looks around to examine the restaurant and realises there is only one young couple in the corner… "Do I really need one…?"

"Yes Sir, I'm afraid it's essential to have…" The porter conjures up an apologetic but merciless smile in a gentleman style.

Peter spots the porter wears the white gloves and top hat on the small table besides him still bears some snow flakes that melt gradually down. Another Italian song starts to play from the "old school" speaker on the wall above the paintings with Italian rural motifs of family life…

Behind him - as a shadow - emerges charismatic reddish hair, full bodied waitress with deep blue eyes - the woman in her mid 50's - she moves like black cat - slowly as if the world has slowed down around Peter. Their eyes meet for a brief but fatal moment! For the first time, since Peter arrived to this frozen Bohemia, his face get a slight red warm colour, as if the hot springs of Karlovy Vary have finally entered the valleys of pain - his deep face wrinkles…

The couple in the corner starts kissing.

Peter observes the menu. He comes to the "BEVERAGES" section and checks the wines.

He stays there for some time…

Peter thinks, 'You can make an exception, Peter. Just today! Only one bottle and then no more… You have a reason! … it's a unique occasion…' Then he utters a sigh…

The waitress comes to his table with an honest smile, "If I could recommend… Our Chef makes the best Sicilian Ragu in the world! How about that? And if you'll have it really spicy, there won't be a need to spice up the life with wine anymore!"

Peter smiles, "Very nice, I'll have that. Where are you from?"

She answers a little shy, "Romania."

"Oh, the country of Mr. Dracula…"

"Yes! Exactly!"

"…and the Chef?"

"Italy."

"The owner…?"

"…is the Chef."

"I see. And the porter at the door?"

The waitress starts to wonder and being cautious, "It's a bit complicated…"

"You are very kind, what's your name?"

The waitress scowling," Ugh! You're asking a lot of questions! Are you a detective?"

Peter with serious face," I'm sorry if I'm too nosy. It's perhaps…"

"My name is Layla and now let's get back to business. What will you have?"

The place gets bit colder for Peter, suddenly.

"My name is Peter and I'll have: this unbeatable Sicilian Ragu, a mineral water San

Pellegrini…or no, perhaps some local…"

"Mattoni? I would recommend - Egeria!"

"OK, Egeria then and… a black coffee… Please, Layla."

"Great, thank you."

Layla brings the food.

Peter tastes the food and calls Layla back: "The food is cold!"

"Cold?"

"Could you please heat it up for me?"

The Italian Chef Sylvester Cavallo sits on a chair and reads Italian Newspapers swearing over the football related article. As an Italian stallion Sylvester Cavallo is a hot blood, is in his mid 40's and comes from Sicily (Palermo) in Italy. He has a black mustache, darker face and fiery eyes. He is small, slim and very energetic. Sylvester can be kind hearted too, but no-one really knows, when the Chef can explode in a fury. From his calm talk he can instantly switch to a devil. He swears in his anger as he nervously reads the news. However, his bad mood rather derives from the current state of things: His and his finance's restaurant does not do well so far, in fact, they are closer to the bankruptcy than they would like to admit!

There is a bottle of great "Barolo" two half-empty big red wine glasses and the wooden board with the selection of cheese, chestnuts and mango chutney. On the table sits another cook - it is an energetic (rural harsh beauty) Italian woman in her late 30's - his fiancée - Aida de Luca. She – same as Sylvester - comes from the city of Palermo. They grew up together in a violent neighbourhood, they went to the Hotel school together and they came to Karlovy Vary together. Their relationship is a super strong emotional bond. They would not hesitate to kill one for another.

Aida nervously bites her nails and drinks the wine and picks a chestnut from the small wooden board. "Sylvester! We need guests! If we don't do something fast…"

Sylvester, looking at the article, "Cazzo!"

"Sorry?"

Sylvester glances at Aida,"Sorry, what did you say?"

She gets back to him furiously,"We're running out of money!"

"Honey, we'll figure something out."

"You've been saying that for months, go and double check our restaurant! Now!"

Sylvester is somehow detached as his mind is still occupied by football. But all of a sudden he says,"Line Up!

Aida is smiling suspiciously,"What?"

"Line Up!" with confidence in his voice. "One good friend and business man did advice us to hire some people to Line Up in our restaurant to generate the ambience of busy dining place."

"It must have been that generous Chinese multimillionaire who never tips Layla or Mr. Tea! I bet, he wants to come with his wife to eat for free!"

Sylvester laughs, raises his glass and clinks with Aida's glass. They drink little wine and laugh together.

"It might be…but the idea is good, no?…In fact the idea might be worth millions…in the long run…no?"

Aida,"…yeah…worth millions out of our pockets….Cazzo!"

They both laugh, hug each other and kiss.

The kitchen door bursts open and Layla enters the kitchen with a plate in her hand raised high. The Italian lovers look up, when Layla starts to shout,"Guys! It's cold. The customer is complaining."

"Oh, OK, tell the customer, we are very sorry and we will heat it up real quick!" says Aida.

"OK", Layla puts the plate with unbeatable Sicilian Ragu on the table, picks the small piece of cheese from the board and runs back to the restaurant.

Peter sits behind his bottle with mineral water and observes the bobbles jumping up to the surface. The couple in the corner keeps kissing. They seem to be inexhaustible in eating their heads off. Peter feels lonely while observing the paintings on the wall and he is also looking at the door, where the porter, Mr. Tea, stays in front of the restaurant with the menus in his hands. There is no point, because the weather conditions trap people in their homes.

But Mr. Tea is vigilant and if he will spot a dog he will try to lure it inside. There it is - the taxi arrives - the group of people pops out - and Mr. Tea manages to talk them in! The porter from the competition on the opposite side shows Mr. Tea his fist - but it is apparent - they are friends in fact! They both smile.

Mr. Tea shakes his arms in apology.

Layla burst the door of the kitchen open again with the plate in her hand raised high.

"Guys! It's still not hot enough! That customer complains and threatens to leave the restaurant. Also, he warns about speaking badly about us in the press!… that he'll write "a nice" review in "Trip Advisor"…"

Aida starts to swear "Va fan' culo! Layla, please tell him, we're really sorry and we will do our best to satisfy him as soon as possible."

Then the chef starts to getting a red face due to anger,"Layla, where the heck did you go first with the plate? To the restroom and then to the guest, or what?"

Layla replies being upset of Sylvesters words,"No, Sylvester, I went from the kitchen to the table. The guest is a bit gaga!"

" Allright! This time that dumbass will get what he wants!"

"This time just make it real hot!!"

Layla puts the plate with unbeatable Sicilian Ragu on the table.

"…and, on a brighter note - we have a big order! 12 main courses, 8 salads, 9 soups!"

Aida with a bit of relief,"Great work Layla! Well done! Make them drink a lot as well!"

Sylvester getting into better mood as well, "We will prepare for them some complimentary starters! Something bit spicy and salty to make them drink! Layla, did you ask about any dietary restrictions, allergies?"

"Sure, just like you taught me!"

"…and?"

"All good!"

"Great!! As to that complaining guy - tell him I will come personally - to serve it really hot! He'll learn his lesson!"

The chef Sylvester takes a silver tray, puts it into the oven, which he sets to 350 C.

Then he turns back to Layla."Now, the big order…What's it gonna be?"

Layla starts reading:" twice Sicilian Ragu with Tagliatelle, twice Pizza Napolitana with extra…but Chef, better you take this paper where I wrote everything they ordered, so you can work it from the top and will not forget anything."

"Layla, actually I am used to get the dishes announced and start to produce them, insTead of reading it on a paper. But you are right, I could easily forget something with an order that big…"

Waiting for the heated dish, Peter observes the photos he did take in his hotel on his mobile phone.

Layla's voice gets him distracted, "Sir!"

Peter switches off the phone swiftly and looks up. There is Layla standing with the empty plate, besides her the chef Sylvester - holding a silver tray with the Sicilian Ragu

Tagliatelle on it.The vapour rises high to the restaurant ceiling as it is apparent - this time it is seriously hot.

"Sorry Sir, I'm the executive chef, you have a problem with the temperature?"

"Yes indeed, the food was cold!"

The chef cannot believe what he hears and just lowers the tray with the food next to the ear of Peter. With a short move the hot tray burns into the ear of the guest.

"Ouch" shouts Peter.

"So sorry, I didn't mean to do that, the hot tray just slipped out of my fingers…", remarks the chef.

"I guess it won't be cold this time…" Sylvester continues.

"You bloody chef bastard, of course it'll be hot when you cookit on the tray before serving on it."

"That is exactly what I wanted to hear - you got your hot food."

As Peter leaves the restaurant, he realises the snow blizzard got even stronger and the temperature must have gone deeper down below zero. His coat is not as thick as he was never used to such weather conditions back in LA. He touches his slightly burnt ear with annoyed grin. "Bastard!"

The porter, Mr. Tea waves at Peter with his hands in white gloves. "Come back again, Sir!"

Peter turns back and with a bit of sarcasm, "Definitely!"

"Good night, Sir!"

As he heads to his hotel in the darkness lit by the green light of the street lamps, he starts to have a feeling he is being followed! The sound of another pair of shoes press the snow.

He stops walking for a moment to double check… Silence. The snow flakes bombard his face.

Peter continues walking. He can see the lights of the hotel in between the tree branches.

Then again those steps in snow behind him… Peter starts running. But as he is old, he quickly runs out of oxygen! He stops and turns back – The shadow?!

The silhouette of some monster approaches him.

Peter grabs the heavy set of the hotel key from the pocket of his long coat. That is his gun now. A couple of dogs bark furiously in the far distance. In the tree tops sit hundreds of crows cackling softly and the shadows of the naked branches, cast by the green light of the street lamp, resemble the black veins of the night phantom!

Peter's sight is not best and he looks for his glasses. It is a man with a hat. He runs grasping his breath barely. Peter prepares for the fight for his life or the money. His cowboy hat is bombarded by the shimmering snow flakes. Sudden bursts of wind - play a squeaky creepy melody on the rusty agricultural machinery thrown into the slopes of the river.

Peter steps forward to face the enemy with the courage. It is the porter from that Italian restaurant - Mr. Tea!

Mr. Tea stops in front of Peter Willington trying to catch his breath. There is some black thing in his hand. Peter looks closer at it.

Mr. Tea,"Sir, your wallet."

He hands the wallet to Peter. Peter takes a deep sigh in the relief.

"Oh thank you so much! Mr. …?"

"Mr. Tea, people call me: Mr. Tea"

Peter looks into the wallet - to double check - all seems to be alright there - then he spots that Mr. Tea observes him…after a hesitation he pulls out a banknote…

"Forget it!… Got to go."

Peter,"Wait…"

"Have a good night! Was an honour…"

Mr. Tea runs back - with his hand keeping his hat on his head - leaving Peter standing there under the lamp with the banknote in his hand and the wallet in the other.

The blizzard turns gradually into a massive dark white snow storm.

"XXX"

The only night club in Karlovy Vary starts its life, when every other place is closing for the night.

There is a Japanese girl called Yuki Hizashi in her early 20's dancing at the strip pole but she is not naked. Some Russians sit on the white sofa, they look like mafia guys and between them their boss. The bottles of best quality vodka are half hidden in the pile of melting shining ice in the wine buckets and silver bowls.

Multiple trays with toasts, eggs with caviar, salmon sandwiches are placed on the bar tables. The men smoke cigars and cigarettes. One of the drunk men shouts at her to dress down finally as the music goes on. But she does not follow the order. She keeps dancing keeping her cool. One of the man approaches her and puts a banknote behind her pants.

Then he returns to the sofa. The other drunk man shouts again. The boss tells him to shut up. A security guy enters the salon and whispers something into the ear of the leader, which makes him to stand up and to follow the security guard out of the room. They go through the corridors and pass the main dance hall where the DJ plays for the masses of dancing guests. They continue through the kitchen to arrive at the back door, where other mafia men hold a young man with mustache. The boss asks the security guy to go out and guard the door from the kitchen side. The security guy leaves. He waits in the kitchen, observes the cooks preparing meals, looks around and when he is sure that none of the staff sees him, he puts his eye close the key hole. He can see one of the guys pointing the hand gun towards the unfortunate young man's head. One of the mafia men turns back towards the door and the security guy moves his eye away from the key hole and looks around the kitchen. The pans are in the fire and the meat is boiling. The vapour swirls under the ceiling and the security guy can hear the 2 shots even in that noise in this busy hell kitchen!

Back in the private salon, the drunk bad guy stands close to dancing Yuki with the knife in his hand shouting at her to dress damn down! The boss returns accompanied by the security guy. He sits on the sofa between the guys, cleans his hands in the buckets with ice and vodka and the melted cubes turn slightly red. The security guy hands him over a paper napkin and the boss dries his hands. Then he spots the bad guy threatens the dancing girl Yuki and hints to the security guy to fix this issue. The security guy - after a small fast fight - pacifies the rascal and drags him out of the room again through the corridors and the kitchen. The bad guy with the freshly acquired bloody bruise under his eye shouts at the security in Russian that he will kill the guy!

But the security man kicks his ass and the drunk man falls down the stairs into the black rubbish bags near the garbage bins in the courtyard behind the kitchen.

"Don't take it personally! Sober up! Ivan."

"I'll kill you! Personally."

The Japanese dancer walks out of the club crying. She walks away, stops at the bus station, sits on the bench, pulls up a cigarette, sets it on and inhales deep – staring across the street.

She searches in her bag and pulls out the book: *"Justice: what's the right thing to do?" by Michael J. Sandel*

She takes the lighter and sets the book pages on fire. Then she drops it on the floor into the snow and observes it burning. A sudden burst of wind opens the book to reveal the warning letter from the Charles University of Law in Prague. The figures for Student fee to be paid are eaten by the fire too. Zeroes after zero.

The snow flakes slowly emerge falling somewhere from the dark sky…

There is a Christmas tree in the snow thrown by people behind the bus station and the silver decorations dance away of the naked branches in the cold wind.

A dog barks from the far distance and its reverberations sting Yuki under her painted nails like the sharp needles. The black taxi finally arrives. Yuki steps inside.

"PRE-OPENING"

Peter walks the stairs down to enter the wine cellar. There are no wines, no bottles in there - just empty racks and real cold air. The walls are sleazy wet. He hears some noise up there above him… Peter stands in the middle of the room with low ceiling for a moment and listens. Silence. Then he spots a small wooden door with big metal handle. He comes closer and takes the handle to open it.mThe door are heavy and hard to open. Peter must use his full strength to push the door open. He struggles greatly. Finally gets in.

The Darkness - cold creepy stale air hits his nose - no light - no bulb - no button to switch… Peter can immediately feel the great moisture here. Suddenly, the woman's laughter breaks the silence, like a surprising lightning strikes from heavy ominous clouds moving fast from monstrous mountains.

There…from the darkness it came…the hotel officially greets Peter! He touches the place where his heart is and throat. Then he searches for something in his way too many pockets.

There it is! - Quickly he grabs his mobile from the last of the pockets - *"how typical"* he thinks -, but this one slips off his nervous fingers…down on the floor…down the stairs into that darkness - into that scary room…

By the noise of falling mobile phone - he can judge there are just a few of the stairs… He enters the room carefully touching the wall and goes slowly down.

He hears steps or some undefined sound.

There definitely must be someone in the room! Peter turns back to see the light coming through the open door. It is very subtle light of a blueish colour. The cat is there!

Peter releases a sigh of relief.

He turns back, squats a searches for the mobile phone. Finally he finds it! Peter switches the mobile on and turns the "Flashlight" on. It is compelling and lights the room enough for Peter to comfortable walk in here and see the stuff. The room is spread into many parts with extremely low ceiling and many pillars. There are many racks along the walls… and there are wines…the dusty bottles of wine!

Now, Peter can hear the sound of water dropping down from the ceiling. He has a feeling as he was in one of the Alan Edgar Poe's horror cellars. He grabs one of the bottles carefully.

It is covered in spider's web and dust. There is no typical label on it, just a small tag - like on the thumb of the dead…

"Pinot noir, DO Gran Reserva, 1916, Tarapacá"

"Manuel Zavala - Melendez"

"Chile"

Peter smiles… and speaks to himself,"I need to hire the best sommelier ever. This will be an awesome hotel, great cuisine and old best wines from all the corners of the world! but something freezes his smile…

He hears the tones of a piano.

The melody flows through the door down the stairs to him from somewhere in this hotel labyrinth. He listens to it.

"Why?" he asks himself.

"The hotel is welcoming me tonight!" he replies to himself.

Peter walks with the bottle and glass through the hotel corridors lit only by the moon light - following the sounds of the piano. He is here already one week and still there are places in this hotel, he has never been to. But Peter was not lazy these days and started to find people to make the place incredible.

Peter goes to the reception area and sees a young, long haired, beautiful receptionist there - she seems to be of the Asiatic origin - but she wears a bright make-up, which makes it difficult to say. Her almond eyes are definitely Japanese, "What's it gonna be, Sir?"

Peter charming,"A room for two…"

Peter was able to employ the porter from that Italian restaurant - Mr. Tea – he carries his seriously oversized luggage up the stairs with the great struggle, breathing heavily. Peter follows him, and as he sees the fierce battle between his biggest suitcases in the world and the unfortunate bellboy, he starts pushing the bellboy to help getting that damn suitcase up… faster…

Peter is wondering and asking Mr. Tea,"Why doesn't the damned lift work?"

"The power went out, Sir! Because of the storm…"

Mr. Tea stops for a moment trying to catch his breath,"What's the room number, Sir?"

"601, which is a great apartment and I chose it due to the adequate size and the beautiful view over the valley. Are we getting there anytime soon?"

"Oh, this is the top floor, Sir…oh God!"

"Let's go! Move your ass, are you a Bellboy or shall I call you "hell-boy"?"

The housekeeper Layla, the waitress from that Italian restaurant, works the bed as Peter enters the room followed by Mr. Tea. She is wearing her new uniform and is flirting with Peter not leaving her eyes from him.

Both - Peter and bellboy Mr. Tea - sit each on one of the large suitcases and observe Layla preparing the bed and cleaning the room. Peter asks Mr. Tea to leave,"Mr. Tea, I will take care of the rest with Layla, you can go downstairs and have a look, how to handle the electricity for the lift. It will help all of us."

A little later Peter sits lonely in the empty restaurant and the young Maître d'hôtel approaches Peter - asking for the order,"Good evening Sir, what can I order in the kitchen for you?"

"Sicilian Ragu with Tagliatelle and freshly grated Parmesan cheese, please. And ask the chef not to make it too spicy, I love to taste the ingredients of the

Ragu and make sure that the food is really hot – but only temperaturewise." Peter touches his ear.

With a smile the Maître d' returns, "The chef said, he'll kick your ass, if you'll ever complain about his food again, since he always makes sure it is real hot, Sir!!"

Peter is angry and in shock the same time," Kick my ass? That's what he said?"

"I am afraid, that is exactly what he said, he will kick your goddamned ass, Sir!"

Peter is looking around the empty restaurant and starts his lesson," Did you hear it people? What this young asshole just said?"

Peter drops the napkin angrily on the table. He stands up, pushes away the waiter and walks to the kitchen.

"I'll teach the guy some manners!"

"Sir!"

"What?"

"Better not..."

"Why?"

"Our CHEF is a bit mad...sometimes...a bit gaga..."

Peter waves a hand and walks into the kitchen.

As soon as he stands in front of Sylvester Cavallo he calms down, as he knows it will not be clever to start a fight with the Italian, but he needs to know, who is the boss.

"Sylvester, I have heard, that you have an issue with my wishes for hot food. Is that true?"

"Sir, I always provided hot food in my career and you should not mention it anymore."

"Well, I see it different, but please keep your mouth shut, when it comes to the boss, who is paying you and who got you out of a miserable position in a loss generating restaurant."

He leaves the kitchen, leaving behind a thinking chef and a Maitre with mouth wide open.

"That is what I call management and self-control", Maitre starts. "We will have a great time here Sylvester, this style is something new."

"You are right Maitre, but get your ass out of my kitchen and let me work!"

At night Peter dreams about the situation, but it is totally weird,'There are cooks with blurred faces holding shaking Peter on a steel table and the chef – Sylvester Cavallo sharpens his knife while swearing in the mixture of Italian & English. Peter thinks, his last minute just arrived! But suddenly - as secret agent - Mr. Tea - with the machine gun arrives and starts shooting the cooks one by one in slow motion. Their blood sprinkles the stainless steel kitchen. Knives fly. The cooks fall in pain down to the floor. The big blood lake spreads across the marble floor and flows through the open door out of the kitchen.

Peter together with Layla hold the chef Sylvester and Mr. Tea cuts off the ear of the screaming cook. The black hotel cat licks the blood. The blood flows through the restaurant. There is a boat in the restaurant and the crew in it. The boat sails to the ballroom. Peter is the captain.'

And he wakes-up, exactly knowing what to do. He gets dressed, grabs the wine found in the cellar and walks down the stairs to the lobby and then enters the ball room where the grand piano stands - waiting for him. The room is spacious and has a soaring ceiling. Peter switches on some of the lights. The immense space is suddenly lit by purple and blue colours. The architecture is stunning and Peter feels overwhelmed by the beauty of it.

Peter puts the dusty bottle filled by history on the piano and sits behind it. He starts to play.

Closing his eyes, he feels that there are guests sitting behind the tables listening to his play. The guests are the future staff of this hotel. They even wear the uniforms. Each uniform - in a style - as per department. And...there is his wife who sits on top of the piano.

"You told me you won't be drinking anymore!"

"Yes I did! And I don't!"

"So what is this bottle doing here?"

"I was on my way down to the cellar to put it back and just stopped by to play some piano!"

"Good boy." The wife disappears and he is opening his eyes again.

He finishes his play and Peter walks down to the wine cellar to put the dusty bottle with sigh back into the rack. Immediately turns around and leaves the wine cellar, saying to himself, "Sorry, but I should not come back here, it is so painful not being able to drink all these excellent wines. But our guests will love them."

He slowly closes the heavy door and goes back to his room, where he falls asleep immediately.

"SAMIA SAHAR"

Samia is in her mid 20's and comes from a small village in Morocco, she currently works at a call center in Mumbai in India as Sales Manager - Team Leader. Samia has a problem with the weather conditions as she hates the hot temperatures. Therefore she stays at work longer after the usual business hours. She is a diligent hard worker with the sense for detail and justice.

Samia has a secret lover on the internet and spends some time chatting with him. Both lovers keep their true identity hidden! She supports her family back in Morocco and she misses them a lot. When she assumes that no one is around, she sings - her voice is soft and pleasant to listen to.

She likes spicy food, Indian TV dramas and enjoys to be surrounded by many people, family, friends. She prefers to keep her life simple. She loves to relax in a Hammam and enjoys cooking for the others. Samia makes the most delicious cakes in space - at least the others say so.

Oashni an Indian girl is crying, she and Samia are sitting in one of the small working spaces of a call center agent, one can call it a box. The rest of the call center works as usual, only Oashni and Samia have to solve an urgent issue of a customer together.

"Calm down, Oashni."

"He said, I'm stupid!"

"I'll talk to him later! Don't worry."

"He's a real asshole!"

"Let me talk to the customer now." Samia clicks the pictogram of the speaker on the screen to put the sound back on.

The customer is wondering,"Where the hell were you?"

Samia taking over the microphone," Sir. We'll get this all figured out. Really quick."

"Who are you? Again another agent! Damn! That's some service, typical call center! You call the "Free Number" and then you spend a bunch of time and that is also money! I WANT MY MONEY BACK! OMG!"

"Sir. I do understand your anger, really I do! If I was in your place, I'd want my money back too. I'm the manager and me and my colleagues will do every-thing we can to fix your computer, right now."

"Oh, at least somebody who speaks the English I can understand! That's a good sign of better times...I hope. I bet, I reached some call center in India or somewhere..."

"OK. Let's start now. My colleague already told me about the connection issue with your laptop. What we need to do now is the following: Go to Control Panel - -"

"OK"

"… and then Network Connections…"

"…oh…where is…OK, I'm there!"

"Good! Now, right-click on the wireless network adapter and choose Properties."

Silence.

"Sir? Are you there?"

"Where to click?"

"Right click! Click the right button on your mouse!"

"Where?"

"On P R O P E R T I E S, Sir!"

"Ah…"

"You got that?"

"Yes!"

"Now click on the Wireless Networks tab and click the Add button."

Silence.

"Sir?"

"Yes, I have it."

"and finally, go ahead and type in the SSID for thewireless router…"

"Where I find the SSID?"

"On the bottom or back of your router."

"Just a moment…"

Silence.

"OK, have it!"

"Now, set the Network Authentication to Shared!"

"Yes."

Silence.

"It works! Thank you so much! What is your name you said?"

"You're very welcome! I didn't give you my name…"

"Where are you from?"

"I'm not allowed to provide that, Sir."

"Oh, I'm sorry, you know, the sound of your voice is very calming…very nice tone of your voice. You're a professional!"

"Thank you."

"You know, I am a filmmaker from LA…"

"Aha…" Samia is getting the idea quickly.

"Oh, what's your mobile number?"

"I am not allowed to provide you with that information, Sir!"

"You know, I'm always on the lookout for young talent and…"

Samia cuts him short," It was a pleasure to help you, is there anything else we can do for you today?"

"…and we're probably or most likely going to do the production of a feature film and looking to do the casting anytime soon… do you have any email, Skype? WhatsApp?…"

"Don't be stupid! Sir. Thank you for your business. Good bye."

Samia ends the call and looks at Oashni who grins.

"Thank you so much, Samia!"

"No worries, sweetheart."

They both smile at each other.

Samia starts,"No. 1 rule, never ever swear at customers! OK?"

"I'll call you!" adds Oashni with a naughty smile.

"If you don't know something, you might also ask customer - nicely - if you can put him or her on hold and get advice from one of your colleagues…"

"True." nods Oashni.

"Everyone knows something the others don't…"

"Yes."

"You're a smart and nice girl, we're all on the same team, we help each other… Oh, it is lunch time, something we should never forget as well – maybe this is rule No. 2, with a hungry stomach it is difficult to be gentle with customers…"

Samia – sits alone in the street restaurant "Talil's diner", which is entrenched between modern skyscrapers disappearing somewhere in the clouds, but that is the closest place to have some decent food for a good price. She eats rice with chillies & lamb and chats with someone on her phone. As per many smiles, hearts and kisses emoticons, we can judge it might be her lover. At some point - as she is excited - she almost drops her phone into the reddish sauce.

She smiles.

There are two men and one woman sitting at the bar and sip mango lassi with plenty of crushed ice through thickstraws. On the banana leaves there are some sweet rice coconut bowls with sun dried figs and other ingredients. One man kisses the girl while the other one holds behind his back the girls hand secretly. Samia notices this and shakes her head angrily. She feels suddenly lonely and writes to her lover, that she has to go back to work soon and types: "Bye for now!"…no more emoticons…

She continues eating her delicious food and drinks water from the bottle, but very little. She never drinks much as she is used to fasting - and not only during the Ramadan. She pulls the Quran book out of her stylish bag and starts reading… Her big beautiful black eyes shift from right to left fast as she feels a spiritual excitement. Samia is a very energetic young woman. She turns her face towards the ventilator and takes a sigh of relief. She touches her sweating forehead and tides up her black long hair. There is a music video playing in the TV hanging fixed by ropes on the palm tree, which provides shadow for most of the tables.

Samia returns to the office and walks through the big hall between the semi closed and open space boxes with the call center agents. It looks like an airport hall - that massive space it is. She holds files and her bag in her hands. Many of the staff greet her with sincere smile as she is both admired and beloved for her character qualities.

Samia is not ecstatic about her situation, but there are not many alternatives and she thinks,'We are all sucked into a never ending rat race. We get sucked in whether we want or not and it eventually kills us! I wish I could see my family more often! Before I became the sales manager and double my salary, I'd been working like crazy - 3 years without seeing my family - 3 long years before I could hug them! Here in India, I did start to sing… ut only when I am alone…when no-one listens… I wish I could work somewhere else. A place with cold weather, but people with warm hearts.'

"ARNOLD BRAUN"

It is an another winter freezing but sunny day. The sky is clean and has the colour of light blue. People walk the streets and enjoy the sun rays, which are today stronger than ever! The smell of morning coffee spreads through the steam of the thousands of the cups across the Cafés across the town. The sound of fresh crunchy croissants - being bitten by the hungry teeth of morning birds - returns from the hills in reverberations. There seems to be no working class existent in this city. All move so slow - as they were flying like the feathers in a soft breeze. The reflections of the sun - in the ornamented windows – hit Peter into his eyes as he admires the tranquil wonders of the silent historical buildings surrounding him like statues. He stops at the kiosk and orders a coffee to go and a croissant. A small bottle of whisky in the window-shop catches his eye for a moment, but he moves away stuffing his mouth with the pastry and sipping hot coffee with pleasure.

Peter arrives at the recruitment agency. The Signs says:

A.B. RECRUITMENT
"Excellent People Do Excellent Jobs"

Peter opens the door.

A man of about the same age as Peter greets him in his office. He holds a big hammer in his hand and there is a nail in between his sharp snow white teeth. The man is tall and slim, with his hair sticking from his head up - like the nails. He looks like an alien and his name is Arnold Braun.

Peter looks around the room to get the first impression of the person he is meeting.

There is a ladder close to the wall and a painting with a deer in the forrest on the floor. The walls are made of wood and one can not overlook the stuffed heads of wild animals and collection of guns hanging on them. Together with the other paintings with nature motifs. They both smile at each other as if they already knew themselves very well.

Peter a bit astonished,"Have we met before?"

"I was thinking the same thing."

They both laugh heartily and shake their hands.

Arnold pulls a chair from his desk," Please sit down. Make yourself at home…"

"Thank you."

"Coffee, Tea…something stronger?"

"Coffee will do me just fine, thanks!"

"I must have seen you somewhere!"

"No! I must have seen you somewhere!"

Arnold sits behind his desk and sighs,"That's some winter, isn't it?!"

"Tell me about it! I arrived recently from the sunny State of Louisiana…"

"I see…"

Arnold picks the phone and calls his assistant to bring hot coffee.

As he speaks with her - he asks Peter, if he wishes to have it black, stronger, with milk or without, sugar?, white or brown?, perhaps sweetener?… The two guys instantly fit together and they enjoy the interaction. Not like 2 gays, but rather like two old friends, who went together through - both harsh & happy times.

Arnold takes the word,"So, tell me…What's it gonna be? How long are you in town? In the Country? Let me guess. You'll love it here!

"You want to know it really?" Peter takes a brief look at the bigger picture of the room once again,"Are you a hunter or what?"

"Above all, I am the best headhunter!"

They both laugh again.

The assistant - a beautiful young girl - enters the room carrying a tray with the coffee, donuts and water.

Arnold kindly,"Thank you sweetie!" Pointing at the doughnuts,"Are these…"

The assistant answers immediately,"Home made? Yes, I made them myself. They're delicious…at least people say so… Hope you will like them!" twinkling to Peter.

"Oh you're so kind! Thank you so much!"

"You'll love them!"

The assistant smiles and places the plate with the doughnuts onto the table and the coffees in front of the gentlemen."…and some water too, should you get thirsty. The coffee is hot and strong! Where are you from, Sir?"

"New Orleans, Louisiana" He stands up. "My name is Peter."

"Samantha. Nice to meet you too."

Peter sits down,"Thank you. You're very kind."

"…so I'll leave you alone with Arnold, if you need anything…do call me, alright?"

"Thank you Sam!"

The assistant leaves the room and Arnold looks at Peter.

"So what you say?"

"I'm not sure what do you mean."

"About her!"

"I see, yeah! Listen, Arnold, I need to hire 300 employees for my hotel… Could you help me with that?"

"You can count on me! When do we start?"

"Let's start now!"grins and sips at his hot coffee.

"I think I have already the right Executive Housekeeping Manager and one great Bell Boy…"

Peter touches his ear and cripples his face,"…and maybe the Chef too!"

"That's great, by the way, legal paperwork will be needed. We need to take all the legal aspects into the consideration! This country is getting pretty tough regarding such matters…"

"…and I thought it was still like in the 90's here…"

"It is not!"

Peter is getting serious,"But, what worries me the most - at the moment - is security. You know, that place…my hotel…it's a massive property with a lot of valuable stuff inside! …and at the moment - the only inhabitants of this vast hotel complex - are a cute black hotel cat and myself…and who knows…maybe some ghosts…"

Arnold laughs.

Peter grins,"…well…in the silent dark nights…you don't want to be there on your own… really!"

"I do understand! Do you have a gun?"

"No, I do not!"

"Just between me and you…if you need one…"

"I guess, we should start with a couple of security guys."

Arnold opens his notebook and writes a few notes,"…and you will need a good lawyer too… to start with. I know one!"

"Great!"

Arnold making more notes,"…and a smart accountant!"

"Perfect! But first the security!"

Arnold in German,"Aber sicher!"

"Are you German?" wonders Peter.

"Well, after 25 years spent here, I guess I'm more Czech than German…"

"Great, you know the place very well then…Then I feel I'm in the right hands, Sir!"

"Spot on. With me on board, you've got nothing to worry about."

"SEBASTIAN HUNTER"

The roofs of Paris are covered by snow. Sebastian sits in his old car and speaks to himself, "Today is Friday and I travel by car from my village house - as I do every weekday - to the bank in Paris. I am bit late, because today I don't want to go there, because I am not in the mood at all, because maybe I'm still drunk and because I want to kill my boss! And if I'll speak with him, I might just strangle him! And if I'll see his ugly white face, which reminds me so much of a scull, I might use my perfect, well trained side-kick, to decapitate him on the spot!

The veteran car moves through the streets until he stops in the underground garage of the bank. Sebastian, wearing a long rain coat, gets out of his car and walks quickly through the garage into the bank offices. He takes the stairs by 2 or 3 per step.

Arriving at his office next to the security room, he opens the door and checks if the two seriously overweight security guys, one black & one white, observe the monitors. They eat burgers, fries with ketchup and drink hot coffee from big mugs. One security guard observes on his laptop some movie by one eye and the other works on crosswords in today's newspapers. Sebastian, sighs and quickly closes the door. He throws his stuff into his office and starts to make his swift round through the bank, like he always does in the morning. He walks through the main office, the bankers feel annoyed by his hastily moves through their territory. They look up from their computers - some angry - some with curiosity.

All this is also seen on the monitors in the security room.

"Hey, Tony, look!" says one of the security guys.

"What's up" replies the other one.

"Our Boss looks a bit angressive today..."

Both security guards stare at one of the monitors – with their mouth wide open - just to see that their Boss Sebastian Hunter, grabs one of the computers and smashes it against the wall.

From the hall Sebastian enters the directors office, without asking for any permition to enter. The director sits behind his big desk in the massive chair. They formally greet and shake their hands. But Sebastian pays particular attention to that handshake to make sure his grasp is more firm and applies killing pressure, so his Boss bursts screaming at once.

"What to heck are you doing, Seb?!"

"What I've seen will hurt you more than this handshake, if I disclose it... So leave Agnes alone, do you understand?!"

"You're crazy, did you forget - Agnes is my wife!"

"Maybe on paper, but that's about it!"

"Get out of my office, now!"

Sebastian pointing his finger at his boss."Don't you fucking touch her again! If I'll see more bruises on her face or hands... I'll come back to rip your ears off!"

The director is yelling, "Get out!"

Sebastian leaves and closes the door carefully keeping his temper on level calm.

The boss swears, picks the phone and dials. He speaks to his wife, "Really?... You're not sleeping with him anymore?...We just had a nasty argument...Yes... Yes, if he comes again...Of course, if he does something to me, I'll call the police... Yes...immediately!"

The office door burst open again - Sebastian is back!

Sebastian furious,"One more thing...Today is my last day at work. I've got something else!

Consider this as my verbal resignation."

"I am calling the police, I'll see you in court!"

"Well, in that case, I'll use that tape...And by the way...you can rest assured... that I might use it at any time just for the pleasure of fucking you up."

"Fuck off!"

Sebastian smiles and as he turns away - as he is about to leave the office - he puts his trousers together with pants halfway down - showing to his boss his ass..."You won't see my white ass anymore!" Then he puts his trousers back up and smashes the door.

The boss runs to the door as they are being smashed right in front of his nose. He punches the door with both hands swearing. The voice of his wife from his phone calls him back. He comes back to the phone."Yes, it was him! ...Do you want me to call the police?...What, if he's on his way to you?"

He stands up with his phone on his ear and looks out of the window down at the street. Seb's veteran car departs off the bank property into the streets of Paris.

"AUDITION"

There is classic telephone standing on the massive dark heavy wood office table.

The snow crystals, glued to the window glass, shimmer in the moon's silver-blue light. Peter Willington sleeps on the sofa in his suit and cowboy shoes on. His position is pretty funny - he lays on his belly with his head leaning against the arm of the sofa. There are piles of papers and files spread across the wooden floor, on the table, all over the room.

There are several identical clocks on the wall behind the table showing the different times in different timezones:

NEW YORK - PARIS - MOSCOW - MUMBAI - BEIJING - AUCKLAND - NEW ORLEANS

The hotel cat walks slowly across the table onto the window sill. The cat turns its head, for a short moment, in the direction of the sofa, where Peter sleeps. We humans would see just a little in that darkness, but the cat sees a slightly blurred bright image. Then the cat stares - without a movement – out of the window.

After his nap, Peter gets up and sits behind the table on which, the cat sleeps with his body positioned in a circle. He can hear suddenly two human voices and steps.

Layla, accompanied by Mr. Tea, appear in the door.

The cat opens his eyes, turns his head and glances in their direction.

Layla in good mood,"Good morning boss."

Mr. Tea adding,"How did you sleep?"

"Morning guys. Good. How about you?"

"The breakfast is ready…"says Layla with her smooth voice.

"Oh, good! I'll come in a moment."

Mr. Tea asks,"Coffee or tea?"

"Nothing against you, but I hate tea. Coffee please! Black & strong. Thank you!"

Layla and Mr. Tea hesitate their standing in the door…

"I'll be there in a moment."

"It's just…you told us this a couple of times today already…"

"This time I am coming for sure. I promise!"

Peter looks around to surveille of the mess in the room. His sight falls on the clock with the sign "MUMBAI" under it. It shows the time 9 p.m.! Peter opens his eyes wide and moves swiftly to "PARIS"…

"Good God! Is it really 4 o'clock in the afternoon?"

The cat stands up - off one file he did sleep on - and jumps down, runs out of the office.

A picture on that file strikes Peter's eye! Peter picks it up and checks the details in the Curriculum Vitae – Samia Sahar.

He does study it with an unexpected interest. She looks attractive and her professional background is quiet impressive.

In the section "A bit about me" he reads the following:

"The spicy food, Indian TV dramas and heartily people, family & friends keep me going with a reason. I prefer to keep my life simple. I love to relax in the Hammam and enjoy cooking for others. People say that the cakes made by me are the most delicious in the universe :)."

The other page contains the accompanying letter, where the applicant expresses her interest in the position of Sales & Marketing Manager in Peter's hotel. There is a phone number at the bottom of the page. Peter suddenly realises the papers smell nice and he touches his nose with them softly. Without a reason - tears scroll down Peter's wrinkled old face.

"KARLOVY VARY BY AIR"

It is a bright sunny winter day. A helicopter circles above the city of Karlovy Vary, which is surrounded by small hills with forrest – everything is covered by the glittering snow.

The Chinese multimillionaire, Jonathan Lee in a purple suit and his wife in extravagant outfit sit in the helicopter accompanied by a real estate agent and of course…by the pilot. They sip Champagne from the stylish Flutes as the taste of Champagne is greatly affected by the shape of the glass! They enjoy their life and what the future will offer to them.

Jonathan points to the window,"How do you like the view, dear?"

"Hey, Jon, you see that massive building down there?" pointing with her finger.

"Yeah."

"That would fit into our business! A hotel!"

"Yep. Great addition to our portfolio of Casinos. Funny…I've never thought of this one…"

"…so now you have it! Something to think about, Jon!"

The real estate agents remarks,"I am sorry to say, it has been sold recently… Ma'm…"

"Ohh, what a pity…Why is it we always come late…Jon… Tell me!"

"Hmm…"

Provoking him more,"oh…do you remember that couple, who bought that stunning spacious villa in those Caribbean Islands?"

"Yes, yes…that was an amazing one!! True, true."

The world fades grey for Jon and his wife suddenly. The real estate manager has a strong empathy for the rich and is a hungry wolf - he smells the big opportunity here! He drinks an another glass of that expensive golden elixir and concocts a charming optimism triggering smile."…but cheer up guys, you know I'm the best at what I do! I'll think about it and see what we can do."

The rich couple glances at him with cold hope in their faces, they are very relaxed from the outside view, but inside Jonathan is already calculating and thinking of a strategy, whereas his wife just wishes, that "her Jon" is finding a solution to get her idea realized. The real estate agent looks out of the window and for him the world shines bright now - empowered by bubbles and phantasies!

"JAMES & JANE"

The same day, after a long time of haze, darkness and uncomfortable blizzards, Peter Willington cleans the heavy snow off the road to the main entrance of the hotel. He wears a funny winter hat and ear pieces listening to some music. As he works hard, he finds something interesting in the snow! It is a bottle of "Becherovka". Peter smiles and picks it up to examine it closer. He opens it and smells,"Wow, smells good!"

The cat observes Peter from one of the windows.

A taxi arrives.

Peter stops working and stares at the arriving Taxi with the bottle in his hand. Three people exit the car: the taxi driver opens the door for a lady and from the other side jumps out a man in his mid 40's.

James Willington comes to shake the hand of his father Peter."…and you did claim, that you'd given up drinking for good, dad! Let me smell it!"

Peter happy to see his son,"I just found it in the snow here!"

"You're funny guy, dad. You always made very elaborate excuses."

"Glad you came, son! How did you persuade Jane? Tell me!"

Jane approaches the two men. "He promised me a child! After all these years…"

"That's a great decision, James - son! Just wondering…do you really mean it?"

James laying his hand around Jane's arms and smiling,"Yeah! We finally decided, dad!…and what place would be better to bring new life into the World, than this amazing hotel! How did you find it?"

"It was a good deal. A great investment!"

Jane curious,"so…when do you want to open it?"

"I guess you should taste the Spaghetti Bolognese I've been cooking since this morning. Let's go inside!"

"Oh, I'm so excited, I want to see everything and I'm so hungry!"

"Imagine I came here also hungry and tired from the flight, but the only thing I found were old bisquits and some coffee powder…"

Peter, James and Jane sit around the round shaped table and eat. James and Jane taste the Becherovka.

James tries to test Peter,"Are you sure you don't want some, dad?"

"Hell, no!"

Jane is much more interested in other things than the habits of her father in law,"So, what is your master plan, Peter?"

"Well, first thing we have to do, is to hire the core staff along with a well established HR professional who'll recruit talent for the general staff.

James enthusiastic,"Let's do it!"

"Oh, by the way, I did already hire our HR Manager! Great guy! And amazing hunter! His name is Arnold Braun, German origin, means punctuality and correctness, that is what we really need.

James with a smile,"Wow, I'm really getting excited about it! But something different Dad, do those old cellars here have some particularly fine wine?"

"They sure do! I will show them to you as I want you to have a look yourselves!!"

Pushing back his chair,"Let's go everybody!"

"ROJO"

To have his excellent wine cellar well proposed to the customers, Peter decided to hire a excellent Sommelier & Cellar Master. To test the applicants, Peter asked to prepare the boardroom for a wine tasting. The room is lit by many candles and a group of people sit in their winter clothes around the table.

The room enters a thin underweight man in his mid 40's with long black hair tied up into a pony tail. He has round shaped red glasses on his eyes and a long black coat touching the wooden floor. His steps make a crackling noise. His name is Señor Ramirez de Ribes alias Rojo, he comes from a bankrupt old Catalan aristocratic family. He has communists beliefs, but sometimes behaves like a fascist. He likes to interfere personal safety circle distance when speaking face to face. Sometimes he touches his opponents chin as if he would like to hold the scull in the palm of his hand - like Prince Hamlet in William Shakespeare's play…or perhaps rather like a predator in the jungle…Rojo likes 2 colours - devilish red and cold mortuary blue. He likes blood and wine and he thinks he is the alien… from Ridley Scott's movies.

Rojo collects small statues of film monsters and heroes and wears T-shirts - predominantly - with the "Alien" motif on them. Rojo is also a photographer and his hobby is astronomy.

When he was younger, he was the vocalist in a "heavy metal" band. Above all - he is obsessed about wine and indeed is true a Master Sommelier - educated in one of the best schools called the Burgundy Wine School located in Beaune, France.

It is already dark outside despite it is only 5 o'clock afternoon and snow flakes bombard the window glasses.

Present are: Owner - Peter Willington, his son GM - James Willington, son's wife Jane, HR Manager - Arnold Braun, Housekeeper Manager - Layla Dragunescu, Bellboy - Mr. Tea and the cat.

The shadow enters the room first and then the thin creepy man follows. The cat displays exaggerated response - as he is scared - and hides under the table.

Rojo greets politely,"Good evenining Ladies and Gentlemen…"

Peter excuses,"Please forgive us the conditions. The power went out."

Arnold takes over," Thank you for coming. How was your journey Mr. Ramirez de Ribes?"

"Sir, just Rojo please, the last name confuses everybody including me. I am Rojo for everyone. To answer your question, the journey was ok, just some strong turbulences above Paris……glad we finally landed…"

Layla stands up to help Rojo from his coat,"Please let me take your coat, or do you want to keep it, as it is really fresh in here?

"No it's fine, I prefer cold weather. The cold wind…" he speaks very loud, as he still listens to noisy metal music and has headphones on. Rojo wears a T-Shirt with the scary motif of the alien from the Ridley Scott's film "Covenant". Behind his belt with many steel spikes he has an "old school" walkman. He switches off the noise,"Sorry, I had it on all way and forgot about it."

The people - sitting around the table - look down at themselves - with the message, 'OMG. Where the heck this guy comes from?!'

The snow falls in clusters onto the roof of the hotel. The moon is covered by heavy clouds that are approaching fast. A storm is about to come. The first strike of the flash hits the forrest surrounding the hotel and the noise of the storm encircles the massive building in its reverberations.

Rojo is pulling up a basket with a dusty bottle of wine placed vertically in it,"Here, this is for you… it's a Rioja from my private collection."

Layla leans over and wants to grab the bottle from the basket…but Rojo is protecting the basket with the bottle,"Oops…hold on!! I'm sorry madame…It needs to stay in the vertical position, as there is a sediment on the bottom, it is called "depot". The bottle shouldn't be shaken."

Peter is comfortable with the explanaition,"Oh it is very kind of you, Mr. …"

"Señor! Señor Ramirez de Ribes, but as I said before, please call me simply Rojo. This is my nickname. Since my childhood, I'm used to it… Nice to meet you Mr. Willington, great to see you all!"

The people in the room again exchange "eye" messages 'the way that man behaves - elegant & noble - is simply not coherent with his appearance'

Mr. Tea brings the big wine glasses and places them onto the table, one glass in front of each person.

Rojo pulls a decantation glass bottle and sommelier set of cork openers, instruments and small knifes in a dark wooden box out of his suitcase and places it onto the table as he was about to run a magician show. He grabs one of the candles from the table with a rather rhetoric question,"May I?"

"Sure, please do!"

Rojo opens the bottle carefully pulling up the cork. Then places the white clean napkin over the decantation glass. The lit candle is now directly under the top of the bottle as he carefully and slowly pours the wine through the napkin into the decantation glass. Rojo's eyes resemble the eyes of the fanatic communist revolutionary - as he was about to overthrow the authoritarian government of Cuban president Fulgencio Batista.

Rojo starts the decantation process and talks,"You know, each Spanish region's wine is as fiercely independent as its people… We Catalans have a culture that differs greatly from our Castilian, Galician or Andalusian countrymen, Catalonian wines have little in common with those from the rest of Spain…

Mr. Tea moves closer to Rojo to witness the magic with shimmering eyes. "Catalonian wines tend to be full bodied and high in alcohol, due to the grape varieties and the region's warm weather - conditions. But Catalonia's best wines also feature intense minerality derived from vineyards planted on granite, chalk and fractured slate soils. However, this wine-diamond comes from La Rioja! Yes!! This one is from my family's private collection… This expensive and sought-after wine is made from 70 percent Tempranillo, 12 percent Garnacha, 13 percent Mazuelo and 5 percent Graciano. This very special wine is made only in exceptional years! Oh…You will fall in love with this wine! I am, so sure! You will get trapped, my dear…There is no escape from Marques de Murrieta: Castillo d'Ygay Gran Reserva Especial year 2007. This particular year was only released to the market in 2015 – after long 8 years."

Mr. Tea suddenly stands up and runs silently away from the room followed by the cat, who is the only one in the room, who knows why…

Rojo is continuing the never ending decantation and real Spanish torture of the people in the room.

James thinks,'This guy is crazy!'

Rojo as if he was not present,"…and during those long 8 years - this eternity life elixir – was being created. Now, let's talk business!"

Peter interrupts,"Oh wait…I thought we would taste the wine first…" but then he freezes as he realises, he did stop drinking some time ago and feels the two pairs of burning eyes - side look - of his son James and his wife Jane - on himself…I mean, the people at this table are excited to taste it, I am sure! Am I wrong?"

Peter looks around just to see thirsty children in the boardroom lit by many candles - everybody freezing due to the electricity outage.

Jane with her eyes focusing on the wine,"Oh, I would love to, it seems to be an exciting wine…You are a true connaisseur, Señor Rojo!"

Layla adds, "Yes please! I can't wait any longer!" and stares at the manly hands of Rojo…

Peter Willington notices Layla's affiliation all of a sudden and feels somehow uneasy about it…

Mr. Tea burst the door open accompanied by the cat. In one hand the wooden board with a selection of cheese and their appropriate condiments. In the other hand he carries plates and small forks.

The cat has a big slice of cheese in his small lovely mouth.

The room becomes vivid in great expectations!

Rojo turns to Mr. Tea,"A great idea, young boy!"

Mr. Tea freezes a bit as he examines the message underneath, the tone and wording… He is not young anymore! He is an old experienced man, despite he looks young! He gifts to Rojo an ominous alert look.

Rojo with the smile of "this evening" winner,"This particularly precious wine now needs 2 hours to breath!"

The people at the table look angry. Only Rojo and the cat enjoy the moment.

James annoyed,"2 hours? OMG, I will die! You are a fanatic, man!"

Layla with excitement,"You are not fanatic but fantastic!!"

Peter back to business,"Mr. Rojo, what are your salary expectations?"

"Certainly not cheap, but a very good value it is, for the quality it delivers…,"Rojo smiling at the dusty bottle.

"Tell us Señor, please, how does it taste?!" Layla ask curious.

"My biggest pleasure, madame!"

Most of the people's faces in the room get pale. The Spanish torture is about to continue for 2 more hours - ideally…

"THE DEER HUNTERS"

It is a sunny winter day. The land is covered by a thick layer of fresh snow. There are two hunters with guns following a deer in the forrest. They move real slow and quiet. There is an absolute silence in the forrest and if one could hear the sounds of frozen trees, it would definitely be here. The two men are, Jonathan Lee and his new advisor but also regular customer of one of his Casinos in Karlovy Vary, Juan Alexandro Polpo. There is one - black guy - who slightly drops behind, it is Lee's bodyguard Bono Eins. He wears a big red hat with pom-pom and looks bit funny as he struggles to make his steps in the deep snow between the massive tall trees.

There is an owl - that sits on one of the tree branches – and which observes the black guy down below.

Bono seems to be exhausted but more and more annoyed by the snow as he gets trapped and nearly falls! He sighs.

The two guys turn towards him with angry faces.

Juan puts his pointing finger to his lips in the gesture "Keep silent!".

The black guy - raises his right hand up in the apologetic gesture. He has thick red gloves on and red sunglass. His face is ornamented by the short well groomed frozen beard.

There is a sudden move of a shadow with big horns ahead of the 3 guys – a bit far from them - in between the trees and shrubs.

Snow starts falling again and big flakes slowly land on the hats of Jonathan and Juan. They prepare their guns.

Jonathan looks through the scope, which is equipped with a graphic image pattern (a reticle) mounted in an optically appropriate position in the optical system to give an accurate aiming point – the deer. He whispers,"Beautiful! Fucking beautiful!"and then towards Juan,"Juan!"

Juan crawling slowly, closer to his boss,"Yes Boss?!"

"I've seen today's article, Juan!"

"What article?"

"About the hotel Egeria…"

"Yes, Boss and?"

"They're looking for a GM's Assistant."

"I see! I get the idea! You want to move one of your pawns into position! Right?"

"That's exactly, what I am planning and going to do!"

Jonathan's eye moves back onto the focus of the rifle. The deer stands there - lovely framed - and stares right into the focus now. The snow flakes fly in the air as if they were the most beautiful bird's feathers, so light and so pleasant to be touched by.

Juan leans towards the ear of Jonathan and whispers, "The hotel Egeria will be yours"…but Jonathan does not hear anything as he is now fully focused on the deer! He stops breathing.

Then he just remarks, "I know!"…and pulls the trigger.

The shot tears apart the forrest silence brutally and the birds fly up off the branches in an attempt to escape and sail into the grey sky.

The deer falls dead into the white snow sprinkled by the red drops of blood.

Bono sticks a little branch of the tree into the mouth of the deer to check, if it is definitely dead. Yes, indeed it is.

"KEY PEOPLE"

Peter Willington, his son, his son's wife, the accountant Rachel Goldstein, the lawyer Petr Cimicky and the head of housekeeping - Layla Dragunescu sit around a square table with piles of papers, notebooks and mugs of coffee on it. They do eat sandwiches. In front of them – next to the flip chart - stands recruitment agency owner and remote hotel HR manager Arnold Braun in his typical black leather suit and white turtleneck. He holds an apple in his hand and chews a portion of it.

The hotel cat grabs and steals one of the sandwiches and runs away.

Laughter burst out into the morning break silence.

There are words on the big white paper of the flip chart, written by green marker pen.

THE KEY PERSONNEL

CHEF
CHEF ASSISTANT
PASTRY CHEF
SOMMELIER - THE CELLAR MASTER
SPA MANAGER
SALES & MARKETING MANAGER
BANQUETING MANAGER
RESTAURANT MANAGER
F&B MANAGER
HR MANAGER / Arnold Braun
ACCOUNTANT / Rachel Goldstein
LAWYER / Petr Cimicky
THE HEAD OF RECEPTION
THE HEAD OF HOUSEKEEPING / Layla Dragunescu
SECURITY CHIEF

IT MANAGER
REPAIRMAN
GARDENER
WINDOW DRESSER
MAÎTRE D'HÔTEL
CONCIERGE MANAGER
THE GENERAL STAFF

BELL BOY / Mr. Tea
COOKS
COLD KITCHEN COOKS
DISHWASHERS
RESTAURANT WAITERS
BARMEN
BANQUETING WAITERS
SPA PROFESSIONALS
DOORMEN
WAREHOUSEMAN
SECURITY GUARDS
ROOM SERVICE WAITERS
DOORMEN
HOUSEKEEPING STAFF
PIANO PLAYER (ext.)

Arnold starts,"Now, which is highest priority, Peter? James?"

"I guess the Chef! And.." while Peter is touching his ear,"I know about someone!"

"THE LAST DAY BEFORE HOTEL LAUNCH"

It is a freezing, but cloudless day. Peter Willington holds in his both hands a big mug of hot black coffee and stares down from the window of his hotel apartment. He can see many "ants" running in front of his hotel and thinks,'The atmosphere is rather tense, because tomorrow, the first guests will arrive…oh …along with the first star guest… that - once famous - Hollywood actor and a former boxing champion! …so early…are we really ready? I'm excited about it, but I also feel nervous! Please God help us!'

The complete hotel staff is gathering in front of the hotel Egeria. All together 300 employees - some of them see each other for the very first time - like the soldiers in the battle of Thermopylae, except, they don't have real shields and spikes. They wear different uniforms depending on the department they belong to. The managers try to coordinate their teams, but it still looks like a wild confused crowd. The chaos is in place until a photographer with his assistant arrive.

The banqueting manager - a woman in her mid 20's - black long hair tied up into a pony tail hands over some pink scarfs to all staff.

Peter opens his eyes wide,"What the hell…"

He puts the mug noisily on the table and runs out of his room, grabbing his coat on his way.

Peter approaches the banqueting manager and grabs one of the pink scarfs to hold it in front of the banqueting manager's surprised eyes,"Whose damn idea was this?"

"It was my idea, boss."The banqueting manager says.

"Throw that shit away."

"But..why?"

"Because I have said so!"

"I thought - you know the colour - these days - is so in…"

"Forget it! Throw them all into the bin!"

"It was the Sales & Marketing department's decision!"

"Don't argue with me, just do it!"

"You're the boss!"

"Better you don't forget it!"

The banqueting manager shakes her head in disbelief and collects the pink scarfs back swearing badly in Italian. The chef Sylvester helps her out with collecting & telling her to calm down.

The photographer starts with moving the members of the staff - like the pawns on a chess board - and her young boy assistant sets the lights. Very soon, all will be ready to go!

The photographer surprised to the banqueting manager,"Where did all the pink scarfs go? Put them back on, people will look great and fresh on the photos!"

Peter hides behind the bell boy Mr. Tea, feeling guilty. The banqueting manager looks around in looking for her boss…

Mr. Tea smiles and says to the photographer, "This is the Egeria launch and we're not sheep, so there's no need to label the livestock! Madame."

Peter grins behind Mr. Tea.

Peter to Mr. Tea, tapping his arm, "Well said, Mr. Tea, well said!"

The photograper looks at Peter,"You Sir, you're the owner of this hotel, right?"

"That's very true, young lady!"

"Come forward to the first line - into the middle - where you belong to!"

"Me?"

"Yes, Sir, you, come forward - quick!"

Peter feels suddenly shy, but slowly crawls through his staff to the front line. The photographer's assistant approaches him, takes off his coat and starts to tide up his hair a bit and adjust the suit…tie…shirt… Peter feels bit uneasy about it.

"That's ok, boy, that's fine!"

But the boy continues his work with soft arrogant smile as if he was enjoying it. Peter leans towards him and whispers to his ear,"Get the fuck away from me!" Then he glances at the photographer to double check, if she does not have any suspicions. The boy's face gets the features of an insulted girl and moves away.

Peter takes a sigh of relief.

At the back line of the group, the Maître d' hotel forms his subordinate waiters with a smile and kind snapshot notes. He is the youngest and thinks he is the most confident, best & sharp looking, with elegant manners, the only one. He adjusts for example one of his colleague's bow and says,"Now you look perfect, soldier! Next time it will be hundred push ups!"

Or - he comes to a blonde waitress with the longest pony tail he has ever seen, he grabs it to his hand and says,"I would love you to beat me naked with that whip, baby!"

She laughs and replies: "Don't be stupid, better go to the toilet and jerk off!"

"As long as you go with me…, will you?"

She hits him back:"I prefer real men with something to play with. Not small boys…"

He returns: "Oh baby, I am a big man! Trust me!"

She laughs.

One of the colleagues of the Maître d'hôtel - the tallest guy - taps the head of waiter in the row down before him with the words, "You're getting bold my friend! Make sure you don't spoil our photographs!"

People start laughing and the unfortunate waiter feels insulted. His face gets red. He is to weak to resist and better says nothing.

The photographer orders the crowd to smile bright! And as she takes the first pictures, the Maître d'hôtel puts black leather gloves on, as he does not want to freeze and get sick. Then he glances with soft grin at guy, who has just bullied the poor waiter in the line below him, and as the photographer takes another shot - he gives a short distance - yet powerful - warning punch to the side of the bully's belly. The tall guy screams, makes a grimace and turns towards the attacker - the Maître d'hôtel tells him with smile, "…just wanted to double check your ribs! How well done - they are…" and laughs in a distinctive, his very own, style. Besides…he is confident to receive and sustain the pain of the punch too…

After everybody has left the shooting to prepare the hotel for the next day's opening, the photographer asks Peter to join him and to choose the best pictures of his staff.

People's positions, their body language and their facial expressions in the photos change. This reveals some certain facts and predictions…

On the photos they see:

1. In the front line the Security Chief Sebastian Hunter and GM's wife Jane stare at each other's eyes…
2. The tall guy in the back top line has a funny grimace in his face and the Maître d'hôtel stares at him with laughter.
3. The tall guy in the back top line has a painful grimace in his face and the Maître d'hôtel stares at him with laughter.
4. In the front line the Security Chief Sebastian Hunter and GM's wife Jane stare at each other's eyes and they see the angry eyes of GM James Willington
5. Owner Peter Willington hides behind the bell boy Mr. Tea.
6. The photographer and in front of him the staff on the stairs - all perfect and smiling.
7. The banqueting manager & chef Sylvester with their hands around each other's arms standing there proud with the pink scarfs on their necks…
8. The owner with the hotel cat in his hands - the cat looks at Peter and Peter smiles at the camera.
9. The Sales & Marketing manager Samia Sahar stares angrily towards the direction, where Peter stands - throwing away her pink scarf.
10. Samia and the hotel cat in her hands smile at the camera.
11. The Executive Housekeeping Manager Layla Dragunescu hugs with the owner of the hotel.
12. Layla strangulates Peter with the pink scarf and laughs. Peter looks angry and scarred.

13. HR Manager and GM James Willington shake their hands in the gesture message: "Well done!"
14. The final best photo of the smiling staff frozen in a jump in the garden with their hands up.

The chef Sylvester approaches GM James Willington with worrying face - telling him, "The power in the kitchen went out…"

James pulls a mobile phone out of his suit pocket, staying cool as usual.

"Sir, that special salmon from the Scottish family farm - the one for our VIP - is spoiled…"

"No! Tell me that's not true!"

"I'm afraid it is!"

James Willington drops his mobile phone back into his suit pocket. They both stare at each other thinking whom to blame for it. The cat enters the scene and drops another dead mouse into the snow and looks up at those two - and the two glance towards the cheerful crowd as they were searching urgently for the first aid.

The owner Peter and Layla discuss something as they walk into the hotel.

The security chief Sebastian and GM's wife chat standing by the cocktail table and drink mould wine served by one of the waiters. They smile at each other.

GM James sees it - his wife with that security chief…! and his face turns pale.

Sylvester puts his hands on his hips and stares down to the ground thinking.

The two electricians arrive in quarter of an hour and work hard to fix the electricity in the kitchen. They look very similar - as if they were 2 brothers. The chef walks the kitchen up and down like a tiger in a cage. GM's assistant Juan Alexandro Polpo walks in and asks Sylvester: "So how is it going? All ready for the opening?"

"Oh, better don't ask me!"

Juan makes a quick surveillance of the kitchen to witness the cooks moving stuff, preparing stuff, running chaotically from place to place.

"I hope you know, what you are doing…"

"That damn electricity! The salmon – delivered fresh and alive from the Scottish farm - suffocated due to lack of oxygen."

"So what? What's wrong with the fact that its dead? It wouldn't be much more alive on the plate…would it be?!"

"It was dead too long time…"

"I see… That's not a good start, not at all…"

Mr. Tea appears in the door, "Hey guys, what's up?"

"You'll need to go fishing tonight, Mr. Tea!" says Juan with a smile to him.

"Says who?"

"Just kidding!"

"Hey, Sylvester, I'll think of something!"

"Really Mr. Tea? All the shops are closed tomorrow!"

"What if I catch a Rainbow Trout?! Could you prepare it in such a way that they can't tell?"

"Forget it!"

"Why?" comes from Juan.

"I'll tell you, what you can do! Come with me guys to my office."

Juan and Mr. Tea follow the chef to his small office. They close the door and they discuss their plan.

"VIP NO. 1"

It is early morning, the streets are empty, the vapour leans out of the underground canals lit by the silver blue moon light. The sun on the other side already wakes up and slowly rises from behind the predominantly Renaissance buildings.

A man in his mid 80's, however still pretty well built walks with his grand daughter through the streets and admire the architectural beauty of this magic place. The man is a once famous Hollywood actor and former boxing champion from Philadelphia.

He speaks to her with deep voice,"I've read that this town was established in 1370 by King Charles IV and was built up during a variety of architectural periods, however most of the architecture of the city dates from the Renaissance and later, we are talking 19th century. Most of the earlier architecture of the town was destroyed either by floods, fires or war."

"Oh Grandpa, tell me again about, when you were an actor!"

"Later little girl, later. Now let us enjoy this beautiful town…"

The man glances at her and then shifts his sight somewhere through the buildings far beyond the horizon.

For relaxing his body and soul he asked for some treatments in the hotel spa and as a VIP the team has prepared a mud bath for the beginning, where he closes his eyes in full relaxation. The pleasant music supports him to fall asleep and he starts to dream, 'From the haze emerges a film camera on a dolly with cameraman and director. Their faces are blurred … Two boxers fight in the haze of a boxing ring… he sits - being now old - in one corner and his opponent in the other. He can not see his opponent's face. The old man tries to zoom onto his face. He realises that his opponent has a white scull instead of face from flesh and two deepest black holes where he should have the eyeballs! The old man sighs. Sweat and blood covers his old broken body. He looks up as a beautiful "ring girl" enters the ring carrying a sign that displays the number of the upcoming round - the number 10. She walks in slow motion towards him and whispers something to his ear.'

The next morning at the restaurant, the VIP table has been prepared in the corner to guarantee utmost privacy.

"Good morning, Grandpa!" and the actor is turning towards the voice from his grand daughter arriving to the table. He smiles and with invisible tears in his tired, kind eyes,"Yes sweetheart?"

"…will there be a concert tonight?

"Yes! A concert will be tonight!"

"…and fireworks?"

"…and fireworks too!"

"..and carousels?"

A bit astonished about the question,"…carousels…? Oh, no my child, but very soon we will go to some other place, where it's warmer."

"OK, I understand!"

"Good. Now, try to eat some of those cute pancakes with berries, will you?"

He pours the maple sirup over the pancakes on the plate in front of the small girl. The waitress comes with the kettle offering some more hot coffee. The old man nods. The waitress pours the coffee and the old man scrutinises her elegant soft skin young hand. Then she comes to the small girl, leans kindly towards her with brightest smile,"Would you like me to bring you some chocolate?"

Then she turns to her grandfather,"Can she have chocolate Sir?"

"Sure she can! Very kind of you! Thank you!"

"SALMON FISHING"

In the early morning hours two men were driving to the hotel "Guardian", GM's assistant Juan Alexandro Polpo and Bellboy Mr. Tea. They are now standing in the car park of the hotel, they sip hot coffee from paper cups. Juan plays to be a bit afraid,"Are you sure, you want to do that?"

"Juan, what else can we do? Everything is closed…"

"Well, I guess it's still better than fishing at night on a frozen river."

"I'm not so sure about that!"

Mr. Tea undresses the winter coat to reveal his cook outfit. He puts the white hat on and is about to leave the car.

"Good luck, Mr. Tea!"

"Yeah, thanks, I'll need it!"

Mr. Tea - dressed as a cook - sneaks into the hotel "Guardian" and follows the kitchen smell and soon is between the busy kitchen staff.

Suddenly the Chef grabs his arm without even looking at Mr. Tea,"YOU! Come with me!"

The Chef drags the unfortunate Mr. Tea to the kitchen range with about dozen of pans with boiling food, sauces, soups and stuff.

"Take care of this!"

Mr. Tea stares at the pans on the stove - his eyes wide open.

Outside Juan observes his watch nervously, "Where the hell is this guy?"

Mr. Tea mixes the sauces and more orders for breakfast specials come in! He is trapped. Luckily, back in his job for Chef Sylvester Cavallo in the Italian restaurant, he did help a lot in the kitchen. Anyway, the Chef of the hotel "Guardian" and the other cooks keep shouting at him - as he is slow. And more orders keep coming in. Mr. Tea is lost and his heart pumps the blood through his shaking veins faster and stronger. He sweats in his reddish face. He has a sensation, he will faint anytime soon in this hell's kitchen. He whispers, "God, if you exist, please, help me!"

At this moment, the tall overweight waiter - who looks like the devil in person - bursts the door open, shouting,"The group is already here! 101x times Scottish salmon with Champagne-butter sauce!"

Mr. Tea spots two young cooks-trainees, "Hey guys - get me that Scottish salmon, will you!"

"We don't know, where it is…"

Mr. Tea looks at the Chef in the search for help. At the very same moment a senior cook arrives with his set of knifes,"Go with them, I'll take over!"

Mr. Tea to the youngsters, not knowing where to go,"Guys, come with me!"

The Chef observes Mr. Tea with suspicion and Mr. Tea feels that he is endangered, so he grabs those two trainees, "Let's go!"

On their way he spots an old but fast dish washer, "Hey, where's the fish? I'm the new one here…" But the dishwasher does not speak English - he speaks Ukrainian only.

Mr. Tea, "OK guys, follow me!"

On their way to the stores in the cellar, Mr. Tea spots another cook, who helps them to find the way. Finally they arrive to the sea food fridge. Mr. Tea stares at the piles of boxes with the variety of fish. The trainees hide behind him.

Mr. Tea questiones himself, "So which one of you is the Scottish salmon…?"

The youngsters also stare at the fish in the boxes. Nobody knows!

Juan stares at his watch in the car and shakes his head, "We're not going to make it…".

At this moment, Mr. Tea bursts the door open! Mr. Tea looks fat – or better pregnant - as he struggles to fix himself into the seat inside the car.

"Where were you?"

"Don't ask me!"

"Did you steal it?"

"I earned it!"

There is various action in the hotel as it is already lunch time. "Hotel" jazz music flows lazily from the speakers. The hostess checks the reservations in the book placed at the restaurant reception desk. The Maître d' hotel approaches her to flirt…

At the ballroom, the banqueting waiters are busy preparing the round tables for the Gala Dinner for the official hotel Egeria launch.

The Pyrotechnicians prepare the fireworks in the garden for the grand opening night to come.

The guests arrive at the reception to check-in.

The car with Mr. Tea and Juan moves fast on the road to the hotel Egeria - getting, time to time, real close to going out of the control.

"Either the chef will kill us…or…you will…Juan!"

"Don't worry. I used to drive in Bogota - no rules!"

"But this is snow…"

"Don't tell me about the snow…"

"You're really crazy, man!"

Juan drives the car real fast and in such harsh winter conditions he risks they will go into the skid at anytime!

Mr. Tea navigates, reading from the navigation app in his mobile phone, "500 metres turn right!"

The cooks work their socks off as the chef Sylvester Cavallo conducts his orchestra. He shouts and swears in Italian. He wants to have everything more than perfect! But there is another reason why Sylvester is so anxious - the damn

Scottish salmon! Sylvester checks the orders and makes sure all is being prepared on time. But the disturbing thoughts come to his head,'Where is Mr. Tea? Perhaps he will need to apologise to their first VIP!'

The first 2 guests arrive to the restaurant. It is a young couple. They speak between themselves in Russian. They check in with the hostess. The Maître d' hotel welcomes them at the desk, helps them from their thick winter coats and asks them to follow him to their table at the window with the best view. He helps the young lady with the chair. Then he hands them over the two menus and the wine list.

"What would you like to drink, please?"

The man looks briefly into the menu and asks the waiter, "We're going - most likely - to have a steak - the beef steak, for the main course. What wine could you recommend to us?"

The waiter looks down searching for their feet to examine the quality of shoes they wear. These seem to be around 100 Euros. The girl wears a golden ring with a gem. Her hair is nicely stylishly made and the small bag she did put on the table was definitely expensive. However her watch is not known brand. The man is very well groomed and his suit perfectly fits to his apparently trained body. The couple seems to be bit nervous - it looks like they are on a date - perhaps not the first, but most likely on the 2nd or 3rd one. They are Russians and Russians - in general - prefer French wines. These two seem to be rather sales professionals than business owners. Something around 30 Euros per bottle would do. But perhaps he wants to impress her. Let's shoot for…

The waiter smiles and replies, "Some of our best Cabernet Sauvignons or even Cabernet Franc French wines perhaps…I can strongly recommend – Olga Rafault Chinon "Les Picasses" - 1993, which is an extraordinary vintage – which stands for consistently delicious wines."

The man, "We'll have that! And a large bottle of still mineral water, please choose for us, thank you!"

The Maître d' hotel sends his runner down to the wine cellars. The young waiter stands in front of the heavy medieval door to the wine cellars and hesitates for a moment. The Cellar Master & Sommelier opens the door and touches the face of the waiter. The waiter steps back with anger.

"What do you want from me, boy?" asks the Sommelier like a witch.

"Olga Rafault Chinon "Les Picasses" – year 1993"

"But when do you need it?" as if he does not want to give it to the waiter.

"I need it…now…"

"Hey wait, boy! When it is going to be served?"

The waiter becomes nervous,"Well…now…"

The answer comes in a teacher's tone,"The wine is a 1993, sleeping in the old cellar racks, covered by dust and cobwebs, waiting for a real opportunity! Do you really think, I'll let it go just like this?" cracking his fingers," Besides - this wine needs to be in room temperature and needs to be decanted! And what's even more important, it needs to…"

Now the connoisseur moves his face extremely close to the face of the poor waiter, who does not have a space to step back anymore! Right behind him is the cold stone moisturised wall of ancient cellars, "…breath!!"

The cellar master grabs boy's face into his hand, as if it was a scull in a Shakespeare's drama. "Do you understand my boy?!"

The boy nods and pushes away - abruptly - the thin long hand of the monster.

"…but please, give it to me now, the guests are waiting…"

"I'll go with you! Now, boy…Come with me to get it!"

"Where?"

The Sommelier makes a few steps back and shows the small door of the secret cellar. He pushes the heavy door open slowly, shows the way,"There!"

The waiter is scared,"I'll wait here…"

"You want the bottle?", the Sommelier grabs & drags the fighting poor boy inside like a spider does,"Come and get it! Allow me to introduce you to the secrets of wine…!!"

The chef picks the mobile phone and calls Mr. Tea but the signal gets greatly interrupted. He can hear Mr. Tea, but can't understand every second word. Sylvester repeats the call several times between checking the hot plates with the meals on the display - before they can go.

The sommelier decantes the wine and explains to the young Russian couple - in Russian, why do they need to wait for some time, before they can drink the wine… He does apologise for the inconvenience and suggest they could start with some aperitif…like perhaps two small shots of Becherovka or best quality Russian vodka…. The runner stays behind the sommelier with red face.

The Maître d' hotel taps on the arm of waiter and whispers: "Hey, what the heck are you waiting for? Go to the kitchen for the orders that are ready to go - table 26 – here are the orders from each of the guests" and gives a small paper to the runner, who has also reddish eyes,"so you know, who gets what. Don't mess it up! Understood? And hurry up, otherwise the chef is gonna kill you!"

The restaurant gets surprisingly filled quickly as many guests just walk in without a proper reservation… The VIP together with his grand daughter arrive at the desk as well.

The VIP hands a 50 USD note to the Maître d'who is smiling as always,"Thank you very much Sir, thank you young lady."

"Thank you old Sir!"

The once famous actor laughs.

"Please follow me to your table. We have prepared it at the window, so you can enjoy the view."

While placing the guests,"We have prepared the Scottish salmon with spinach as requested, would you like some starter before?"

"Well I am getting old and do prefer only one dish at lunch, so no thank you for me. But maybe my grand daughter?" looking at her.

"Grandpa, you know that I have to look at my weight, so no for me as well."

"Something to drink?"

"Just plain water will do."

The Maître d' hotel writes down his notes quickly,"ok…got it!"

The Maître d' hotel makes a short bow and steps back almost hitting the GM James Willington, who approaches the table to greet hotel Egeria's first real guest - star!

The Maître d' hotel enters the kitchen with the menu and approaches Sylvester,"As for Scottish salmon, well, unfortunately, we do not have it!"

"But you had told me, you'll have two portions…"

"I'll go with you, to speak to the guest. Let me just wash my hands and change my clothes."

The car moves fast on the road to the hotel Egeria and the car stops in front of the hotel's carpark gate. Nothing happens - the gate stays closed. Mr. Tea presses the buzzer. No response.

"They're asleep again!" shouts Juan,"I'll have them fired - all of them!" and to Mr. Tea, "We will have to run, to make Sylvester happy!" Saying that Juan already leaves the car and Mr. Tea does the same, the leave the car where it was – blocking the way to the parking, but the fish is more important at this very moment.

Sylvester thinks already about how to apologize, when his thoughts are disturbed by the yell of Mr. Tea pushing the kitchen doors open,"Chef, here is what I found, is there a Scottish salmon within this..?" and several fishes are poured on the shiny polished steel kitchen table by Mr. Tea.

"Caro Mio, yes of course here is the salmon we need", taking the salmon aside.

"Sylvester, sorry, it took longer than expected, but I hope you will be able to cook it still to perfection!"

"Buon Lavoro!! Where did you get it Mr. Tea?"

"It's a long story…"

"I owe you a big favour! Grazie mille!"

"No worries, Sylvester!"

"You are the best. Don't worry, I will cook it and our star guest will love it!"

"THE OPENING GALA"

The hotel owner - Peter Willington is sitting relaxed on the couch in his apartment. He is wearing evening social clothing, his shoes are well polished and he reads from the paper:

"Dear guests...ahh...no...!"

He shakes his head and his sight falls onto the black cat sitting on the table close to his computer monitor.

Peter addresses the cat, "Ladies and gentlemen, dear guests, dear hardworking colleagues...is it better?"

The black cat nods slightly, "Meow!"

Peter smiling, "Thanks bro!"

Peter continues, "...after the months of preparations, we have gathered here, to celebrate the launch of our hotel Egeria - together. And I am eternally grateful to all of you, for your highest professionalism! The beginning of this year was hectic for everyone - so much to be done - and no role was too small or less important...oh...I'm not good at it...perhaps I should ask my son James to make the speech...?"

Peter turns back to cat: "What do you think?"

The cat shakes its head slightly and narrows its eyes down.

Peter grins, "Ok, Ok!"

Peter wants to continue reading but someone knocks the door, "Enter!"

The door slowly opens and two heads appear - his son James with his wife Jane.

"Hey, where are you dad? Everybody is waiting..."

"Hey, son, don't you want to do that speech...? Besides - you're the GM, aren't you!"

"Oh no, dad, I'm not going to do it! Come on! You'll be great! You're the best!"

Jane supportive, "Yes, no-one can do it better than you! Besides - you're the owner!"

"I'll sleep here! I'm not going!"

Peter hides his head under the pillow. The cat jumps down from the working desk and in a few more jumps he lands on that pillow pushing him to leave.

The three Willingtons arrive to the Ballroom, where they are anxiously awaited. James pushes Peter directly to the microphone on stage. Whispering in his ear, "You are great Dad and the faster it is over, the more we will enjoy the evening together..."

Peter is standing on the stage, rises his glass and smiles romantically -for a moment - at Layla and then at the guests and the VIP with his grand daughter.

"Long live the hotel Egeria!"

All guests and staff rise the glasses of champagne. The owner of the hotel leans towards his VIP guest and whispers something into his ear.

At the same time Jonathan Lee, in his red suit, who also got an invitation to the opening, whispers into the GM Assistant - Juan Alexandro Polpo's ear," I need you to help me to acquire this amazing hotel, Juan! By any means…"

Juan makes a devilish grin and then turns back towards the stage and raises the glass, while his eyes meet with the eyes of the always suspicious owner Peter Willington.

Juan smiles. Peter does not smile.

The Chinese multimillionaire turns back to his wife and kisses her on her cheek and they talk about something…

The small orchestra starts to play and their leader joins in by singing.

The cat watches the scene from the comfort of the hotel hallway window.

The guests enjoy themselves, some dance, some just observe the stage with the band. The team works hard serving the food and drinks.

Then James gets on the stage and asks the guests to join him on the terrace to watch the fireworks in the garden.

It is a great success, the people love to see the beautiful pictures the pyrotechnicians were able to produce in the sky and as a special effect, they play some great, well-known music to it.

The cat sits in the window and observes it, but when the noise hits really hard - he jumps from the window and hides behind a corridor table.

The guests return to the ballroom, where the band plays on the stage and a young girl sings. She is the grand daughter of the VIP, who has a great voice and the band immediately recognizes her talent. They play some popular songs together and the girl likes to be on stage with the professional musicians. The guests love it.

The stars twinkle on the clean indigo sky above the hotel Egeria.

What a start.

"THE QUEEN OF CLUBS"

Two famous youtubers arrive from LA to the reception. As they approach it - they perform street rap encouraged by a small but powerful speaker. One of the guys has a wireless microphone. They come to the young beautiful receptionist Yuki Hizashi. They move the mic close to Yuki asking, "Hey, girl, ya wanna free-style on our beat?"

The other guests - some elderly parents with their kids and the kids of their kids - look up towards Yuki and the Youtubers, as they check out with Yuki's handsome Czech colleague - Jiri Mlady.

Yuki keeps her coolness," Freestyle? I don't do free style…"

The one with the dreads tries to encourage her with his smile,"Come on."

The other with the microphone,"Do what ya feel".

Yuki is confident and ask a bit shy,"…can we do it somewhere low key?"

"…yeah…maybe right here…?" pointing to the corner pillar of the hall.

"..I am trying not to be seen…"

"Ah yeah. I feel ya, I feel ya!"

The three move to that nearby corner pillar. Yuki holds her hand before her lips that might suggest she is bit nervous over all.

The rasta youtuber holds the speaker and pushes the button to play a new beat. The other holds the microphone in front of Yuki.

The music starts and Yuki looks down to the floor. The YouTubers start dancing to the rhythm, smiling and encouraging Yuki to begin her solo.

> "…today I came late
> the boss will kill me
> yeah
> back there in Japan
> one finger losing
> but this is not Japan
> this is Vary
> Charle's city
> built by money"

The pro rappers are astonished and get into the groove with Yuki,"Yeah! Keep it going!"

> "I hate this city!
> I love just money!
> So I can pay my…

dreams to come in
to the level,
where I can fuck it!
All!"

Yuki puts her hand on her mouth watching the small kids with worry.
"Yeah, put your hands in tha air!", comes from the youtubers unison.

"…to say to my boss…yeah…"
"…come on yeah!!"
"…to show the finger…"
"…dat one…in da middle"
"Yeaaaaaahh!!"

Everybody - who are present at the reception - laugh, because they see, what
Yuki does not… …the hotel owner enters the scene - his face is rather serious.
The youtubers feel the prey, but also want to save the situation Yuki fell into,
due to them and they needed to jump in immediately. "Hey there, boss man, you
wanna freestyle for us?!"
Peter does not want to spoil the fun, especially if the happy family, coura-
geous Yuki and her colleague Jiri look at him. So he grabs the microphone and
hesitates for a moment listening to the beats and starts,.

"…and I'm the owner
of this hotel…
I'am maybe older,
but not a fun spoiler…"

"Yeah, yeah" comes from the youtubers showing their appreciation.
The family laughs! The receptionist Jiri laughs and cries, not believing his
eyes. Yuki opens her mouth in heartily happy smile.
Peter is encouraged,"…but if my hotel…
Youtubers,"yeah, yeah, keep it comin'!

"…but if my hotel…
…gets too noisy…
Yeah, yeah…
I will close it!
No more drinking!
No more dining!
No more sleeping!"
Youtubers with a laugh,"Yeah, yeah!"

> "..and you two guys…
> ..in room three four…
> I will lock you!
> …for the nights FIVE!
> Give me high five!"
> Give me high five!
> Give me high five!"

All are dancing and putting their hands to a high five.
Peter stops - exhausted - but laughing as he started to dance with all people.
The only comment of the youtubers,"Y'all are bangin'! Dope!"
The family applauds in the excitement. Juan Alejandro Polpo arrives to the scene and claps his hands with sarcasm. He smiles, but his smile is the one of a snake, if just snakes could smile.

"TOO MUCH FOR AN OLD MAN"

Peter Willington is in his apartment about to go to sleep, but he does not feel well, feels cold. He sets the temperature up, but it is still not enough. The long fingers of the winter sneak somehow to the room and Peter can almost see their creeping shadows. He can hear the sound of merciless Siberian wind, penetrating the microscopic window crevices. The tall trees behind the hotel shake and squeak as if they were some ancient forrest monsters ready to attack with their jagged branches. There is a snow white owl sitting on one of the frozen branches of the spruce and monitors the hotel.

Peter stays close to the window wearing a thick warm hat and a winter coat - he observes the trees dancing in the wind. Peter calls the room service, "…and please get me some medicine, I feel, I have a cold…yes…lemon and honey… yes….everything….thank you! Put it on that special account, as usual… great."

The waiter prepares the tea in the room service kitchenette. He puts the box with the pills on the tray, gets the honey and lemon and gives the bill into the brown folder. A telephone rings. The waiter picks it up and makes notes, "Yes, mam…sure…room 212…twice club sandwich, a bottle of…yes…I'll be there in about 15 minutes, 20 at the latest! Thank you for your order, mam."

The waiter runs with the tray with tea, honey, lemon and medicine out of the kitchenette. The phone rings behind him once again!

The waiter stops, "What the hell is going on tonight?!"

He wants to return, but spots his colleague returning from his "cigarette break".

The waiter shouts at the smoker, "Where the hell have you been for so long? If you you're stoned, don't fall in the sink like you did the last time!"

"Shut the fuck up!" reverts a deep voice from the kitchenette.

"Yes, mam? What can I do for you?" follows - echoing through an empty corridor.

The waiter with the tray goggles and continues to deliver the first aid to the patient Peter Willington.

Peter swallows the pill and drinks it with the tea. Then, he hides under a blanket in his winter coat and a thick hat. Occasionally his hand emerges, grabs a monstrous mug with hot tea, his head emerges like the head of a well-aged sea turtle, sips the tea and disappears back in the blankets. After a few repetitions the blankets remain covering Peter. He fell asleep finally.

The snow storm follows shortly after the unexpected flash cuts the sky behind the windows purple. The light bulb in the table lamp bursts broken.

"ZERO"

Hotel Egeria GM's assistant sits alone behind the Roulette table. If there was not him, it would be a dead table. The small ball stops and - Juan Alexandro Polpo angrily smashes the bottle against the wall. His number did not arrive!

Immediately, he apologises to the waitress, who did swiftly arrive to double check - what is going on. Also the security guard approaches fast. Juan asks the waitress to get him Rum, "Sea Dog" preferably - the whole bottle of it.

Juan is - a well known - notorious player in this casino owned by Jonathan Lee, but he is also Lee's advisor, everybody knows. Juan turns back to the table. The small ball spins on the ball-track as if it would never stop...like the time... Juan glances sadly at his few remaining chips.

"Place your bets!" announces the black female croupier.

Juan gazes hungrily at the full beautiful lips of the woman moving in a slow motion. They have the round shape, like a circle...They are about to fashion words, "No more..."

Juan pushes all his chips onto the number zero like a flash and smiles like the devil.

"...bets!" the croupier spits out.

The small ball runs fast - like our Earth around the Sun. The waitress brings the bottle of desired rum and a new glass with thicker walls. The croupier looks now like an abandoned statue in the reddish sands of the planet Mars. The small ball slows down, but keeps running, as if it would never stop. The young exotic waitress opens the bottle and pours a sea of Rum for the dog. Juan, "It'll be the ZERO!"

The croupier wakes up laughing.

The waitress puts her thin - honey skin - hand around the brave arms of Juan. He closes his eyes, drinks to the bottom and places the empty glass onto the table noisily. The guy at the slot machines - behind Juan's back — screams, "Yeah!" and the wonderful clinging music - of the coins waterfall - starts to play.

Juan opens his eyes, just to spot the small ball balancing, for a moment in a slow motion, on the edge between the numbers. The miracle triggers a victorious smile in Juan's pale face!

It is the Zero!

The black woman croupier frowns as she witnesses how - Juan kisses the exotic waitress on her cheeks, who just could be 50 or 15.

Juan walks the night streets drunk and sings something in Spanish. The almost empty bottle in his hand. He spots a taxi. Juan raises the bottle up, but the driver does not take him, Juan has to find his way home on his own.

"POKER STARS"

The next day Jonathan Lee has a poker round invited to his villa. There are the following people present in the poker room:

> Juan Alexandro Polpo, hotel Egeria GM's Assistant,
> Jonathan Lee, Fortune 500 Guy,
> Bony Eins, Lee's bodyguard & best friend,
> Jan Pesek, Russian Mafia Lawyer
> and Elmar Meyrink, Bank Manager & Psychiatrist

They play the "5 Card Draw" poker. The walls are lit by a crackling fireplace and few candles, placed throughout the room. A black panther pretends sleeping on the sofa. Time to time it opens its eye slightly. A raven sits on the window. There is a big aquarium with golden and red fish. The statues of Egypt Pharaohs, Ancient Greek Philosophers and Chinese Warriors cast shadows onto the poker players and the walls surrounding them. Behind the windows - a snow storm hits the city, once again – this is a cruel winter.

There is a tempting pile of money bills in the middle of the table and loaded guns in the holsters. Juan closes his eyes and tries to penetrate the brains of his opponents. The banker counts the cards in his mind. He sees the cards, the numbers and some strange pictograms.

The panther opens its eyes wide, yawns showing off its long sharp yellow teeth, stretches its legs to reveal the pawns and claws. Its long whiskers are the antennas and its ears the radars to help to evaluate, if the prey at the poker table is worth eating. But his belly is full of the best quality beef meat cooked by Jonathan's private chef. He dreams of time when he was scraping the meat of antilope leg bones with his tongue, rough as sandpaper, to make them shine in the sun. When he was spotting the female panther - and was dragged by an invisible overpowering force to the beast. It was time to play. They were playing, being entirely sprinkled by the antilope's warm blood. This sunny Kenyan afternoon felt like the whole sweet eternity to them.

The panther stands up, feeling lonely and abandoned. It jumps down from the leather sofa and elegantly lazily walks to the leader of its Coalition. It stops next to Jonathan Lee, puts its heavy head on his legs and roars. Jonathan smiles and teases its ear. His cards are not so bad over all, he has a high "full house" with (3 Queens and 2 Kings. The banker - dealer - Elmar Meyrink asks him, if he really does not want to exchange some of his cards. Jonathan's face resembles an oriental mask from the Chinese opera.

Jonathan in his mind,'But if I get rid of one of the Kings and draw that last Queen - the Queen of Clubs…it could be even better…'

Jonathan's eyes shift unconsciously towards Juan, who sits to his right. Juan has got his eyes closed and face turned into a marble bust. His artificially coloured white hair shimmer in the erratic light of the crackling fireplace. A pendulum clock swings back and forth. Its time keeping element releases merciless sounds – the beats that carve the loaf of our space into the myriads of frozen frames. Just in case some future time traveller decides to pop in for a peek. Here and there. The dealer Elmar Meyrink observes the players and says,"Being a rather talented psychiatrist, I have a perfect view into know what's going through their minds right now. I inherited from my ancestor - a famous writer and obscure financial speculator - rather extraordinary abilities.

A photographic memory, a telepathy and also the ability to some extent to forecast the future. Lately, I've started to play with a telekinesis as well. That's, why Jonathan pays me so well! And I did help him, several times already, to secure great deals and to win them."

The dealer Elmar Meyrink gives to Juan's marble bust the silent screaming look,"GIVE UP, YOU SON OF A GUN!"

But behind Juan's eyes a complete different picture is drawn, 'Juan sits on a throne. A steam train arrives. The cowboys step out of its doors - carrying big wooden boxes secured by heavy iron locks. They lay them down in front of Juan and open them breaking the locks by hammers, spades and axes. The boxes are full of golden coins. But it is not their glimmer that strikes King Juan's eyes, but rather the woman in black that steps out of the wagon to walk the red carpet being simultaneously rolled out by black and Chinese slaves dressed in indigo blue striped teared dirty uniforms.

The elegant woman, who looks like the Queen, walks slowly - accompanied by the noise of clinging chains, firmly fixed around the knuckles of the workers. The Queen comes real close to King Juan, she holds a Spanish flamenco fan made by five poker cards "The Royal Flush in Clubs". But then, she pulls out a big hammer - in order to smash Juan's marble face into pieces!'

Juan opens his eyes and sees the reality in his hand the "Queen of Clubs" is missing to get the "Royal Flush in Clubs".

Jonathan gives Juan an open nasty look - in the fierce attempt to cut his brain by the sharp stream of fire running from his rich greedy eyes. Juan again closes his eyes and stops breathing. He is aware of the hellish touch of his boss's mind and it feels like an excruciating eternity. Juan does not breath, does not make a single movement.

He has a bad vision,'A dark basement. The walls, the floor, the ceiling covered by black teared plastic bags. The last thing Juan sees, is a chain saw and the barrel with the pictogram on it - a red triangle with the scull in the middle - it's acid!

Jonathan and Bony Eins put a plastic bag on Juan's head. Juan shakes as he suffocates.'

Back in the poker room, Jonathan speaks to banker Meyrink, "Yeah, I'll take one more."

He discards 1 card of his pair making the leap of faith. The dealer Elmar Meyrink throws the requested card elegantly to Jonathan's position at the table. Jonathan grabs it and unfolds it close to his eyes. He remains still. The eyes do not show anything. Juan observes Jonathan's eyes breathing slowly – being careful - not to release any unintended noise. Juan is a very sensitive sneaky sleazy guy and in his guts he feels, Jonathan did not get what he needed!

Now Meyrink asks Juan, "You fancy more or two?"

Juan discards one card and stretches his free hand with its palm wide open, "Just one."

The dealer Elmar places the card under the stag and returns Juan a new card from the top. The players stare at Juan, but he does not check the card and sits quiet. The eyes of the predators move onto the black man Bony Eins. Bony Eins has his sunglasses on - as always. Jonathan knows, he even sleeps with his sunglasses on!

Bony Eins discards 2 of his cards, "Give 'em to me!"

He gets the cards and it is perhaps the good deal this time as his sunglasses reflect the flames of victory. A soft smile escapes his full lips. Bony Eins, "Hmmmm…"

Jan Pesek, "Three for me, please."

Jan Pesek - the young man himself - accepts the cards as well and as he checks them, he sighs as he felt the sudden sting of medusa.

The banker Elmar Meyrink whispers, "…and one more for me as well…"

The young man checks his cards and shakes his head, "Fold" and discards all his cards face down to table.

Juan thinks, 'One is out - four remain.'

Jonathan with powerful voice, "Raise!" and he throws 500 Euros onto the pile of the bills as they were just used paper napkins.

Juan, "Call" and he throws his last money into the middle of the table.

Bony pulls out 500 Euros from his pocket and matches the bet.

Jan Pesek gazing at the banker, "FOLD" and he drops out of the current hand, opens the can of soda nervously and drinks it.

Now Jonathan, Juan and Bony are the ones remaining in the game.

Juan again counts for himself, 'Three players remaining!'

Jonathan pulls out 1 Euro and drops it onto the table.

Juan searches in his pockets, but finds only 50 cents and looks around as he was in the search for help. Jonathan laughs as he remembers, Juan had sacrificed all his coins to that tobacco machine in his Casino. The banker Elmar pulls out some coins and throws them into the middle, "That's for Juan"

Bony Eins matches the bet, "Call".

Juan, "Let's see 'em."

Jonathan observes his both remaining opponents and his mind gears up - analysing the situation faster. Jonathan smiles and raises by 1000 Euros.

Juan gives banker Meyrink a look, "Could you lend me some...", but the dealer stands up remarking, "I'm going for a smoke!"

Jonathan, "Sit down! You can smoke here..."

"No Jonathan, I am going out!"

Juan is disappointed, "Fold!"

Bony Eins matches the bet and then he takes his Rolex watch off his wrist. He places them carefully onto the money bills in the middle.

Jonathan with wide open eyes, "Hey, bro, I gave you that for your birthday - How could you...?"

Bony Eins grins at his boss.

Jonathan, "Fold!"

Bony Eins grabs all the treasure from the middle and smiles.

Jonathan is annoyed, "Hey, that was the last time I give you a present like that!"

Bony for the last time checks his cards - he does not have anything there - he was bluffing. But he does not show his cards. He does not show his happiness. And he does not make fun of anyone.

Juan tries to steal the cards from Bony, "Show me, what you had!"

Bony catches his octopus hand, "Come on!"

Juan to Jonathan, "He's gotta show us his cards!"

"No he doesn't."

Juan tries to grab the cards from Bony once again.

Bony shouts, "Let go!!"

"He was bluffing!" Juan to all.

Bony keeps the poker face, his eyes laughing behind his sunglasses, takes back his Rolex watch and picks all the banknotes from the table.

Jonathan to Bony, "Hey, could you walk the panther?"

"Sure, boss."

Bony takes the panther out to the garden and walk in the snow to observe the stars. They are embraced by the silence of frozen trees.

Bony to his four legged friend, "So, what ya say bro?" The panther feels a creeping hunger and licks the leg of Bony.

"FORREST"

It is early morning and Peter Willington does some jogging in the deep snow within impenetrable darkness of the forest. The fog slinks intertwines between the naked tree branches frozen to temporary death.

He wears a thick warm cap and a flash light attached to his forehead. As he runs, he spots some shadow moving not too far from him! He speeds up. Then he sees it again! The white transparent Satin Veil - there!! He hears a woman laughing.

Peter speeds up his run even more, being scared to death. Suddenly, he stumbles over! For some time Peter lies on the ground and tries to catch his breath. Then, he touches his back with the groan of pain. Peter swears, "Shit!"

He closes his eyes in the expectation - as if something, really terrifying, was about to happen now to him. And it really comes! Someone puts a blanket over him!! Softly… Deadly… With silent breath.

The blood in the old man's veins turn into the red ice! The pain is replaced by something much more ominous… Peter grabs the random timber, hidden under the snow pillow, and prepares for the fight. Then, he hears steps in the snow. The shadow - the forrest's invisible entity - steps over his body and disappears in the forrest. Peter can still hear the reverberations of the crunching snow. He looks up and keeps turning his head with the flash light on it - fast and erratically - as he is in great shock.

The pain in his back is gone and he stands up real quick.

He hears the laughter from a distance again.

Peter starts running back towards the hotel. And then it happens - the light of his flash light goes off! The batteries ended their life.

Peter to himself, "Of course, just a perfect time."

Peter stops - because the darkness got now even denser, thicker. In this particular moment he could even touch it! His heart beats fast. And then stops. Something did touch him! He turns, but there is no one… No one, he could see, no one he could touch! He searches for his mobile phone hastily and finds it, but the device slips from his hand down into the deep snow! The thing that happens to Peter quiet often. He searches for it, crawling on his knees in the deep snow. Then the alarm of his mobile phone triggers off and the black snow is now lit blueish. Peter grabs the phone real quick and attempts to switch the alarm off. He spots the "Envelope" pictogram blinking - there is a new message…He opens the message, 'It's time to wake up Peter!'

Peter wakes up in his bedroom of the apartment and sits on his bed, breathing heavily - as he did just escape from that nightmare. The alarm is on and noisy. Peter sighs, grabs the phone and he manages to switch the alarm off. He lets his body to fall back to the bed and his face turns into a grimace instantly. Peter sits up once again and touches his back as if something did sting him. He looks down onto the sheet. There is a small tiny - but sharp - tree branch… The old man takes it with his fingers in disbelief.

As Peter puts his feet into the slippers, he spots something interesting on the floor. There is a little bit of mud and water and another thing. He picks it up. He examines it closely, trying to adjust the focus of his eyes - as his sight worsens day by day. The haze dissolves to reveal…

"HEAVY DUTY - CHINESE SUITCASES"

Once in a while, the hotel Egeria has groups from the Far East as their guests…

Mr. Tea is in his element to organise a smooth luggage distribution of the arriving group. He moves the trolleys from the Lobby out of the hotel - one by one.

Mr. Tea - in the black perfectly fitting suit, black magician's hat and white gloves - prepares the golden trolleys at the place where the busses should stop.

"…as for me, this is the first time I'll have to meet such a challenge!"

Then - finally - the bus arrives. It is a 65-seater Double Decker one, which can not drive up to the hotel.

Mr. Tea runs down the drive way to tell to the tourleader to walk up to the hotel with her guests and that he is going to take care about the luggage. "Welcome to the Egeria, unfortunately, this bus is too large to drive up. Reception is just a few meters away, so please go check in. I will handle the suitcases!"

"Ni hao." Smiling tourleader and in awful English,"When is the bus going to drive up the way, why do we stop here?" Apparently, the tour leader did not understand the words Mr. Tea was using. Mr. Tea decides to use a non verbal communication. He points his finger in the direction of the hotel and invites her and the group to join him to get there by walking.

There are some voices from the group which Mr. Tea interprets as being annoyed. It seems, the guests are reluctant to leaving the bus without their suitcase. Mr. Tea is in his element, pushing the guests towards the hotel reception. Then they seem to understand and walk there.

Mr. Tea - runs back pulling one of the trolleys to the bus, where its driver already started unloading the suitcases. What he did not expect, was the amount and size of suitcases. His one trolley - was for sure - not big enough. Thus he had called another bellboy to bring one more. Yet it was still not sufficient!

Nevertheless, by pulling the incredibly overfilled trolleys up to the hotel, the bellboys showed the human capabilities once more - "Where there is a will, there is a way." - as the Chinese proverb says. Sweating like hell, he and his colleague arrived at the hall and they knew they had to do another trip… Two Chinese ladies, lined with trunks, started to yell complaining their ones are missing! Mr. Tea is in his element to promise, that he will get them from the bus. So he picks two other guys to get the trolleys and walk back to the bus, where the driver still waits, but ready to leave as soon as possible. The bellboys, led by Mr. Tea, collect the rest of the luggage to bring them up to the hotel.

Mr. Tea shows the suitcases to those two panicking ladies. The ladies do not recognise any of them and Mr. Tea wonders, where their suitcases were lost. He speaks to the tour leader, but she has no clue. An investigation is about to begin

- the receptionist Yuki enters the scene - still red in her face, uncertain about her freestyle rapping performance. She wants to know, where the group was before and if all suitcases were identified.

"Could you please tell me, where have you stayed before? Or…is this your first hotel in Czech Republic during your trip?"

"We come directly from the "Four Trees" hotel in Prague."

"And did you find all of the suitcases?"

"No. Two ladies miss their luggage!"

Yuki is now turning to the two ladies, "Are you sure, your suitcases were loaded into the bus, back in Prague…?"

The two ladies don't understand a word and give the "Dog's Eyes" look to their tour leader. The tour leader talks to them in Chinese explaining, what the receptionist had just said to her. The two ladies are furious with their hands, lament and repeat things twice as they seem to be twins. They look a bit funny in their exaggerated make up.

The tourleader is doubtful, "They claim, they had seen last their suitcases in the corridor of the hotel in Prague…"

Yuki is very consequent in making decisions, "Just a moment, I'll call the Four Trees hotel in Prague immediately!"

"Thank you so much!"

The receptionist walks to her desk and calls to the Four Trees hotel in Prague.

"We have 2 ladies here, who were your guests last night - from a Chinese group. They are missing their suitcases." She starts smiling, "Really? You did find them…Just a moment please."

Yuki covers the phone speaker by her hand and turns to the group saying, "They said, the suitcases were so heavy, that the bellboys refused to carry them down to the bus!"

Then Yuki returns to the call, "OK, we will send a driver to collect them… Our driver will be there in two hours at the latest…Thank you so much!...Yes… You too!...Have a lovely day."

Yuki speaks to the group "They have said - better send a truck! And that they look forward to getting rid of those suitcases."

The two Chinese ladies glance at each other. They look rather serious.

"SALES & MARKETING"

The hotel Egeria sales & marketing department consists of two offices, 1 small boardroom plus a small kitchenette. There is a team of 4 sales & marketing professionals, 1 graphic designer & photographer, 1 accountant and 1 legal advisor - lawyer. The team is led by sales & marketing manager Samia Sahar.

As in every such sales environment - things don't go always smooth. It is caused by the famous - infamous office politics…

The pressure to fill the hotel rooms, boardrooms, ballroom and wellness center up to its full capacity - from the owner & top management - is enormous. The competition - especially here in Karlovy Vary – is fierce, indeed! There are so many excellent hotels over here and yet the hotel Egeria aims for the stars. The strategy is to bring "shining & exposed" people from all the corners of the world to attract the influx of guests.

Pavla, one of the sales representatives asked Samia for a meeting and the meet in the Boardroom, as Pavla requested the meeting to be 1 on 1.

Pavla is angry and starts her verbal attack, "Jana has the absolute worst table manners ever! I can't sit close to her, Samia!"

Samia listens.

Pavla glances - through the glass window of the office – at her colleagues in the main office room…just to meet the eyes of Jana! By coincidence? Perhaps not!

The eye touch is real cursory, but stings painfully both antagonists!

Samia in her mind,'In a sales environment - more than anywhere else - can long time fondness turn - in the blink of an eye - into the years of silent hatred. And vice versa. All this - intertwined with small talk, backstabbing and somebody else ruthlessly scrambling to the top. Oh, why I don't I sing better?! Or why I don't I bake cakes in my "one day - Inshallah - privately owned" bakery?! Or both, haha…'

Pavla continues to let her anger out, "She chews like a cow and, as if that is not bad enough, she talks with her mouth full! In front of customers! Even while she's on the phone!"

Samia laughs softly in a disbelief,"Oh common, Pavla. Take it easy. Focus on yourself! At least, that's how I do it… by focusing on myself."

Pavla continues not willing to listen, "She chews so loud, I can even hear her when my door's closed. Oh, she's also - always - looking for someone to pick-up her lunch or Tea or whatever else she doesn't feel like doing."

Samia is getting serious, "All right, I'll talk to her."

Pavla smiles as if she has won a battle, "Thank you so much, Samia!"

"No worries."

Pavla walks out of the boardroom meeting with the face of a poker player. She sits at her desk right next to Jana. One could cut the thick deadly silence between the two.

And suddenly, Pavla says to Jana, without even looking at her, "Oh, have you seen that action movie…"

The response is silence.

Pavla glances at Jana. Jana has got her eyes closed and looks like an ancient statue. The eyebrows painted thick black, eyelashes extreme long and bloody red lip stick all over her face.

Pavla continues, "…with Leonardo DiCaprio?"

Jana opens her eyes, "…hmm…eh?"

She gazes at her super long decorated nails.

Pavla never gives up, "Catch Me if You Can!"

Pavla grins.

Jana replies annoyed, "Hmm…I'm busy now!"

Jana opens a can of soda, crunches crisps and chews an extra large baguette. Jana is extremely thin and the more she eats the slimmer she gets. She is of a smaller height and has some nasty authoritative manners. Jana is a young, but already experienced woman in her mid 20's.

Pavla glances at her - few times - with a great disgust. Pavla is a tall and seriously overweight woman in her mid 50's. Pavla moves closer to Jana as she was about to put some bigger pressure on her colleague. Pavla is an invader.

Jana picks the phone as she was about to call the police or security chief, but she just does this to discourage her opponent from the sudden strike.

She calls her boss Samia, "Hi Samia, this is Jana… I would like to have a word with you immediately, if possible… ok lets meet in the Boardroom in 5 Minutes, I will finish my email… the topic?.... well that is something I can only tell you personally… Ok, see you then…"

In the Boardroom Jana is already waiting for Samia, who comes 2 minutes late. When Samia enters Jana starts, "Pavla is the worst coworker I have ever had!"

With acted surprise Samia, "Oh really? Why?"

"She's an attention-seeking sociopath! She constantly invades my personal space."

"The approach you need to take is to disengage and just do your work."

"Oh…that's easy to say…but you wanted to talk with me about something?"

"Well…She opens her diary. Yes I did, I just wanted to go through the sales forecast for the next quarter, that's all… But…now I see - I've overlooked an upcoming meeting with a client."

Samia closes the diary and smiles at Jana and leaves the Boardroom.

In the evening the "lost" suitcases arrive to the Egeria. Unloading one of them from the trunk, it falls down and opens in front of the main entrance. What made the suitcase so heavy was obvious, cutlery of the "Four Trees" hotel, a crystalline vase which bursts into thousands of pieces, bathrobe and other stuff. So Mr. Tea calls the Security Chief to take over. The Security chief calls the police which arrives minutes later.

Sebastian Hunter is waiting at the reception desk and gets the room number the twins are accommodated. He shows the officers the way to the lift and then through the corridor. He knocks at the door, but with his masterkey, he opens the door immediately, so the ladies have no chance to hide or leave the room via the window.

The picture Sebastian and the two policemen get was to expect. The two Chinese ladies are already packing stuff from the Egeria to take with them. The two robbers look up from the newly bought suitcases they freeze when they see the security chief and policemen. They know their tour is over, definitely and start to shout and swear at them something in Chinese. One of the policemen calls for a female officer to search the ladies before arresting them and as the police walks them in handcuffs through the lobby to their car, the two youtubers pass by with their speaker playing loud and shaking their microphone. One of them asks the group, "Hey, you wanna freestyle for us?"

The Chinese ladies cover their faces with their hands and swears at him.

"Hey, you wanna go with us too?" is the answer he gets from the police officer.

The other youtuber grabs the arm of his mate, "Don't!" – and drags him away.

The hotel owner arrives to the scene, still being sick, but he does not have strength to investigate what has happened here. He just stands there in his thick hat and winter coat and observes the set.

Mr. Tea comes to him and asks, "Boss, do you feel alright?"

"No, not alright! Not alright at all!"

"Go to Chef Sylvester and ask him to make you some strong spicy garlic soup."

"Yes, that's a good idea my friend."

"You'll be alright!"

Peter is curious, "What has happened here?"

"Eh…just two small robbers from a big country, tried to smuggle some Bohemian hotel artefacts."

"They didn't want to pay for their souvenirs?"

"Their suitcases arrived from the Four Trees hotel in Prague completely filled with forks, spoons, knifes and much more."

"I see…" Peter laughs.

"And they did seem to want to continue their endeavour in your hotel too!"

Peter shaking his head, "Not in our hotel, not in our hotel!", and to Mr. Tea, tapping his arm, "Well, keep an eye on our dear guests, my friend. I've got to go to see our magician Sylvester, maybe he could help me to feel better."

As Peter passes the reception, he spots the two youtubers turning the head of Yuki once again.

"COOKING WITH SYLVESTER"

The kitchen is swamped - as always at this time of the day. The executive chef invites some of the hotel guests once per week to peek over his shoulder during the work. This time - there are three ladies putting the gourmet aprons on. The chef Sylvester also distributes the Chef hats to them.

Sylvester welcomes the guests to his kitchen and begins, "…and now, ladies, you shall know - exactly - how hard working in the kitchen is! For a moment, please carefully observe my colleagues as they work and ask whether they need some help. Is that understood?

The ladies nod.

The chef is in action and the orders come in, one after the other. He uses a microphone to announce the orders to the other chefs. The ladies chefs talk with each other, like the ladies do, about everything and everybody. A bit of complaint is also in their tones, as they thought they would cook. All of a sudden the situation changes. A loud yell under pain from the back of the kitchen.

The executive chef runs to the cook who had hurt himself. He holds his left hand in a towel. The blood soaks through the towel already and drops fall down on the floor.

Sylvester is worried the moment he sees the blood, "What happened here?"

The cook under pain," I just cut off the tip of my ring finger. But it's still hanging on by a flap of skin."

The blood sprinkles from the wound.

The kitchen gets even busier with incoming orders.

The owner Peter Willington arrives to the kitchen as well – in the hunt for Sylvester's garlic spicy soup - the miraculous medicine.

Sylvester shouts, "Cretino, idot! How often I have told you to be careful?! You have to go to the hospital right now to save your finger!" and turns to another colleague, "You, go with him to the emergency room, I'll call an ambulance to pick you up."

The two cooks leave the kitchen while the chef calls the ambulance.

The three guests are in shock, from what they have just witnessed and do not have a single word.

The chef Sylvester approaches them with a devilish smile and mean voice,"Ok Ladies, You thought you weren't cooking today… Wrong! Now you'll cook since you'll be replacing the two gentlemen who're on their way to the hospital. Please, be careful, that I don't have to call the ambulance for a second time today! Though, at the same time, I want to see, whether or not you're fast enough."

The first lady is overweight, has well-groomed nails, make-up and a modern hair cut. She is already annoyed, "Hey, we're the guests and you're the cook! Is that not so Chef?!"

Sylvester snickers, "Maybe so, but this is my territory! And besides, several times today didn't you claim to me, that you're much faster than my team?!"

The chef turns to his colleagues in the kitchen, "Guys, stop for a moment, guys…I would like to introduce to you our three new team members - they will replace, temporarily, Pavel and

Jirka."

One voice from the back, "I pick the small one!"

The cooks laugh.

Sylvester replies, "Fatti una pugnetta!"

The second lady who is small, thin and energetic, is ready to start, "OK, tell us what to do!"

"You have just seen what my colleague Pavel did… He was preparing the meat in the walk-in. Luckily, all the meat mise-en-place is ready. Now, anytime I call for a dish, you bring the meat to the saucier post, which is here in the main kitchen," pointing at the table next to the stove, "This will be done by one of you, feel free to choose who it will be."

The second lady whispering,"I'll do it, but can we please have a cigarette first?"

Sylvester does not believe what he hears and shouts,"No!"

"Ok" whispers the second lady back.

Sylvester asks with an aggressive tone, "What's your name? - that way I know, who to shout at!"

"I'm Rebecca."

Sylvester turning to the two remaining ladies, "Jirka was on the Saladier post, just prepare the salads as you saw before - that's an easy task - isn't it?"

They unisono answer, "We'll manage."

"What are your names?"

The first lady with a strong voice, "Eileen!"

The third lady is tall, beautiful and serene, "Svetlana"

"Great!"

Sylvester to the whole kitchen turning around, "Let's keep going, ladies and gentlemen!"

"One Filet Steak, One Porterhouse." Chef shouts into the microphone and awaits the answer. "Did you understand, Rebecca?"

Shy voice answers, "Yes I did."

"Why didn't you say so?" and shouts to all ladies, "Please answer with YES, SIR! ..or.. YES, CHEF!"

"Yes, Sir!"

"And hurry up, we need to cook that meat."

"Yes, Chef!"

Rebecca brings two pieces of meat to the hot kitchen.

The cook on the saucier post looks angry at Rebecca and shakes his head in disbelief, "Sorry, wrong! Please bring the right ones, they're in the walk-in, second tray from the left… and third from the right."

Rebecca runs to the back and instantly returns with the correct meat.

The cook now kindly but with a hint of sarcasm, "Thank you! Good thing the boss didn't see that."

Sylvester through the PA, "One salad "Nicoise", one mixed and one mixed without "Raddicchio". These are starters, so get them done A-S-A-P!"

Eileen and Svetlana again unisono avoiding Rebecca's mistake, "Yes, Chef!"

The two ladies do their best and finally bring the three salads to the boss.

Sylvester with a reprehending voice, "Thank you. Those took you ten minutes to prepare, I needed them in five. If it happens again you'll have extra work!"

Eileen with her strong voice conters, "Why are you being so mean to us when we're trying to help you? We are guests, our money pays your salary. You have no right, whatsoever, to shout at us! Do you understand?!"

"Then leave MY KITCHEN! Thought you wanted to see how a real kitchen works – real hard work…hard life!"

"Svetlana, let's go!

Both ladies glance angrily at smiling Sylvester and leave the kitchen like two small girls.

Sylvester to himself,"Bitches, never did a hard day's work in their life, I guess." And then into the microphone, "Rebecca, time to leave, your friends are already sitting in the Café sipping their Latte machiato."

Rebecca rushes to the chef.

Rebecca kindly, "Thank you, it was a pleasure to work with you."

Rebecca leaves the kitchen with a smile. Sylvester's smile follows her. Someone taps on his arm. It is the hotel owner Peter Willington who addresses Sylvester in a weak voice,"Could you please make some nice spicy garlic soup for me?"

"Yes, boss!"

"Oh, don't boss me all the time."

"OK, go to bed, I'll have someone to bring it up to you. And if you are sick, you shouldn't be coming to my kitchen, spreading your germs! I've already lost two guys this evening."

"Oh I am sorry, I didn't mean to…"

Sylvester gesticulating like the Italians do,"Don't be sorry. Go! Go! …to bed! Mama mia!"

The chef looks fierce and Peter runs away from the kitchen and hears the Chef from his back with overacted Italian accent, "Have a good night, BO(Z)!"

Peter Willington stands in the lift still wearing his winter coat and thick cap. The lift goes up.

Peter to himself, "My employees aren't people, they're monsters! They'll eat me alive!"

Peter puts his hands deep into the pockets and his body shakes. He frowns at sudden. He pulls one of his hands out of the pocket. Peter examines the thing he did pull out of it. It is that card of "Queen of Clubs". He shakes his head and puts it back. Peter hears some voices singing, he moves his head as if he wanted to listen closely. The singing does not come from the lift speakers. It is not the hotel music. The lift stops and the doors open. The singing gets louder as he walks out of the lift. He stops for a moment and listens, then continues through the corridor towards his apartment.

A little later it knocks on the door and it is being opened with a key from outside. It is Layla, who brings the soup.

Peter is smiling to the unexpected room service waitress, "This was a strange day, indeed."

"Tell me about it! We do need to increase the budget for Housekeeping department. We do need more people."

"Oh no, Layla! Let's not talk money before sleep! Please."

"Then when?"

"Tomorrow."

"You said that yesterday and we needed more housekeepers the day before yesterday."

"Tomorrow. Speak to James, he's the General Manager!"

"But you control the money. Eat the soup, it's hot and it's good for you!"

Peter sips the soup, "Oh, it is good! This soup is good! You know, sometimes I wish, I was a Buddhist monk living high up in the Himalayas."

"Why is that?"

"Just kidding! They don't have soup like this up there!"

"Why would you want be a monk?"

"Life would be so simple. No people, no money, silence…"

"I'll go with you!"

Peter grins and teasing Layla, "…and no women!"

Layla slaps his head kindly, "Stop talking, eat the soup."

Peter laughs, "My Chef shouts and swears at me, you're beating me! This is some business I'm running!"

Layla is about to leave the room but then she stops in the door, "Oh, I almost forgot…", she pulls out a book out of her pocket, "Here, Mr. Tea sent you something."

She returns to Peter and hands him over the book. Peter accepts it with curiosity.

"Oh, what's that?"

"I don't know, I'm not much into books."

"Me neither. I prefer to read a nice woman…"

Layla bursts into a laughter, "I guess you'd better take two of those pills I gave you instead of just one. Your face is red. Your fever must be way too high and you're starting to hallucinate…"

"And my hallucinations are beautiful! I'll die as crazy old man."

"You should understand the benefits of a broken heart."

Layla walks hastily out of the room and before she closes the door "Don't read too much, you'd better get some sleep… Good night."

"Good night Layla. Thank you very much."

Layla walks slowly - day dreaming - through the corridor and observes the paintings on the wall. They all have one in common - the theme is love. She can hear the singing of men and women coming somewhere from downstairs. She shakes her head and walks faster. The singing gets louder. The sound leads her way.

"SLIGHTLY BACK IN TIME"

Every Friday evening there is a wine tasting organised in the hotel's wine cellar. And today is Friday. The Sommelier and the Restaurant Manager invite special guests to taste the wines of the region. GM - James Willington, his wife Jane, GM's assistant Juan Alexandro Polpo and the Security Chief Sebastian Hunter are also present. The guests are already after the 10th wine to taste and – as the tasting is always made professionally – they are writing their comments on a piece of paper.

All of a sudden, one of the guests starts to sing the Chianti song. He is having such a volume and accuracy in his tones that the glasses on the table start to vibrate. The others look up from their papers and enjoy the beautiful voice of the gentleman as he continues. There are also the young youtubers from L.A. between the guests.

The singer vigorously,

"Hoch die Gläser, hoch das Leben, hoch die Liebe, tralalala!
Auf die Sonne - Auf die Reben - Auf die Liebe, tralalala!
Lasst uns lachen, lasst uns trinken, lasst uns küssen, tralalala!
Wenn uns gold'ne Stunden winken und wir wissen, tralalala   "

Getting into the rhythm the guests start to clap their hands to the melody. It is apparent that the singer must have some experience from the opera. The security chief Sebastian Hunter crawls out of the room hastily.

The singer continues encouraged,

"Ja, ja der Chianti-Wein, der lädt uns alle ein.

Drum lasst uns glücklich sein und uns des Lebens freu'n, beim gold'nen Chianti-Wein!

Ja, ja der Chianti-Wein, da sagt uns keiner nein.

Drum schenkt die Gläser ein, die Welt soll unser sein, beim Chianti-Wein!

Und dein Mund sagt ja in der blauen Sternennacht und das Glück ist nah, weil mir deine Liebe lacht!

Und ein Lied erklingt, das in uns're Herzen dringt und wir lauschen zu zweit jener Stimme so weit und vergessen die Zeit!"

Layla arrives to the cellars and stands listening in the door.

The singer turning to Layla continues,

"Unser schöner Traum führt uns über Zeit und Raum und die Erde versinkt, wenn das Lied still verklingt bis ein Ruf zu uns dringt

Sebastian Hunter arrives back with a violin in his hands and immediately starts to play to accompany the singer! Finally the tenor invites the guests to sing along, at least the refrain.

"Hoch die Gläser, hoch das Leben, hoch die Liebe, tralalala!

Auf die Sonne - Auf die Reben - Auf die Liebe, tralalala!

Lasst uns lachen, lasst uns trinken, lasst uns küssen, tralalala!

Wenn uns gold'ne Stunden winken und wir wissen, tralalala"

Everybody loves it.

GM's wife Jane smiles at Sebastian Hunter - their security chief, as he plays the violin. Sebastian smiles back at her.

All applaud.

"Ja, ja der Chianti-Wein, der lädt uns alle ein.

Drum lasst uns glücklich sein und uns des Lebens freu'n, beim gold'nen Chianti-Wein!

Ja, ja der Chianti-Wein, da sagt uns keiner nein.

Drum schenkt die Gläser ein, die Welt soll unser sein, beim Wein!"

"BOGOTA SLUMS"

The tin roofs of favelas are loaded with big used tires and concrete blocks on them to keep them in place in case of severe wind. It is raining. The abandoned dogs bark and kids play in the mud. A wet rat runs across the street. A hungry goat digs in the broken bins for some left overs. Colourful plastic bags fly in the wind and an old man on the bicycle rides through the busy streets. The man looks a bit like homeless and a bit like someone who is on his journey around the world. There is an overloaded cart attached to his rusty bicycle and flags sticking on the rods fixed to the handlebars. One flag is made of the transparent yellow flag and the second one is the one of Germany. There is another flag on the rod mounted to the cart behind the bicycle. The flag of free Tibet. The kids run behind the mysterious traveller and yell.

Some throw stones at the rider from the different world. Some try to stop his bicycle by throwing tree branches through the spices of the fast spinning wheels. Right in front of the rider a bull emerges and the old man on his "Bicycle Harley" is glad he had thrown away that red flag. He manages to turn into the narrow corridor between small half-broken houses, where the beast can not fit. But the wild rabid haggard dogs decide to chase him as if they were sent by the bull.

The sudden loud noise of the gun shot tears the haze and rain. The rider glances back to see one of the dogs falling into its own blood and mud. The kids laugh behind him. The old traveller suspects, the bullet was assigned to him and speeds up his pedalling. Another shot whistles, narrowly missing his ear, and tips a bit of concrete wall off - well ahead of him. The wheels spin around like hell. The rider looks back to see that one of the kids holds a machine gun this time! He can already hear and feel the power of it - well in advance.

He speeds up and flees to one of the lousy houses made of rubbish, it is the house of Maria Angela Polpo, the sister of Juan. She is first afraid, but then is merciful and invites the stranger in.

He is very thankful and Maria offers him soup, which she serves him in a clay bowl. He sips it under the observing eyes of Maria and her two daughters Iris and Xuxu. He likes the soup very much, as he was not expecting to get any food this night.

The two small girls do eat as well, but with their eyes fixed and distracted by the old man with big white mustache and white long thick oily hair fitted into a long pony tail. There are several scraggy cats staring at the bicycle rider from the shelves, wardrobes and windows. The rain hits the tin roof hard as if the water drops were the nails penetrating the tin cover of the coffin. But in the same time - it sounds pleasant - it sounds pleasant to the lonely rough broken warm hearts like the one of the foreigner.

The man looks exhausted and very old. The young woman and small girls have Indian features in their faces - especially the eyes and the skin. The man looks around the room. It is full of colours - blue, orange, green, yellow. It brutally contrasts with the outdoor environment of the favelas. The man feels like at his own home. For him - this is the paradise! He smiles at the girls and at the young woman. They smile back. No words needed. The girls examine the foreigner and Maria Angela tries to guess the age of that man.

Maria Angela in her mind, 'He must be well over 70, perhaps even 80…but he seems so virile…he looks like one of the Indian - Shamans…from the villages in the deep jungle.'

The man finishes his food and bows to Angela Maria and small girls - expressing his sincere thanks. There is a medallion hanging on his neck. He pulls out a wooden Chinese box and opens it to reveal what is inside. Coins, photographs, an old pocket onion watch, a green glass transparent ball, a golden ring with emerald, a few raw diamonds, golden nuggets, an iron cross - military decoration, some buddhist book, a small buddhist prayer mill, a rosary made of wooden bowls, a seashell and many more little mysterious things like the pack of old well used yellowish playing cards or another silver locket.

The small girls come closer and with astonishment dip their small tiny fingers into this treasure. They play with the stuff and the smiling wizard lets them to do so freely. One girl opens the locket to reveal an old picture of a young woman. She glances at the old man. The rider's smile switches into a serious sad look. The other girl picks one of the coins and scrutinises it. The coin is from the year 1943 - it is the German coin. It says "Reichspfennig", and there is a number 1. The girl turns the coin. On the other side there is an eagle holding the swastika in its claws and the sign above it "Deutsches Reich". The girl puts the coin back and picks the green transparent ball. She holds it close to her eye observing the mysterious rider through it. There is also a small letter - half burnt, yellowish, dirty - apparently ancient too. Her sister grabs the pack of playing cards and runs away. The man opens it and reads. From his eyes drop the Tears down. The young woman observes him. The other girl runs away too dropping the green transparent ball down on the wooden floor. She chases her sister. The small green ball keeps rolling across the room. One of the cats jumps down and hunts it. The old man folds the letter and puts it back, then picks one of the raw diamonds and the golden ring with emerald and hands it over to the woman. She does accept it with smile. The traveller then closes the mysterious box and puts it back to his bag.

Angela Maria serves him a hot tea and the man rolls himself a cigarette. The woman offers him the leaves of "Coca". The man smiles, nods, puts some into his mouth and chews it. They both drink tea and the man smokes the cigarette getting more and more relaxed.

Whilst in the neighbouring room… There is a small tent on the floor in the middle of the bedroom. It is lit by a pocket lantern. The two shadows indicate the two small girls are inside it. One of the girls holds the cards and the other one holds her free hand having her eyes closed.

"Now, Xuxu. I will think about a card and I'll send the image of it directly to your head. When you'll see the card in your mind just pick it! Pull it out of my hand."

"OK, Iris. I'll do that."

Iris is staring at the card "Queen of Clubs", "I am now focusing on the card."

Xuxu stops breathing, "OK"

Iris's eyes are firmly fixed on the card "Queen of Clubs". The girls hold their hands. Xuxu has her eyes closed and sits still as if she was the ancient Aztec statue hidden in the deep green jungle. Xuxu slowly moves her free hand and touches the tops of the playing cards by her tiny fingers.

Iris stops breathing in her excitement as well.

Xuxu pulls the card finally and opens her eyes slowly. Iris smiles bright, "Yes! We did it again!" both start to breathe heavily.

The sisters both stare at the picked playing card and the "Queen of Clubs" stares at them.

In Peter's apartment, the table lamp is on. The whole hotel sleeps, except of its owner Peter Willington. Peter has his winter coat and thick cap still on and is covered by many blankets. The book from Mr. Tea in his hands with his head gradually falling down on it.

His eyes close slowly, still able to capture the last sentence on the current page "Awareness itself, descending from a state of pure consciousness and being absorbed by the object perceived, becomes the mind."

Peter falls asleep.

At the same time, just a couple of streets further down in town, a luxury minibus stops in front of the night club where some girls already wait. They enter the car and the girls dive into the comfortable leather seats and Jonathan Lee distributes the flute glasses with Champagne. Next to him sits his wife Jenny. Bony Eins, Elmar Meyrink, Jan Pesek and Juan Alexandro Polpo - all are inside as well. There is one particular woman that strikes the eyes of Bony - the black haired elegant girl all in black! He drags her to himself, "Come here, don't be shy, baby." She laughs and does not resist. He takes a closer look, her long black hair shine indigo blue. He intertwines her hair by his thick long fingers hidden in the bloody red glove. The girl's eyelashes are extremely long and fiercely black. Her lips painted black too. The make up consists of dark shades of purple and silver dust. She wears a black leather costume and an artificial fur. Bony with his deep voice, "You look like the Queen of Clubs, babe!"

Jonathan gets alert.

The minibus moves off the club entrance and sails the winter streets of Karlovy Vary down town as a boat in the snow waves.

"SECURITY - WHAT ELSE?"

At the same time inside hotel Egeria...

The hotel cat walks slowly through the corridor of the cellar. It hunts something! It is a mouse.

At first, the mouse stands still and listens to the sounds by its sensitive ears, tries to detect some unusual smells by its nose with long white whiskers. Is it the cheese or the predator?

It stands on its back legs, catches the signals and analyses them. Then, starts running fast and the cat follows.

The security guard sleeps on the sofa having the remote control in his one hand and the other in between his legs. Apparently he enjoys a good nap. The big TV is on - some black and white detective drama. There is a big bowl of fruits standing on the floor besides the sofa and a half-empty plate of chocolate cookies. The paper cup with the rest of black coffee stands on theglas s conference table. The handle of the door quietly moves and someone opens it real slow. A leg emerges...

The security chief Sebastian Hunter squats silently in front of the sofa, not to wake up the sleeping security guard. He pulls out his mobile and makes a selfie with himself and the sleeping security guard in the background. Then Sebastian walks silently out of the office and closes the door slowly behind him.

In the cellar corridor, the cat jumps and catches the mouse, but the mouse manages to break free from the predator's playful grasp. The chase continues. The mouse escapes and disappears in a small hole in the wall. The cat sticks furiously its paws into the hole, but after short fight it gives up. The cat waits patiently with its beautiful yellow green eyes transfixed onto the hole - the door to hotel mice's "apartment", waiting for the mouse to come out again.

Juan Alexandro Polpo stays at the main entrance of the hotel and makes a phone call, "Hi Maria Angela...you know you're my beloved sister!...That's not a problem, I'll send the money. They want that much?...Listen, I'll send it by the end of the week, I promise." He continues, "OK... and how are the kids?... I miss the smiles of Iris and Xuxu?...Lovely. May God watch over you all for me!...How is mother?...and uncle Jose?...Good, good!...Sorry? Once again... it's windy here...yes, a lot of snow! Freezing!"

Juan spots the security chief Sebastian in the hallway.

"Listen, I got to go now....Of course I'll come back. Yes I will....I pay that all back and we'll move somewhere else...Exactly!...Listen I got to..."

Sebastian is about to open the glass door.

"Everything will be fine, Maria Angela!...Love you too, say hello to the kids, bye...bye."

Juan Alexandro Polpo hides his mobile phone into the pocket and puts the black leather gloves on - in the same moment Sebastian taps his arm.

Juan dislikes Sebastian a lot, as he puts his nose everywhere, which is not good for him and his plans. He turns towards Sebastian. Sebastian smiles, but his smile is fake and he does not like Juan either.

Sebastian sarcastic to Juan, "So, how was the game?"

"What do you mean?"

"Did you get good cards?"

"I don't believe in good cards! You have to make the most of what God deals you. Why aren't you asleep this time of night?

"I can't sleep tonight, after this amazing wine tasting, which made me sick at the end!" Sebastian burps to support his feelings regarding the quantity of wine they had to drink.

"Ah, you surprised me, with your violin tonight…and you surprised Jane too…"

"What are you saying?"

Juan explaining,"I mean, the way she looked at you…"

Sebastian is getting visibly nervous and pulls out a box of cigarettes,"Do you want one?"

"Sure, why not?" accepting the cigarette. He grins and starts singing, when Sebastian lits it for him,"Lasst uns lachen, lasst uns trinken, lasst uns küssen, tralalala!"

Sebastian starts laughing,"Get off my back, will you!"

The cat keeps waiting in front of the "Mice Gate". Cats are extremely patient hunters! The mouse puts its nose out slightly detecting by its highly sensitive whiskers any possible threat.

The cat sits still as it was an Egyptian statue in the desert. The mouse disappears again in the hole. Then, very slowly, the transparent green ball rolls out of the hole just to stop right in front of the surprised cat! The cat taps on it by its front leg's paw to examine the thing. It moves little. The cat taps on it again and the ball rolls fast across the corridor. The cat keeps chasing it.

"BOGOTA BIKER"

In Bogota it is late afternoon, the girl puts the coin back and picks the green transparent ball. She holds it close to her eye observing the mysterious rider through it. But then, at sudden, the small green transparent ball falls off her hand and drops down noisily onto the floor.

The small girl chases the small green transparent ball - together with one of the cats - as it keeps rolling across the room. The girl almost grasps it, but the ball disappears in a small crevice in the wooden floor. The bicycle rider smiles at her and waves his hand in a gesture, "It's fine, don't worry about it!"

Maria Angela sends the two girls to bed and ask the man to stay on the sofa in the living room, as the streets are not safe at night in the favelas, or actually anywhere in Columbia. He is very pleased to have found a good place to sleep and thanks Maria Angela and wishes the girls beautiful dreams.

After a short night, it is early morning in Bogota, the mysterious bicycle rider is getting ready to depart the hospitality of Maria Angela Polpo and her two lovely daughters Iris and Xuxu. The old man with long white mustache sits on his rusty bicycle and accepts with sincere gratitude the small bag with bread and cheese from Maria. She hands him also a plastic bottle with water.

The man stares at the water which glimmers in the blueish light of the fading moon. Then he pulls out some photograph from the pocket of his dirty oily ripped trousers. He hands it over to Maria and smiles. He jumps onto his bike and departs via muddy road up to the hills in the morning haze. Maria observes the flags dancing crazily in the morning wind. The man turns back for the very last time and waves his hand. She waves her hand too.

The young woman, wearing black clothes and black scarf, stands still with the picture in her hands, gazing at the crescent moon. She has a special Indian hat and from the far distance looks like a black Queen.

Then she examines the photograph, it is black&white.

There is a German 2nd World War tank in the desert and young soldiers posing in front of it - half naked - smiling bright at Maria Angela. Some drink wine directly from the bottles. One of the soldiers holds a book of Quran in his hand. On the tank - a small Arabic boy sits, having the medallion on his neck, and holding the small transparent ball in front of his eye.

"HOLLYWOOD VAMPIRES"

It is one of the first spring days and a soft rain sprinkle the roofs of buildings and hits the windows of the Karlovy Vary airport. The first green leaves grow from buds on the branches of trees shivering in the wind. The watch on Peter's wrist shows 6.35 a.m., April the 6th" Peter observes the sun rising and a black thing emerging from a small cloud. His hair waves in gusts of wind.

A small black airplane arrives to the airport. The wheels touch the runway smoothly.

A white limousine awaits the passengers - right at the airport - not so far from the runway. Inside the limousine, Peter Willington, his son James Willington, one waitress and one of the hotel drivers are waiting.

The waitress prepares some welcome drinks, Champagne, orange juice and mineral water.

First, two bodyguards step out, then members of the music band Hollywood Vampires leave the private jet using the stairs. A cameraman documents every step. The musicians smile into the lens of the camera and make grimaces and hand signs.

James Willington and the hotel driver wait for them with big black umbrellas above their heads.

The members of the band enter the limousine and are offered a welcome drink by the beautiful young blond waitress. The elderly long-haired frontman Al Cooper smiles at her, "Now that's what I call - A Warm Welcome - yeah!"

He grabs a glass of Champagne with his long fingers covered by many rings, "Thank you sweetie."

Then he grabs a second glass and - observing her body – adds, "I'll have a pair of those."

The other band members follow their leader. One of them kisses the waitress on her fore head, "Thank you, Love."

"CAFÉ VIENNA VIBES"

The GM's wife – Jane Willington - is a well groomed lady in her mid 30's, she sits alone at the table in Café Vienna of the hotel Egeria. Jane has black shiny hair and her skin is still tanned from the Californian Sun. She is of a smaller height and has a well proportioned body. Her gestures are elegant. Her eyes are pure black supported by a light purple make up and long extended lashes. Jane wears a pink costume, which leaves the top of her breasts naked - leaving a sufficient space to onlooker's imagination.

Sebastian Hunter enters the café walking slowly. He immediately spots Jane and scans her face and body. Her skirt is pretty short and her legs are looking damn good. She drinks an espresso from a small porcelain cup and takes miniature careful bites of the fresh crunchy croissant. There is also a small bottle of still mineral water on the wooden table with a chess board inlayed into the table's desk, so no table cloth or runner on it to cover the beauty of the furniture.

He crawls like the tiger closer to her. She looks up. Her very girly and sexy neck is decorated with a white gold bracelet having a big pink diamond in the center.

Sebastian smiles, showing off his sharp snow-white teeth,"May I join you?"

Jane smiles back and glances at her long pink nails, "Please, welcome.

Jane realises his teeth look like the ones of the vampires and she finds it hot.

Sebastian sits close to her and his predator's instincts immediately kick in.

"Jane, you're very early today…How did you sleep?"

"James went with his father to the airport…To pick up that band from LA…I was going to go with them…But, I…don't feel well…sort of…I'm sick of this weather! I miss California.

"I know what you mean."

"I hate this cold country."

"It was brave of you to come to Europe."

"Oh, I just followed my husband James…Though I'm not certain why… We've been together for a long time…"

Sebastian is hearing the buyer's signalling, "Trust me, Jane, I do totally understand your situation. I was married too…12 years. I always did what she told me to do. And one day she stood in the door and said, "Why don't we have sex with other people? And we can still live happily together in an open marriage."

"Oh, gosh! Did she really say that?"

Sebastian acting broken and sad," Oui mon cher."

Jane and Sebastian freeze in the evolving conversation when the receptionist Yuki passes their table and asks Sebastian, if he would like to order something and that she will hand the order over to the waiters.

Sebastian sincerely smiles at Yuki, "Oh wonderful, my dear, I'll just have an espresso please…no sugar…no milk, thank you so much, Yuki, you're very kind and so attentive."

Yuki replies with a professional smile, "No worries" and leaves them alone.

Jane acting angry, "Bitch! So what did you say to her?"

Sebastian acting as a victim," I said, that I love her so much and asked her, if she already has someone…"

Jane now curious and with compassion,"Did she have someone already?"

Sebastian just nods.

"That must've hurt a lot…"

"The worst thing was…that the eyes I fell in love with…the eyes that were so beautiful…like the eyes of an angel…were - at that moment - as cold as ice…Cold - like the eyes of a killer. I'll never forget that look, full of malice and judgement, those once loving eyes… Filled with betrayal and hatred later."

Jane touches the hand of Sebastian.

Sebastian surprised, "Jane, your hand is so cold."

"I told you, Seb, it's freezing here…"

He puts his other hand onto hers and rubs it tenderly. Unconsciously, both of them move a bit closer to each other.

Sebastian now takes the role of an advisor,"Maybe it's time for a trip home to California? Or maybe even just a drive down to the French riviera or maybe Italy…You and James…" He is testing her, searching for her pain points.

Jane makes a grimace,"Me and James? Oh…"

Their hands - clenched together - get gradually warmer. Sebastian Hunter's knee touches the knee of Jane and it feels warm, pleasant - even it makes them bit nervous as it creates a kind of sexual tension.

The waiter emerges from behind the corner and looks like an assassin with the tray and coffee cup on it. Like a spy from James Bond movies.

They release their hands from the mutual grasp nervously and move slightly away from each other.

The waiter places the espresso in front of Sebastian and can sense that Jane Willington and Sebastian Hunter feel a bit uneasy for some reason.

The waiter, "Anything else? Something for you, Mrs. Willington?"

The word "Mrs." kills the morning day dreaming of Jane and Sebastian. Both Jane and Sebastian have a suspicion, the waiter knows what sparks between the two… The way he did put the accent on the word "Mrs.", the way he scrutinises them with his stare…

Jane with serious and cold voice, "Nothing for me, I'm good."

Sebastian with smile adds, "We are good. Thank you. Please put it on my account!"

The waiter bows, "Thank you" and leaves them alone.

Sebastian to himself, 'The fragile bubble of sweet future promises has burst. The deer he'd deftly stalked, in his crosshairs moments ago, has fled before he could squeeze the trigger and claim his prize. But Sebastian is a skilled and experienced hunter, stalking isn't the only method at his disposal. Sometimes it's necessary to abandon stealth and subtlety and embrace "Sturm und Drang". His prey may have slipped away, now in hiding somewhere, but it can be flushed out into the open. And when it's in the open, thinking it's on its way to safety… Sebastian knows, that he does not have much time this morning, but James and his father are now on their way to the airport. It doesn't have to be today. But, the way she did stare at me during the wine tasting… the way she did touch his hand just a moment ago…she is sending out strong signals. The hunter decides to take the risk and loose the hounds. With a little luck, they'll drive her out into the open where he'll have a clear shot. Sebastian smiles at Jane and says, "You are a beautiful woman, Jane…"

Jane freezes, "Oh, come on, Seb."

Sebastian knowing that this will come, "If I were in James's place…"

Jane resisting, "Well, you're not…"

Sebastian is totally reluctant to "No", "I said, if I were I would take you to some warm sunny island, just you and me, we'd forget about this damned hotel, we'd forget about the cold. Being somewhere warm we'd go back to the times when we were hot. Even if for just a little while."

"Oh, don't be silly, you really think I'm a naive school girl?" Jane continues slightly annoyed, "What makes you think…James and I aren't hot anymore?"

"The way you said   "James and I and then sighed." re-enacting Jane.

"What are you talking about, Seb?"

"Oh, please forgive me…"losing ground under his fees and switching himself into an unfortunate victim, "You know, I'm kind of sensitive, perhaps too sensitive, after we talked about my ex-wife…You know, I just wanted you to cheer up, you looked so unhappy and fragile sitting here all alone. So, I told you that story… and to be honest, I really like you, Jane…I really do think, you look great!"

Jane smiles at the cup in front of her, "I really think, men are sometimes like little kids. They never stop playing games…"

Sebastian knows he has to change his strategy, "I agree with you there…but, if you had just one hour left to live, what would you do? What would you do right now?"

Jane now stares directly into the Sebastian's eyes not believing to what she hears…She waits and she is alert - ready to run away as fast as she can…but, simultaneously, she feels the heat penetrating her body. She has a sensation as if the ticking bomb of her heart was about to detonate and tear this damn world into the pieces.

Sebastian feels the rising tension, he knows they are now balancing on the razor like edge or they will maintain the heat of the balance, or they will fall into the dark cold abyss, lonelier than ever before.

"Sebastian, you know, most people are all talk, that's all they do."

"True…because they're afraid to take risks…"

"Why should they?"

"I agree with you, Jane, one can lose everything by taking risks."

"You see…"

"Kids aren't afraid of taking risks. They can sit on a window sill ten floors up with their legs dangling around below them."

"What's so good about that?"

"They know they're immortal."

Jane rises her eyes from the coffee cup and glances at Sebastian. His face is wrinkled and it looks like as if he had some scars.

"You never give up, do you Seb?"

Sebastian leans closer to her, "Sometimes, I want to give up…"

Jane laughs and Sebastian uses the opportunity to touch her hand again.

He remarks, "Ooh, lala, your hand is warm! Success!"

Jane letting Seb's hand stay on her hand, "Yeah."

Their knees under the table again touch.

"Jane, just a moment please…" searching for something in his pocket.

"Sure."

He pulls out a card key with the number 666.

Jane smiles, "What's that?"

"That's proof. Proof that I'm not all talk and I take risks."

"What the fuck are you talking about, Seb?"Jane is cautious.

"Let's be kids for a moment, ok?"

"OK…"

Sebastian puts his hands behind his back hiding the card key. "Pick a hand…"

"Put your hands in front of me!"

Sebastian follows her order and places his hand on the table in front of her.

"Do you take risks, Jane?"

"I don't know…Why should I? I don't take risks…"

Sebastian begging, "Please, Jane, do it for me!"

"Why should I?"

Sebastian waits for a moment and examines Jane's eyes, her eyes are still cautious, but smile and are playful, "OK, maybe you don't take risks. Maybe you have the most beautiful eyes in the world. Maybe I'm stupid. But, I'm going to take the risk now."

"Come on, cut the shit, why should I?"

"OK, if you pick the hand without the keycard, you can slap me really hard!"

Laughing, "Oh that would be a pleasure!"

Acting as Romeo "But if you pick the hand with the keycard…"

"Yes…?"

"But if you pick the hand with the card key…you'll come with me to my room and…let me have my way with you."

Deadly silence. Jane stares into the eyes of Sebastian. She feels her face gets red and her body burns as she has a sensation of being humiliated. Jane is unable to make a single move and Sebastian Hunter looks to her like a nasty dirty man now. She feels sick. Jane - a woman in her mid 30's - thought that very little can surprise her, but this man caught her by her neck. She wants to run away, but she says instead, "What did you just say?"

Sebastian knows he must push till the very end and speaks quietly, "I'll be gentle or rough…I'll do whatever you ask…Just for today…"

Jane whispers, "Are you out of your mind?"

Sebastian closes his eyes, "Deal?"

Jane feels seriously uneasy and wants to leave, she does not know how to react in such an awkward situation. She observes Sebastian. He's got his eyes closed and two hands stretched on the table, now he looks to her - somehow funny. She has a feeling as if they both returned to their childhood, to its wild colourful phantasies. Jane immerses herself briefly into a retrospection. She starts laughing being pretty nervous.

Jane whispers, "What a sick pervert!" but in her mind, 'It's been such a long time since I've done anything really crazy…or maybe I just slap this pig now.'

She moves her hand slowly and touches the one of Sebastian's.

Sebastian opens his eyes, "This one? Are you sure?"

Jane replies, "I'm not sure, no…but yes…this one…"

Their eyes meet briefly in the expectation what will happen next.

"A NIGHT BEFORE"

Maître d'hôtel - Thomas Koenig - a handsome - super confident - black haired, slim young man, he could be the twin brother of Cristiano Ronaldo, arrives at the reception with a small plate and deliciously looking desert on it. This desert was made by the pastry chef personally and he is a real super star in his field. The decoration looks fantastic.

He comes to the receptionist Yuki and gives her that desert, "One of the guests couldn't eat it…dietary restrictions…"

Yuki surprised, "Oh, you're such a sweet boy…thank you."

Thomas Koenig smiles, "For you, anything…"

Yuki serious, "How's it going in the restaurant tonight?"

"We're really busy!"

Yuki gazing at the desert, "Wow, it looks so pretty…"

Thomas flattering her with a seducing smile, "Just like you…"

Yuki laughs, "Go back to restaurant, Thomas, quick! The guests will complain."

"Can I get a kiss, for the desert? As a reward?"

Yuki laughs to the face of Thomas and picks the phone faking the call, "Hi, is this the police? Yes, there's a boy causing trouble here…"

"Yuki, you owe me a kiss."

Yuki picks a bit of the desert with a tea spoon and pretends she will shoot that sweet bullet at Thomas's playboy face.

Thomas laughs and walks back to the restaurant shaking his head.

"DON'T PLAY WITH THE RUSSIANS"

It is a rainy evening and people rush to do some late shopping on T.G. Masaryk Street. Most of them are on their way home after a hard day's work. Between the shoppers, under a big black umbrella, Juan Alexander Polpo walks slowly. He drinks a coffee from a paper cup. He stops in front of a Russian food store and - with a little hesitation - enters it.

As if he was awaited, one of the shop assistants immediately asks Juan to follow him into their back office, which is hidden behind the racks with imported Russian food products. In one of the back offices two fat guys sit with shouldered Uzzi machineguns and pistols behind their belts. They play dice for "money" and drink milk. They place the Uzzis on the table between the plates with Russian "Vareniki" and plastic bags with "Sushki", which are Russian small crunchy mildly sweet bread rings. There is a pile of "Sushki" rings in the middle of the table - instead of money. The guys are heavily tattooed everywhere possible. A popular Russian tale, "Father Frost" runs on the small old TV, which for sure was there already during the cold war. There is some singing scene in original language. In the scene - the main hero Ivan leaves his home and mother, who gives him some advices how to behave and not to forget her ever.

Juan gazes at such an unusual scene.

The shop assistant, with the round shaped - thin framed -glasses behind him, who looks more like a university professor, remarks, "We Russians drink milk too…" The 4XL built tall guy looks back at Juan chewing the food noisily. Then they switch off the TV uttering sarcastically, "Конец сказки, Юан" (*End of the tales, Juan*).

One of them stands up and searches Juan, to double check any guns, Juan could possibly have on him. The Russian mafia member has tattoos on his hands, fingers and neck. He wears many heavy silver chains, bracelets and huge cheap watches. His head is perfectly shaved and his mustache and beard are roughly 2 days old.

The man is kind and smiles at Juan, "Kag dyela, Juan?" (*Howare you doing, Juan?*)

Juan cautious, "Vsyo khorosho, Volodya…" (*everything is good, Volodya*)

The Russian hints to Juan to follow him, "Davai!" (*Follow me!*)

The security guard leads Juan downstairs into the cellar, as he opens a secret door hidden under the piles of empties and cartoon boxes. The secret door admit them further underground and then they continue walking through a long tunnel lit by few red lights.

Juan enters a dark - by an obscure ambience intersected –room.

The guard breaths on his back, following him and utters, "Не Стесняйся, мальчишка." (*don't be shy, boy*)

One of the walls is made of neither concrete, bricks nor other building construction material, it is a heavy fabric, where Juan has to stop at a place where the curtain lets shine through some light. The guards stand on both sides of Juan and grab the edges of the curtain to open it.

The bloody red heavy curtain opens to reveal the Russian Mafia Boss, sitting in a medieval French chair. His name is Ivan Abelman Kostinsky. The man in his mid 50's wears a white fur. His hair is black like the feathers of ravens and his eyes are black too, like coal. They shine in the light of the many candles dispersed across the spacey room. There is a petrol lamp on the desk, it illuminates half his face leaving the other in the dark. His facial features strongly resemble the typical Jewish ones. In fact, his grandfather was a Jewish astronomer from Lvov and his grandmother a Russian singer at St. Petersburg's opera. The man's thick beard is well groomed. He smiles bright, welcoming Juan, "Я рад тебя видеть, Юан." (*I'm glad to see you, Juan.*)

The boss sits behind the wide heavy wooden table. There is a notebook on the table, an opened thick book – the kind being typically used by the accountants, and some folders. A paper-weight is made of a human stuffed head. The empty look of its glass eyes give Juan a goose skin. Its teeth are substituted by the sharp purple amethyst crystals. Juan spots something strange standing in the corner – coffins…

Juan is speechless…

The Ivan turns to his security guy, "Call Jeanette and ask her to bring us that stuff…"

The security guy with the machine-gun in his one hand does so.

Juan turns his eyes at Volodya with a silent question, "What stuff…?"

Ivan turns to Juan, "I really hope, you have it for me today…? The only acceptable news is good news."

Juan is impressed by the direction and scared, "Mr. Kostinsky, please accept my sincere apologies…"

Ivan smiles, "My dear Juan, please do something for me…Stop apologizing! If you can…? A real man does not apologize."

"I'll bring the money as soon as I have it. I swear…" with a wide smile, "… and stop making promises!"

The security guy Volodya opens the door and a nearly naked woman enters the room with a suitcase. The only stuff she wears are black leather bikini pants and her nipples are covered only by two small crosses made of black tape. Her hair is artificially coloured blond, her eyes are deep blue and lips painted dark red. There is a wide belt with sharp long steel stings around her snow-white neck. Juan is terrified, the things in the room dance around him. The sound of Jeanette's high needle heels puts stamps onto this obscure postcard from the next world.

She passes Juan with a strange smile and comes to Ivan, kisses him long and puts a metal box on the table. Juan does not know, what to observe first - naked Jeanette or the box…? Jeanette opens the metal box and pulls out a smaller one. Juan imagines many things that could possibly happen next. He does not feel well about the situation he is in. Jeanette opens the smaller box and places it on the table on top of a black leather napkin. Then she pulls out a syringe, a small glass bottle with white crystals, a spoon and a German vintage cigarette lighter from 1930s. She places all the stuff on the leather napkin.

The sexy demon starts preparing a narcotic dose - and as she does it, she glances at Juan with a sensual cruel smile - time to time.

Ivan is nervous and getting impatient,"I am not sure, if you will give me my money back, Juan!"

Juan hastily, "I will! I will!"

"I know, you will." Ivan is serious now, "Funny, only when people are tortured, when they are put under a lot of pressure – they do deliver…"

Juan stares at the fingers of Jeanette, they have extensive, creepy nails, "The reason is, I've had some unexpected expenses…"

Ivan snickers, "or losses… unexpexted shopping", with a wild laugh.

"I just need 24 hours to get you your money."

Ivan is acting surprised, "Oh, you must be a magician, Juan. You keep us waiting 2 months and now you can perform miracles - in 1 day? No, brother, no, no. I don't believe in miracles. I believe in hard work. Hard work beats talent, in the long run. But, hard work is not enough, you also need to protect the fruits of your harvest. And trust me, Juan, I am a fierce protector of my harvested fruits."

Jeanette winks at Juan as she heats the white crystals in the shining cosmic steel spoon by the cigarette lighter.

Ivan smiles at Juan and then on Jeanette, "We must make sure, you understand the term "DEADLINE"."

"I know what it means. In 24 hours I'll bring it plus 10 percent on the top."

Ivan serious, "I know you know, what the term means. But, my dear Juan, what we are going to do now - is a bit of a practical exercise… It's time for you to become a man, Juan. So far, you have been a talented student of life. Nevertheless, my dear brother, theory is not enough. And… Do not worry! We are not going to kill you… Not tonight… You know, from my early childhood, I always wanted to become a doctor… You know…to help people…to cure their illnesses… You are sick, my friend and I want to help you, trust me."

The white crystals in the spoon turn into a liquid and first bubbles appear. Juan stays silent and his face turns pale. Jeanette pulls the liquid into the syringe. She makes sure there are no air bubbles in the syringe. The devil comes closer to Ivan and sits on his legs. Juan and Volodya behind him observe this obscure night theatre. Ivan opens his mouth and closes his eyes. Jeanette injects the drug into the man's gums and then she kisses him long, putting her long tongue inside his mouth. The boss opens his eyes wide and his pupils turn into the monster like reddish star-rays. He sighs in a big relief. Ivan stares at Juan, stands up and takes his fur coat off. Jeanette assists him. Then she helps him to wear a long white coat.

The narcotised man is in his element putting the plastic medical gloves on. The special medical googles with the tiny microscopes attached onto the lenses. A surgical mask makes his outfit perfect.

Ivan is approaching Juan, "…but even more than a doctor, I wanted to be a dentist…"

Juan is more than terrified, stands up and steps back towards the door, "Hey, wait! Just in 24 hours + 50 percent more."

Ivan is smiling again, "My dear Juan, I should have told you a story about my former patient Dima before! But we'll get to it…"

"What happened to Dima?"

"Be patient."

Juan makes a few more steps towards the door, but Volodya hits his head from the back with the gun-stock. Juan falls unconscious.

When Juan comes back to life, he is tied up to the chair with black tape. His mouth is opened wide and kept this way by a system of clamps. Volodya holds Juan's head firmly in his bear like hands. The doctor – Ivan - makes Juan's teeth thorough examination with the proper dental instruments and announces to his assistant - sister Jeanette   "11, 12, 13 are OK…14 - Upper Right - needs a root canal treatment…"

Juan opens his terrified eyes wide open.

Jeanette pulls out a small drill of the box and announces happily, "Unfortunately, we do not have any anaesthetics left…"

Juan sighs.

The "dentist" acting annoyed, "What a pity… and shrugs his arms in an apologetic gesture, "I am really sorry, dear patient, rest assured we act as gentle as we can!" continuing, "should you feel you cannot bear the pain anymore, please let us know. However, we will need to continue in order to heal you."

Juan sighs louder and shakes his whole body.

Ivan now with a worried voice, "Mr. Patient, it will be slightly longer session tonight, because the rotten tooth has three roots…"

Juan sighs even louder and shakes his whole body again in a desperate attempt to free himself. The panic overwhelms him totally. He keeps mumbling something.

Ivan in his element, "Sister, the drill please."

Jeanette hands the required instrument to the doctor and they both kiss long. It is apparent they do enjoy every moment. The dentist then leans over the patient, who is in a mental agony already and tests the drill in front of his eyes.

Jeanette smiles at Juan.

The "doctor" drills into the tooth of Juan, who tries to yell, but can only release unidentifiable sounds. Then he pulls the tooth out of Juan's mouth and blood flows everywhere.

Juan's body shakes in great pain.

"FORBIDDEN FRUITS"

Whereas at the hotel Egeria Jane stays in one of the public bathrooms in front of the mirror and gazes into her own eyes. She touches her neck and then she puts her engagement ring down… She walks to one of the rooms and knocks the door…Sebastian walks across the room as if he was a tiger locked in the cage. Sebastian opens the door - Jane is there. Sebastian takes her hand and pulls her into the room. They move closer to each other and start to undress each other. Suddenly Sebastian grabs Jane into his arms and carries her to the bed. He throws her onto it. He undresses her violently and then he undresses himself. She takes her pants off. With short moves Sebastian ties Jane to the bed with ropes he had prepared before. They are kissing each other, they make love and their two naked bodies shake in mutual pleasure…

GM's assistant Juan Alexandro Polpo walks down the corridor and touches his mouth with painful sighs. Some guests did complain about the loud music in the early morning. And now, Juan has to solve the situation. Juan knocks at the door and they open as they were previously not closed properly…

The sighs of the two lovers intertwine with the loud music. Juan enters the room cautiously - and the mirror reflects something he would expect the least - Jane and Sebastian!

He observes them for a while and then searches in the pockets for something. Finally he pulls out his mobile phone and gets it ready to make a picture -- but the battery blinks red, signalising a critically low power. Juan is whispering to himself, "Please, just one…" As he presses the red button to capture the sensitive moment, the phone goes off. "Shit!" he utters inadvertently. In the very same moment he covers his mouth by his hand and makes a few steps back for the fear of being exposed. The sighing stops. Juan silently crawls backwards.

The music stops. Juan closes the door and stands in the corridor without a single movement.

Sebastian stands right behind the door and puts his ear on it, listening - hunting for any suspicious sounds. His both hands are placed on the door. He is completely naked.

Juan is on the other side and feels the presence of one of the lovers.

Silence.

Sebastian touches the door handle in order to open them.

Juan makes a few cautious steps away.

Sebastian opens the door slowly, just wide enough, to see the corridor… It is empty. No traces of life.

Juan hides behind the statue of Egeria. He can see - as the door slightly open - a pair of Hunter's eyes in the cranny. Juan is not sure if Sebastian sees him.

Suddenly, something small emerges from behind the corner! It heads towards Juan. It is the hotel cat. Juan is afraid the cat will expose him. But, the door closes again. And Juan breathes out in relief. The cute animal is rubbing his legs. Juan smiles at it, but his smile turns instantly into a painful grimace as he touches his cheek. Juan's eyes emit fiery anger.

"OLD STUFF"

In the restaurant later this morning, waiters survived the breakfast's peak and the clock hands show 10.00 a.m. Sebastian Hunter is taking his breakfast. Juan Alexandro Polpo joins him at his table. But, he does not eat anything and time to time - unconsciously - touches his cheek. His face is pale and his eyes burn.

Juan detached, "Morning, Sebastian."

"Hi."

Both men observe a few last hotel guests, queuing with the plates at the buffet stations. The chefs assist them.

Juan starts gossiping into Sebastian's ear,"I have an interesting proposition, man..."

"What's that, Juan?"

Juan looks around the restaurant searching for the big ears and dodgy eyes, "Well, I'm afraid..." His eyes meet with those of the Maître d'hôtel, who almost immediately - turns his eyes away, "...that this isn't the best place to talk about it..."

Sebastian is getting curious, "About what?"

"Lets meet tonight around the hotel, then we can talk."

Sebastian suspicious, "All right, see you then..." and stands up from the table staring oddly at Juan. He leaves the restaurant to go directly to a storeroom in the cellar to meet his subordinate Karel Kunkal. He orders him to tidy up the abandoned – long time not touched – hotel repository. To get Karel some help, he calls the banqueting manager Aida de Luca, "Hi Aida, this is Sebastian, could you allocate 2 strong guys to help Karel to get the store in presentable shape? It will be for the benefit of all departments, as there will be a lot of space, when it has been cleaned up.

Aida agrees, "But only for a few hours - as they have to prepare the boardrooms for the "Jewish Chambers of Commerce" members, who supposed to arrive tomorrow from Brooklyn."and she instructs two banqueting waiters, who already work on the preparations, to help in the storeroom, not just to be cooperative, but also to be able to use the room at first hand.

The security guard with the help of two banqueting waiters work hard to move all the old tables, chairs and other stuff covered in dust. Time to time - the banqueting manager Aida turns up to help little, or just for a banter - to make sure the job is done in designated time. The hotel workers dive deep into the cable tangle, electronic equipment clusters and paintings of unknown artists, old TV sets, flip charts, books and files, boxes with the markers / papers / pins / magnets / old menus / old coins and other forgotten things. Just name it!

The boys feel adventurous - as if they were the archeologists, digging in the sands around the Pyramids – in the hunt for the ancient excavations. And who knows…? In such a mess & dust, they might even find the mummy!

One of the boys - a banqueting waiter - a thin tall Czech guy named Leos - finds boxes with old VHS stereo cassettes. These are labeled. He picks one, on which the labes says, *"CAM 44A / CORRIDOR / DECEMBER 8 1992 / 00 - 6 AM"*.

Leos goes to the security man Karel with it to show him what he has found. Karel examines the VHS without any interest, but then picks walkie-talkie and calls to his boss Sebastian.

Sebastian sits in his chair behind the desk and makes some research on the latest security trends commonly used in hotels, other commercial premises or households. He opens the link on his computer "Security Solutions for Hotels and the Hospitality Industry". Suddenly the electronic voice of Karel is heard, "Hello Sebastian, this is Karel, can you hear me?"

Sebastian takes his microphone from the station and answers, "Yes Karel, I can hear you. What has happened?"

"We have found some old VHS tapes from the surveillance system, shall we keep them or throw them away?"

"I will come down later and we will check them first, but is there also a VHS player in the store, you know that this format is not available for years…"

"Yes, boss. We found an old VHS player as well, but if it works, we still have to check… I will have to find the cables as well."

The other banqueting waiter – Ludek - finds an old Spanish guitar. He tries it and it seems to be working well!

After they have finished in the cellar, Karel asks Leos and Ludek to wait with their "treasures" for to the security chief's. When he comes, first thing Sebastian does is, he takes the guitar from Ludek, first tunes the guitar and then starts to play some accords.

He puts the guitar aside and asks Leos, "Please show me the VHS cassettes and the player." Leos already has plugged the player into the socket and surprisingly it works. "Mr. Hunter, we can start watching the films, just after I have connected this screen with the player."

"Leos? Correct what I read on your name tag? Take the cables and start the show…"

They all watch the screen and see an empty corridor…

"QUICKIE"

Jane and James Willington took a short break in the afternoon and are in their apartment. The couple is in their bed. They make love, but James finishes too soon and feels ashamed about it. To Jane it seems more like, he is not interested, rather than less in love… Besides, straight after they have finished this brief afternoon romance, James did receive some messages on his mobile phone and ran away with it to the toilet. Jane is already suspicious for a long time regarding his infidelity!

"THE HUNTING DAY"

Jonathan Lee together with Bony Eins, Juan Polpo and the real estate manager of Jonathan, are accompanied by Jakub Srna, who is the forester for the area near the hotel Egeria where they are now located. They are on the hunt for another deer or - if not deer - wild boar. Whatever comes first their way. They see a deer running towards the hotel as if it went mad. In the matter of fact - the deer comes to the hotel bins to check for the left overs, which tend to be generous and in this tough cold winter helpful!

At the same time James Willington brushes his teeth with an electric tooth-brush. He wears a grey T-shirt. He stares into the mirror, examining his eyes. Looks closer. Suddenly, the shadow in the mirror moves behind John swiftly. He turns back. Steps out of the bathroom. It was his wife! He sighs of relief. Goes back and continues his morning cleansing.

James is talking to himself, "…like other people…I brush my teeth, go to the bathroom, wear clothes…" he goes to the walk-in wardrobe and opens the drawer with dozens of neckties. "…hm…I need a simpler life!" He picks a red one. Then he chooses a black suite.

He goes to the small kitchen of the apartment, opens the fridge with a lot of soya stuff and fruits… He cuts a wholegrain dark bread on the board saying to himself "…and now you wonder, why the hell I just do not got to the hotel restaurant and have a proper breakfast…?"

James drinks coffee from a big mug with the motif of a red kiss on it. There is a short motto below, "*It is better to be first than last!*"

He smiles.

"Well, I guess Jane and I - want to have a place here that feels like home. So it's not like we're at work all the time."

James walks the hotel corridor and listens to his mobile which says, "9. 15 a.m. - Brief meeting in boardroom ANNA".

As he looks up - he faces the big black eyes of a deer!

James in a shock shouts,"What the fuck!"

James's face gets pale! He is frozen on the spot. Both look at themselves without a single movement. The mobile phone continues talking, "10.00 a.m. - meeting with Sebastian on the new security camera system"

Sebastian sits on a high chair and plays the old Spanish guitar. All listen. There is also Jane standing at the door. And as Sebastian plays, she is sucked into a daydream, 'Jane and Sebastian sit on a beach of an abandoned island. The waves hit the shore in the slow motion. The wall of water foam approaches the 2 lovers as they hug each other in the white sand. The sun is low and creates the yellow

- black painting out of the silhouettes of the - low above the ground - crawling palm trees...'

Applause.

Jane wakes-up back to the reality. The people clap their hands in their appraisal of Sebastian's unexpected showcase of his hidden virtuosity. He just grins and his eyes stop right onto the eyes of Jane. Jane wakes up once again and deflects her look away.

In the upper floor corridor a strange scenario is taking place, James and a deer stand opposite each other, no movement at all. Just James has dialled a number on his cellphone and keeps it close to his ear. After the connection is there, he whispers, "Sebastian! Send some of your guys to the 6th floor - left wing! NOW!!" and to the deer, "How the hell did you get in here?"

Then, behind the deer, a couple of drunk people emerge from a room! They laugh as they can't believe their eyes. They are the members of the famous Hollywood Vampires band.

One of them - the leader Al yells, "People of the World, wait for me!"

He disappears in one of the rooms. The noise is to be heard from that room and wheezing. Al finally comes out with a big flat TV screen in his arms. His companions fall down to the ground in the laughter. One of them, "What the fuck!"

The other one, "That's the fucking guy from that TV show! That's him!!"

Al, "The one with the antlers…" now screaming, "Out here in the field, I fight for my meals…"

The deer turns towards Al with his back to James Willington - and freezes again.

Al starts singing, "…I don't need to fight, to prove I'am right…"

The deer puts his head down as he was about to attack Al and the group with its formidable antlers.

James worried about the safety of his guests, "Sir, guys, please…go back to your rooms - now!"

Al continues as he did not even hear James, "…and I don't need to be forgiven!"

The deer manages to sneak through the corridor and jumps over the drunk and stoned members of the band being convulsed with laughter. The deer disappears running downstairs.

Al yells at the running deer, "Keep moving, blood sucker! Run!" he throws the TV screen towards the deer and it noisily breaks into the pieces.

Sebastian arrives to the scene and James shouts angrily at him, "What kind of a security guy are you? Tell me! How the heck it is possible, that we have a deer on the sixth floor of our hotel? Tell me!"

"EGERIA ART"

At the very same time, just in the other part of the hotel Egeria complex - Mr. Tea and the security guard Karel observe a painting on the wall.

It is the painting of EGERIA.

There is a naked woman dictating the laws of Rome to Numa Pompilius. As Mr. Tea is a literate well travelled person, he is in his element to give Karel some insights into the background of this work of art.

"THE LEGEND OF EGERIA"

Mr. Tea explains to Karel, "The naked woman is Egeria, who was a nymph and a goddess of the Roman pantheon. She is associated with water bearing wondrous, religious and medical properties. But most of all, Egeria gave her wisdom and prophecies in return for libations of water or milk at her sacred groves. That man is the second most legendary King of Rome - Numa Pompilius, who succeeded its founder Romulus.

The nymph Egeria, as legends say it, was a Roman deity and lover of Numa Pompilius, who lived between 715 and 672 BC, and who was the successor of Romulus in the kingship of Rome. For him, she was a great inspiration and guided him in his legislation. Her name is synonymous with the conception of a wise counsellor and adviser."

Karel is wondering, "How do you know all this stuff?"

"It's simple. I read it and memorised it."

As both men observe the painting, being hypnotized by the curves of naked Egeria, they hear an approaching noise. And as they turn to see what is going on, they do witness a deer running through the corridor - being followed by the security Chief Sebastian, GM John Willington, famous Al Cooper and the rest of the drunk band members. The strange group disappears.

Both men look at themselves, left speechless. Then they glance back at the painting with their strange feelings - as if they were on LSD. And then, they start running in their frantic chase of the group.

The sun goes down, nevertheless there is still some light giving a sufficient visibility to the scene. The hotel staff observes the deer running towards the forrest. A sudden shot tears the heaven into pieces and the deer dies in his last jump.

After some time, Jonathan Lee followed by his men emerge from the forrest. Juan observes Bony Eins as he takes photos of Jonathan with the deer trophy with his mobile phone. Then he spots something in one of the hotel windows. He is interested and something tells him to look closer. He picks his field-glasses and raises them to his eyes. He can't believe to what he sees...

A man and a woman kiss each other - and they are no other than Sebastian Hunter and Jane Willington!

Juan to himself,"This time I'll get you." He pulls his mobile really quick - zooms in - and takes the pictures. Juan smiles as he scrolls through the pictures he did hunt just now. "Not the deer...That's the trophy of the day!"

It is just after dinner and Sebastian takes Karel to the canteen for a coffee. They have a chat and Sebastian shows pics from Paris to Karel. There are also pictures of the protests and demonstrations of the yellow vests and half naked girls in red. Then - on purpose - he shows the selfie of Karel sleeping in the office and himself as he squats in front of the sofa.

"PICS OF THE DAY"

After work Juan can't wait to get home. He is close to running to his apartment, eager to get the photos of his mobile printed. Having them in his hands, he looks at them and he smiles while he puts them to the safe. For his "excellent work", he opens a bottle of "Sea Dog" and enjoys a glass. He watches the TV news - they talk about the band "Hollywood Vampires" who are about to throw a gig at the Pilsen football stadium.

The band was very generous and gave free tickets for the concert to the hotel staff, so small groups have organized their transport to Pilsen after their shifts in the afternoon. They agreed drop-off and pick-up at the shopping center near the stadium.

Samia and her team shop for some outfits and accessories that would be a fit for the upcoming gig. The girls meet their colleague from the reception - Yuki. Yuki takes them to a Sushi bar. The girls enjoy many plates with the delicatessen and the piles of the small plates rise up.

The girls have fun, being a little drunk from the sake, which they had together with the sushi, they start trying a variety of sun glasses - some of them really eccentric ones. After the optician they enter a toy shop and the girls run with toy guns in between the shelves. They do pretend they take a part in the battle. One of the girls picks a microphone - it's Samia. She pretends singing. Yuki takes photos of all of them, catching the funny moments. Then Yuki finds a toy movie camera and pretends to be shooting a music video.

The other girl picks a toy slate and acts a script girl. The rest does some dancing. A shop assistant looks annoyed, but the young handsome security guy observes the beautiful girls with delight. The girls continue doing crazy things in the evening streets, while walking towards the stadium, merging with other fans in the craziest outfits.

"COOKING WITH THE KIDS"

One of the pastry chefs prepares a tray with ice cream in small glass bowls. When he finishes the task, he takes the tray and walks away from the kitchen. He brings the tray with ice cream to the Salon next to the Café Vienna and immediately gains interest of the kids, who were signed up for the cooking class. They do surround him.

The pastry chef is very much fond of showing his talent to others and one group of guests is loving to work with him – the kids.

In the salon next to the Café the floor is covered with plastic and long tables are placed as working stations for the kids. The chef has placed the ingredients needed on the tables and waits for the rest of the kids. They arrive with their nanny or parents who are filming their loved ones while they are mixing the butter and eggs with the sugar, then they add flower, we know why the floor is covered as one kid has more flower on the ground than in the bowl, where it supposed to be. Baking powder is added, chocolate powder is added. Kids start to taste the dough. Fingers are getting brown from the chocolate. Nuts are added to the dough. Pastry chef shows how the dough should look like. Then he rolls it on the table and takes a glass to cut out circles from the dough. Kids are following his instructions. Then the circles are placed on baking paper covering baking trays.

20 min later the cookies are ready.

During the waiting period the chef explains how to prepare sugar and egg white to decorate the cookies. He is providing all the kids with sufficient decoration stuff. When the cookies come from the oven, they are cooled down. The cold cookies are now ready to be decorated and the children put all their phantasies on them. The kids are allowed to take their work and happily present it to their parents.

Hotel owner Peter Willington takes part in cooking with the kids. He is now back in his full health.

"SLEEPER"

The evening starts and in the basement Karel is looking for a place to get some rest. The security guard finds a new place where to sleep – the storage room they did make tidy today morning. He tells to himself, "OK then, just a quick nap, just a quick one…"

He finds a massive wooden wardrobe - perhaps from the 18th century.

The young man, who loves to eat and sleep, switches off the light and uses his torch to see the things. He opens the wardrobe and hides inside. Then he sets the alarm, puts the walkie-talkie volume up and closes his eyes. Very quickly he falls asleep. He has a dream about Egeria, his dream is an erotic one…

"A DREAM OF THE EGERIA NYMPH"

A beautiful blonde long haired woman with dark blue eyes walks through a pine forrest heading to ancient castle ruins. Egeri realises that she is in the remnants of a spa, when she sees a small pond with springs of warm waters.

A man from the distant planet walks the same forrest, admires it's beauty & uniqueness and approaches the ruins of the castle. It's the security guard Karel.

Karel spots a beautiful creature - Egeria - as she drops her clothes down onto the stones. She stands on the edge of the basin with the hot water. The man hides behind the half broken stone pillar without any movement or breath - as he has become a statue from ncient times.

Egeria is naked, she enters the hot water in the basin and enjoys the feeling. She does not know she is being observed by the stranger from a different planet... The sun illuminates the water and plays the shadow game on the walls of the ruins.

The man - suddenly - unconsciously - makes a move, and from his pocket slips a red crystal off into the dark green pine needles covering the ground below his feet. The fragile crystal breaks into the pieces that shine in the sun rays refracting white light into its multi colour sparks. The sudden noise, kills the peaceful silence in the same time painful & beautiful, it awakes the wonderful creature – the nymph and goddess - Egeria from her day-dreaming. She looks around hastily and yet - as she was from the past dreams of young men - moving slowly and fast at once. Egeria examines the source of the sound.

There!

She had spotted him. A stranger behind the pillar. He looks like a small boy caught doing something wrong or rather something strictly forbidden. She hastes and swims towards her clothes. And as she emerges from the hot water and steam. There he stands, handing her a big towel. The stranger - gentle man... Karel. Egeria loses her fear and let her self to be embraced. She wants to say something, but he puts his finger onto her lips as if he wanted to silence her, but in fact - he touches them to examine - why are they so magnetic beautiful?!

Someone observes them!

It's the security chief Sebastian Hunter. His teeth are sharp and claws long. He has special round-shaped sun glasses on his eyes that release 2 fluorescent greenish rays. They scan the scene. Egeria and Karel turn in the direction of the predator Sebastian, as if they felt - someone else is here. Sebastian instantly turns into the green poisonous snake. The snake moves along the ruins and walls covered in dark green leaves of ivy.

Egeria undresses and drags Karel into the warm spa, and they merge with the vapour rising from the water surface. Karel kisses Egeria and examines her beautiful elegant body by his strong hands. Her skin is so white and honey like.

The snake hangs from the pine tree branch above them. It opens its cold mouth to reveal its long sharp poisonous teeth. The sticky transparent liquid drops down onto their naked bodies. They have sex nevertheless.

The green deadly devilish snake enters the water…

Karel wakes-up with a smile.

As if Sebastian knew about Karel's dream, he searches for Karel in the back-office but cannot find him. He keeps searching as if this was the most important job in the world. He likes to play. Sebastian passes by the swimming pool area and observes two girls swimming there. He glances at his stylish sports watch, which shows 8.20 p.m. Sebastian raises his walkie-talkie, while staring at the young slim girls, they look Asian, but who knows nowadays what nationality they have, "Karel, what is your position? OVER!"

Silence is the answer.

The girls now hug each other and kiss. Sebastian opens his mouth slightly, revealing his vampire like teeth.

The walkie-talkie reverts to Sebastian, "Did not copy. Repeat. OVER!"

Sebastian is frozen by the spectacular view and only utters, "I'll find you, you bastard."

Sebastian almost hits the guests as he makes his way through the corridor. He does apologise with a smile and an elderly couple smiles back.

As Sebastian passes the banqueting office he spots the assistant banqueting manager Jiri Soucek doing something dodgy under the desk. Sebastian glances through the glass door just to see the young man moving the bottles of wine from the paper cartoons into the backpack!

Sebastian keeps walking and pulls a small note pad and a torso of the pencil out of his suit pocket. He keeps walking and writes down this note 8.37 p.m. – Jiri Soucek / the bottles of wine!"

Sebastian even enters the storage room, but Karel is well hidden this time. As Sebastian opens the door and switches the light on, Karel wakes up and through a key hole observes Sebastian sniffing around. Karel holds his breath in the big wardrobe and takes the picture through its key hole. After a while the light goes back off and Sebastian leaves the room and Karel breathes out in relief.

In the very same moment - the mobile alarm, Karel has set on previously - goes on. Karel immediately switches it off, but…the door opens again… Karel's eye is glued to the key hole. His heart is beating fast. The silhouette of his boss dwells in the door for an eternity.

Karel in his mind, 'Well, this is it. He's got to know I'm here.'

The shadow monster Sebastian Hunter raises his hand and the thing he holds in it - is the walkie-talkie! Karel utters, "Shit!"

Karel glances at his walkie-talkie attached to his belt. He manages to put its volume down just in time.

Sebastian Hunter whispers ominously into his device, "Karel… I know you're here…"

Silence.

Sebastian continues, "K a r e l…come out!"

Silence.

"You don't want me to come find you, do you…?"

Silence.

Sebastian makes a step towards the wardrobe.

Karel moves his hand to open the door as he already decided to give up - but in the very moment, Sebastian's mobile rings. Sebastian answers, "Yes my love, sure, I'll be there…kiss, kiss baby…me too…yeah…I'm always ready…for you."

Sebastian closes the door and Karel breathes out knowing it was damn close to being fired.

Karel departs the wardrobe and carefully opens the door of the room. The corridor is empty. He walks away and turns his walkie-talkie back on.

"THE CONCERT"

Samia and her office team arrive to the stadium. They observe with curiosity, how the people are dressed and see that what they have chosen in the shopping mall do perfectly fit. They wear hard rock outfits and sip fruit cocktails - "Umbrella Drinks". The team building is on.

The band enters the stage accompanied by ovations.

Whereas in the hotel Night Club the evening show begins.

Music comes from the speakers and the light is switched down that only one spot remains.

James Willington enters the stage and applause accompanies him.

James takes the microphone and turns to the audience, "Good evening, Ladies & Gentlemen, Welcome to our Club, this is a little show my team and I have put together for you. I am glad to see that you enjoyed our food. No, you don't have to say anything, I can see your bellies from here. But to make you happier, speaking of food, do you know the definition of a vegetarian? - It's someone that can't hunt, can't fish, and can't make a fire".

Laughter from the guests follows.

„Don't get me wrong, it's not that I dislike animals. But, being a food lover I do have to admit that animals make the best food. On the bright side, I suppose that makes me an animal lover as well!"

James takes the smiles of the audience with satisfaction.

„During our show I would like to provide you with some short stories I have heard. I hope you'll enjoy them."

He speaks to the audience in very clear voice, so everyone can understand him,"First, let me tell you a story, one of my friends shared with me. He claims, it really happened to him. I won't reveal his name. Let's call the story "Why I fired my secretary?"

A couple of weeks ago I had my 45th birthday and I did not feel well anyway. I went down to the breakfast and knew, that my wife would bekind to me, she would say "all the best" and maybe have a little present for me. She did not even say „good morning" and in no way she said "all the best". I said to myself, "Ok, the women are like this, but the kids did not forget it."

The kids came, didn´t say a word and left me all aside. As I went to the office, I did not feel well. I went through the entrance of my office and Janet, my secretary, approached me and said „Happy birthday, boss!" After this welcome I felt a little bit better, at least someone remembered my birthday. I worked until lunchtime.

Per minute exactly at twelve, Janet knocked on my door and said "Hey boss, it is such a beautiful day, and it is your birthday, why don't we go to lunch together, just you and me!" and gave me a big hug.

My secretary Janet was very young andbeautiful, not to mention charming. I answered, "That's the best idea, which I did hear today sofar…". So we left. We did not go to the regular restaurant, we drove to a small and cozy restaurant outside the town, to have some privacy.

We drank 2 Martinis and enjoyed the superb lunch. On the way back to the office Janet giggles and says, "You know, it is such a beautiful day and it is your birthday, we do not have to drive directly to the office, do we?"

"No, we do not have to." I replied.

"Lets go to my apartment!" Janet offered.

As we arrived to her apartment, we drank other 2 Martinis and smoked a cigarette.

Janet giggles again and says, "If it does not bother you, I'd like to change into something more comfortable…it's too hot here…"

She gives me a sultry look and adds, "Relax, make your self comfortable…my Boss…. I'll just go to my bedroom and will be back immediately!"

I was able to answer just excited "Sure, do so!" and she left into her bedroom.

After a minute she came back.

She did carry a large birthday cake in her hands… being followed by my wife and the kids - all smiling, singing „Happy Birthday"…

They suddenly stopped smiling when they saw that I was lying on the couch wearing nothing but my socks!"

Laughter and applause by the guests…

"Thank you folks and good night."

James is about to return to his table but an anonymous voice from the crowd shouts, "What happened next?"

The other voices add into a collective demand to know more.

James, as if he was prepared for that, "My friend fired his secretary. Unfortunately, his wife also fired him."

Laughter and applause by the guests follows and James Willington leaves the stage at last.

"ONE TEAM - DIFFERENT BACKGROUNDS"

If a hotel is booked to full capacity the managers need to assist line employees in their work. Layla this time helps the Ukrainian dishwasher named Fedir with a pile of dirty dishes. All chefs already left after a busy night. Fedir is a small thin man in his early 60's. He fights with the dishes like a warrior, he sings some song in Ukrainian empowered by Czech beer (this is allowed in books). The can stands on the small steel table and he picks it up time to time to take a sip. There is also a bluetooth speaker and android mobile standing next to the can. A hard rock song comes out of it loud.

Any repetitive work is hard - especially for a creative person like Fedir is. Back in his home town of Donetsk he used to be an actor in a small theatre. The unfortunate circumstances had brought him fortunately to Karlovy Vary and he can restart his life once again. As Fedir is lost in the fierce battle with the dishes in hot steam surrounding him - we flashback briefly to his story:

Fedir crawls through the ruins of the house. The building is being slowly consumed by the fire flames. A smoke and dust swirl in between the broken walls. The gun shots keep breaking the silence painfully and time to time a hand grenade detonates - not too far from Fedir. He spots something in the dust on the floor - he picks it up.

It is a photograph.

There is a school class on it with their teachers. Just a few steps from Fedir lies a man in agony and blood. Fedir leans towards him. The Unknown Soldier whispers to him, "цигарка" (*a cigarette*)

Fedir does not hear him well, "що ти кажеш?" (*What are you saying?*)

The Unknown Soldier, "будь ласка, сигарету" (*a cigarette, please*)

Fedir searches in his pocket and pulls out a box of cigarettes. He lights a cigarette using a fire flame dancing right besides them. Then he wants to insert the cigarette into the mouth of the soldier but his enemy's eyes freeze as his soul escapes the dead body. Fedir smokes the cigarette. A random bullet hits a mirror on the wall behind him. He turns back with the cigarette in his dry lips.

There is blood on the mirror. Fedir touches his arm and his face distorts into a scary grimace in the broken mirror. Fedir grabs his machine gun and runs away.A sound of tanks chase Fedir in the street full of dead bodies, broken cars and houses in flames. He enters an old long time abandoned cinema. The silence of solitude in the middle of war surrounds him. Fedir steps onto the stage with the machine gun in his hands. He turns towards the empty seats.

Fedir shouts towards an invisible audience, "Go to hell!" and opens fire at the empty seats.

Back to reality, Fedir opens another can of beer and glances at Layla who helps him in the deadly fight with dishes. Fedir raises his can and taps on it with his finger and a question mark in his eyes, "ви хочете пиво?" (*Do you want a beer?*)

"Let's get this done quickly, so we can go home!" Layla continues working.

Fedir smiles at her, "якщо ви не хочете говорити…" (*If you don't want to talk…*)

Layla focuses on the dishes. She pulls a shallow pressure cooker - this one is basically a short silverish pot with a handle - out of the dishwasher. She puts it in front of her face and as she quickly moves it, it makes a scary face out of her beautiful one.

We flashback to Layla's story:

Layla - being a young girl - sits in the wooden dry toilet and from a small window in the door she can observe the church and local pub of the small Romanian village. Some drunk men leave the pub shouting and singing. One of them walks towards the toilet. Layla locks the door from the inside. Then the man disappears from her sight. She breathes out in a relief and tries to finish the task as per the command of her body. Then someone takes and presses the handle down abruptly! And in the small window appears a scary face with the vampire like teeth! Layla yells loud and keeps the handle of the door in her both hands. The scary face disappears and Layla - holding her breath - puts her ear onto the door listening. She can hear the man's steps as he walks away.

Silence.

Layla waits.

Silence.

There is no one around the stand-alone wooden dry toilet. Only the distant hauling of the wolves creep from a dense never ending forrest. The lights in the pub's windows switch off one by one. The barman locks the door, grabs the last drunk man by his hand and they both leave the scene. The door of the toilet slowly opens with crackling squeezing noise. The face of Layla emerges. A shadow of the vampire moves across the wooden toilet walls. Layla steps out and looks around being scared. She then takes courage and walks home. The vampire secretly silently follows her. The girl speeds up her walk. The tree branch crackles behind her - all of a sudden! She turns back and there he is - the vampire monster, right behind her. She yells first, but then switches into a laughter, "Hey, Stefan, you really are stupid!"

He bursts in to laugh too, he is drunk, "I want to suck your blood, Layla!"

"How many bottles of wine did you drink tonight, tell me!"

He comes close to her, hugs her and kisses her neck. Then he bites her with his vampire fake teeth and she laughs, "Stop! It hurts." She kisses him on his nose.

Layla's flashback ends.

Layla, Fedir and Mr. Tea stand in front of the side door behind the kitchen. Fedir smokes and Mr. Tea sips tea from a mug.

There is silence.

They are all exhausted after the busy crazy day and observe the blinking city lights down in the valley below them. Some abandoned dog barks, when they are going to the old car of Mr. Tea, who offered them a lift to the center. He asks to the rest, "Fancy some Romanian gypsy music? Cool stuff!"

He does not wait for their reply and inserts the CD. Mr. Tea starts the engine. Layla in the back seats shakes her body softly to the rhythm and smiles. Fedir pulls out a bottle of Ukrainian vodka and offers it to Mr. Tea, "ви любите пити?" (*Do you fancy a drink?*)

"No, thanks, I never drink while driving!"

"це самогон!" (*this is "samohon" / home made spirit*)

"No, no thanks!!"

Fedir gets serious in his face, "The Best Vodka!!"

Layla reaches her hand, "I'll take some."

Fedir hands the bottle to Layla and murmurs under his mustache to Mr. Tea, "добре, ви нехочете пить зі мною" (*ok, you don't want to drink with me*)

Layla drinks from the bottle and sighs as the spirit is deadly strong, "Oh, that's strong! It's really good."

Fedir continues his mumbling annoyed, "тоді мі неможемо бути друзями" (*then, we can't be friends*)

Layla hands the bottle back to Fedir and he takes a long furious sip. As their car approaches to a sharp double bend, Mr. Tea remarks, "Everytime I drive here, I feel kind of lost…don't know why…"

"The gate to the parallel world opens here for you…" comes from Layla.

"What?"

"There are many versions of us, we live in a multiverse, meaning, there are many versions of you living in the different universes. And sometimes those intersect creating the gates. You'd better close that gate."

"Yeah, I have heard about this theory. But, how do I do it? How do I close such a gate?"

"My grandmother comes to visit me in the next few months. She's a famous witch in our village back in Romania. She can help you."

"I hope she's not a vampire too!"

"You never know…, you know, where we come from…"

Layla shows her teeth off and bursts in a laughter.

Fedir shouts angry at Mr. Tea, "Bullshit" and takes another sip from the bottle. Fedir openly provokes Mr. Tea with his furious gaze. Mr. Tea glances at the back mirror and sees Layla shaking her head conveying the message, "Don't!"

Silence, only the music plays.

Mr. Tea is a wise man and knows that quarrel with a drunk man is a total nonsense. Mr. Tea has a thick skin.

The lights of the night town keeps blinking and the car moves through the narrow road that goes zigzag from the hotel Egeria to the sleeping town. The first days of spring are here and birds refuse to sleep tonight.

"MMS"

The security chief Sebastian Hunter stands alone in the hotel tower - the highest point of Hotel Egeria. He feels like a hero, like the winner of the day. He pulls out of his pocket a white underwear of Jane. There is - by the red lipstick - written "4 SEB, J." He smells to it and closes his eyes. When he opens them, he can see the old car of Mr. Tea leaving the hotel premises. He follows it by his eyes and dwells on the blinking city lights until they go totally out-of-focus and all he sees is a sea of multicolour bouquet. The sound of the departing car dissolves in the depth of the night. His mind is with Jane. He does not think about the consequences. Typical Sebastian.

Silence.

His cellphone vibrates. End of a night-day dream.

Sebastian wakes up, makes a sudden move as he searches for his mobile device. It's a call. It's GM's assistant Juan. Sebastian picks it up, "Hey Juan, what's up?"

"Hey Sebastian, are you awake?"

"Sure, what happened?"

"Nothing major. Just…We need to meet now!"

Sebastian wonders and answers, "I don't have time now, let's talk tomorrow at work."

Juan with strong voice, "We need to talk now! You and me, top secret, our 4 eyes only, behind the hotel, in 30 minutes."

"Give me a break. You can tell me everything at work tomorrow morning. Unless there's some hotel Egeria security issue that needs to be solved immediately. Is that the case?"

"No."

"See you tomorrow then.", but before Sebastian presses the red button, the mobile phone vibrates again, as a MMS message arrives. It's a picture. Sebastian increases its size by his two fingers and his heart stops beating. There is Jane and him hugging each other and kissing in the room on the photograph!

Sebastian is shocked, "See you in 30 minutes."

He finishes the call and squeezes his phone in an anger.

And Karlovy Vary in the valley, which seemed to be the city of angels just a while ago, look like an inferno now. The lights of the town are sharper than ever.

Juan dances around a car on the parking lot, Bony Eins - the driver - awaits him inside with his sun glasses and the red leather gloves.

"LOUD CHECK-OUT"

It is a sunny morning and sky is light blue. The city in the valley wakes up to another work day. The new guests arrive to the hotel in busses, cars and taxis. Mr. Tea leads his army of bellboys into another battle with hardcore size luggages. A group of French tourists exit the bus and walk through the entrance door into the hotel. At some point - out of a blue - the rain of bread balls falldown onto them. Some other foods like toasts, fruits and cookies follow.

The visitors are unpleasantly surprised, they cover their heads - faces and search for the cloud that releases such a strange annoying rain. There they are! Standing on their balconies. The members of Hollywood Vampires led by most active frontman Al himself. Apparently they are drunk and stoned. They throw any food available to them at the tourists and laugh wild.

The French guests swear at the attackers, who are encouraged by that even more. They are ecstatic about the fact they made them angry.

Mr. Tea pulls out his walkie-talkie and calls the security.

GM James Willington walks out of the reception and looks up.

He is followed by the security Chief Sebastian Hunter shortly.

Sebastian shouts at the musicians, "Please stop all this nonsense! Immediately! Otherwise we're going to call the police!"

The response is a laughter and even more heavy rain of food pieces.

Al screams, "Go to hell!"

Little later four police cars arrive at the hotel Egeria entrance. The guests take photos and shoot the videos with their mobile devices, phones, tablets. The police men run into the hotel. GM's wife Jane Willington accompanied by the hotel owner Peter Willington arrive hastily to see what is happening… just to witness that - on the face of Sebastian lands a big cake with cream and strawberry jam.

The bellboys laugh.

Mr. Tea smiles and takes a picture of Sebastian's unhappy face, speaking to himself, "Sometimes Karma hits back."

"DEALS WITH THE DEVIL"

The moon emerges from the shattered clouds in order to lite the scene behind the hotel Egeria. An owl sitting on the branch of the tree and makes its sound as it spots the moving silhouettes down below. Juan meets Sebastian in thefForrest next to the hotel well after midnight. They walk the forrest path and Bony Eins follows them few steps back. Typically, the emotions like the fear, anxiety or uncertainty, are being multiplied in the darkness under the black coat of the night. Even the people we know look different, especially if we meet them in the deep forrest. Their faces, illuminated by the lanterns, look a bit mysterious if not scary - in some instances. Juan did choose such a location to make sure no one will listen to their conversation. As both men, being followed by the black silhouette of Bony Eins, walk the forrest path, a few pairs of black shiny eyes emerge in between the trees. The creepy grunting of the boars reach the ears of the men. They point their lanterns in that direction. Shadows move erratically in the shrubs.

Juan, though being responsible for the location, is scared, "Maybe we should change the meet. This doesn't feel safe. Especially at night."

Sebastian with cold voice, "What exactly do you want from me, Juan?"

"Sebastian, I've got a proof, that you and Jane are in an illegal relation…Now, I need some money from you…what do you say? What do you think about the pictures, I've sent to you? They came out better than I thought."

Sebastian is annoyed, "What?? What the fuck is illegal in it? Are you crazy, man? I won't give you anything – period!"

"Sure…sure", with sarcasm, "I'll give the pictures to Mr. Willington. You think he'll like them as much as I do?"

"Do as you like, Juan. You are sick."

Sebastian approaches angrily Juan and grabs his neck and murmurs angry into Juan's face, "I know where you're from. I know who's after you. Maybe I pay them instead. Hell, maybe they'll even pay me…you're still breathing, but we both know you're already a dead man."

Someone hits Sebastian's head from the back. Sebastian falls down to the ground. The hurt man looks up to face Bony's nasty eye look. Bony Eins, holding a pistol in one hand, pulls out a knife. He places its sharp blade onto Sebastian's neck with the words, "How 'bout I slit your throat?"

Sebastian shakes his head.

"One wrong move and you will bleed like a struck pig."

"I can pay." Sebastian is visible afraid.

"I know."

"How much?"

Bony Eins turns towards Juan with a demonic smile, "I love this question."

Bony Eins back to Sebastian, "An adult heart pumps the blood at several litres per minute. An adult has about 4 or 5 litres of blood. So an adult will bleed to death in just under a few minutes. Don't try this at home…"

"I want from you 4 or 5 thousands, by the end of each month, Sebastian."

"I don't have that kind of money…"

Bony Eins slaps Seb's face softly, "I'm sure you'll find a way, Romeo."

Sebastian Hunter stands up and observes the two rascals entering Bony's car. The car departs the forrest leaving shocked Sebastian in the darkness. The grunting of the wild pigs and noises of crackling tree branches behind Sebastian force the Romeo running out of the forrest. At first, the gang of boers hunt Sebastian, but very quickly they give up, standing in the middle of the path and gazing at man's moving legs.

"MAFIA WORK"

Three young girls dance at the poles of the strip club. They do move sensually in the rhythm of the music. The DJ in the corner mixes the music and a stand-alone couple of youngsters dance there. The old men sit down below the stage and observe them with their mouths wide open. Time to time, the semi naked stripgirls walk between the men, who insert generously the money bills behind their pants. One drunk business man tries to climb onto the stage with a fistful of banknotes falling from his fatty fingers covered in massive gold rings. The man even manages to dance at the pole to the laughter of the audience. Then he tries to kiss the strippers. But very soon the bodyguards arrive, they pacify the man and kick him out of the club.

The Russian mafia boss, Ivan Kostinsky sits with his men in the secrecy of a box. They do observe the photographs of a Swiss top ranked tennis player and check the upcoming tennis tournament informations in the city of Munich in Germany on their mobile devices. The boss analyses the odds on games decided by bookmakers. He taps onto the player with his finger decorated by the big gold ring with black stone, "Vot etot molodyets proigraet dlya nas!" (*This gentleman will loose for us!*)

"THE BLACKNIGHTS"

A wealthy Canadian family arrives at the hotel reception in the early morning, followed by many valets. The family name is "Blacknight" and they are welcomed by the receptionist Yuki, "Good morning. Welcome to the hotel Egeria Mrs. & Mr. Blacknight."

The bellboys quickly accomplish their mission with the help of family's valets.

"If you would like to go to the breakfast after the check-in, it is already served in the restaurant. I am sure you are hungry after the long travel." Yuki adds friendly.

"Oh that is excellent news, our kids are "starving", Mr. Blacknight thanking Yuki for the information, giving her a 50 CAD note tip.

The family does not even go to their rooms, they immediately go to the restaurant.

Erick - the junior of the Canadian family, drinks juice and counts the biscuits as if they were money, medicaments are strewn on the table. He gets seizures sometimes as he suffers a mental disorder.

His mom Karen is a kind woman, but his dad Ronald is having the same goal as the rascals do, making an illegal deal, they came to the hotel for a bad purpose, they want to assist with the acquisition of the hotel and are partners of Juan Alexandro Polpo & Jonathan Lee.

Ronald to Juan, as he passes the table, "Hey Juan, how's our deal going?"

"Yeah, everything is going well, let's meet tonight around 9 p.m. - in Jonathan Lee's casino".

"All right, see you there after 9."

After breakfast Erick strolls the Hotel garden enjoying a joint. The birds are on the lookout for the worms! Suddenly Eric spots a beautiful girl by the river next to the hotel. Their eyes meet. The girl is Lavinia Angel, she is one of the hotel guests. She runs back to the hotel, as she is afraid that maybe this man is in the fact some lunatic or the forrest ghost.

Little later Lavinia enjoys her coffee in Café Vienna and suddenly Erick Blacknight arrives. Both seem to be surprised.

Erick charming, "Good day, pretty river lady, may I join you?"

"Yes, you may," with a stutter in her voice, "thought you were a ghost in the forrest, but I see you are not…"

"Thank you!"

It is the beginning of a long conversation and it appears that Lavinia likes Erick a lot and is just about to fall in love with him. But he starts to get tired, the long travel takes his tribute and he needs a rest, "Can we meet again tonight at 7 p.m. outside of the hotel - in that lovely garden - my lady?"

"Yes, of course."

At 7 p.m. Erick awaits Lavinia with a colourful bouquet.

"Hey Erick, sorry I'm late."

"No worries." Giving her the flowers.

"Oh you are so kind," she is so happy…

They stroll around the hotel, talk and laugh, they have so much fun and enjoy the romantic scenery.

"WHERE IS ERICK?"

In the evening, the Blacknight family searches for their son and ends up at the reception alarming the hotel staff – "Their son Erick got missing."

The reception alarms the security and also the owner family. The parents, Karen and Ronald are joined by Peter Willington to look for Erick in the hotel garden. They are fearful and sad that maybe something bad could have happened to him due to his mental disorder.

Suddenly, one of the hotel waiters emerges shouting, "Oh My god! We found Mr. Erick Blacknight unconscious close by that well outside."

Everybody runs to that place to see Erick conscious and smiling. He was found by the former hotel employee Mr. Albert Pohadka who was walking by. Albert helped Erick by giving him water and talking to him. The Canadian family and also Peter Willington are very gracious to Albert and invite him to the hotel. Soon, Peter Willington is about to know, that Albert used to work in the hotel and knows about many things that happened at the Egeria.

Karen with a soft voice, "Where have you been, Erick? We were distressed!"

"I was with Lavinia today. She's so beautiful!"

Ronald embarrassed, "Erick, please... stop that nonsense... There is no Lavinia..."

Ericks looks up with the sadness in his eyes.

Karen to her husband, "Oh, Ronald, of course there's Lavinia..."

"I gave her flowers and we talked and walked in the garden...but..."

"But?"

"She had to go..." Erick goes on.

Ronald turns to Karen, "Oh, I have to go too...to that meeting..."

"SIRI"

A small private black plane awaits its passengers at the Helsinki airport. This night big white snow flakes fall down from the dark heavy clouds. A small group of people enter the plane one by one.

A little blonde girl gazes into the forrest surrounding the airport while climbing up the stairs to enter the plane. A pair of yellow eyes in between the frozen trees observe her hungrily. The beast is waiting…

It seems everyone in the private small plane sleep - except of the pilot, of course, and the small blonde girl Siri. She sits behind the table and plays a game of chess with herself. Siri - despite her age - is one of the best chess players of the World. Her parents and assistants, who accompany her on the journey to the tournament in hotel Egeria in Karlovy Vary, sleep.

"BAHRAM"

Hotels in China have no floor number 4 and people tend to believe the number 4 is a symbol of death. However, the rest of the World doesn't care. An aspiring young chess master accommodates himself at the hotel Egeria in the room 404. He is from Iran. The hotel owner Peter Willington - having had not best experiences with the room number 404 - tries to avoid selling that room and usually he claims the room is being under construction. But, for the young Iranian chess player, the number 4 – is the lucky one. What can you do…?

Iranian chess player Bahram Zarathustra is a young university teacher of astronomy and occasional actor in his mid 20's. He has a thick black mustache and shaved head. His eyes are yellow with a bit of greenish lines that look like the rays of some star - the colour & pattern, very rarely to be seen between human. He wears a long black coat as he enters his room. He does not have any suitcase with him, only a black metal box. The mysterious man makes a thorough surveillance of the room. Never letting his small thin box go out of his hand that wears a black velvet glove. The man has only one hand, the other one is an artificial one.

That hand he can operate by his mind. There are special sensors attached to his forehead and tattooed - electronic chip like - black lines run down his cheek and neck disappearing under the tall big collar. Bahram spots a big spider crawling across the marble floor and squats down observing the monstrous insect with a great disgust. Using his artificial hand he pulls a huge steel pipe lighter and points it at the spider. The wizard Bahram whispers ominously, addressing his words to the creepy insect, "If you want to shine like sun, first you have to burn like the sun." And he presses the trigger of the lighter. The powerful stream of blueish flame turns the spider into the dust instantly. As Bahram keeps squatting and meditating over its unexpected victim, the expected visitor crystallises in the air behind him.

The red monk without a face says, "I am at your disposal my Lord."

Bahram utters without turning around, "Thanks for coming."

The Iranian chess player stands up and walks to the table. He places the box onto it and with a sigh of an obsession he opens carefully the box revealing a chess set.

The red monk disappears, but his words disperse the silence of the room 404, "You will reach the final of the tournament, but that small devilish girl Siri is even stronger this time…"

Bahram is curious, "Oh, tell me more…"

The red monk groans, "Hmm… She signed it…at last."

"And I thought she never will…" disappointed Bahram.

"Everyone does…"

"Not everyone…" disagrees Bahram.

"Well, you did…and now - so did she…like so many before…and thus shall it ever be…for all eternity…"

"It's irrevocable."

"Yep," confirms the red monk, "Once someone lets us in…There is no going back, indeed. Is it worth it? I don't know. Surely, you must know…and also Siri…"

"What's backing her now? Is it stronger than you?"

"Well, I'm afraid it might be stronger than myself…Unfortunately."

"But you promised in our agreement…" Bahram wonders.

"I know…but I have an idea, how to make you prevail, in this contest as well…"

"How?"

"We kill her! You go down to the wine cellar and get that rat poison…Then, the night before the final match, you go to her room, when everyone is asleep… when all will sleep…you put that poison in her"forrest fruit" purée she loves so much… Then she'll be dead. In two shakes of a lamb's tail."

Bahram disagrees, "That seems a bit complicated and dangerous…Listen… We signed an agreement. So do the fucking job on your own. Otherwise…our agreement is voided and you can suck my…"

The red monk starts laughing and interrupts Bahram, "Hey, hey, Bahram, you never have had the slightest sense of humor. That was a joke, you dumbass… Let's play!

"But, you said the entity, that signed Siri, is stronger than you…didn't you?"

"Keep your pants on! I know that demon well – it is the WOLF. You humans, should know better than us…how to deal with wolves…"

"We'll turn the wolf into a dog."

"That's it…"

Bahram pulls the chessboard out of the box and sets the pawns, "Tell me more."

The red monk materializes once again, slowly walking towards the conference table.

"ALBERT"

Siri couldn't sleep in her room and decided to sneak out for a night walk. She grabs the chess set to take it with her, of course…

Siri sits at the stone table in the garden lit by the stars and the moon and plays chess with herself. A shadow emerges from behind the shrubs. It's the old man Albert Pohadka, he approaches Siri supporting himself by a walking stick, "What's a little girl like you doing here by herself after midnight?"

"Couldn't sleep, tomorrow I'm playing in the Chess finals…and…you?"

"Well, for the very same reason…I used to work in this hotel some time ago… and, of course, I've seen things. Things that still haunt me."

"Even a ghost?"

Albert smiles mysteriously, "Something like that."

"Do you play chess?"

"Well, I used to. But if we were to play you'd certainly win."

"Well, if you beat me - which is very unlikely - you have to promise that you won't tell to anyone!"

Albert ominously, "I can keep a secret…"

"Have a seat. Let's play."

Albert sits down opposite of Siri and she set's the pawns.

Albert wisely, "I'll tell you a story, it happened in room 628 right here in this hotel. Meanwhile, you can think about your first move…"

Siri is gazing at the pawns lit by the soft moonlight, "How about a "Ruy Lopez" opening?"

Siri moves her white pawn to e4.

Albert moves his black pawn to e5 and starts telling the story

"Dogs are the „beast" guests… There are guests which have a special relationship with their pets, respectively dogs have a special influence on their owners. We recognize that dogs, along with their owners, are most welcome at all properties. Though we don't say so publicly, we feel that there are four kind of dogs

    a.   Small, nasty, behaving badly
    b.   Big, nasty, behaving badly
    c.   Small, well trained
    d.   Big, well trained

Those Cs and Ds never cause problems. Neither do their owners. Bs are the wildcard. Not only do they and their owners cause problems, they're dangerous as well. So dangerous, in fact, that their owners often can't control them. These cause the most trouble.

This is a story about a Dobermann named Axel, who was taking over the hotel property the moment he entered the door with his owner, an Italian gigolo type businessman. He thought this monster would gain him some respect by proxy. Axel was able to bark so loud, that guests were turning around in the restaurant, also when Axel was not even in the dining room. So actually the dog received the respect himself, not the Italian guy, who more looked like incapable then providing the wished authority. The „duo" had booked a suite for 3 weeks, so from the check-in the staff counted the days down to their check-out. The room attendant was so afraid to enter the room that she asked the Executive Housekeeper to agree with the owner, that she gets the information when Axel has left and only then entered to clean.

One day the regular room attendant was sick and a replacement from Ukraine took over her shift and forgot about the potential „meeting" with Axel in the suite and quickly entered with the „Good Morning, Housekeeping!" call. As she closed the door, she heard a heavy raspy breathing behind her. She turned around to see 85kg of bad attitude inside a slobbering Dobermann waiting for her next move. She freezes. Axel barks louder. She covers her ears. Axel takes this as a sign of weakness and moves closer, barking louder. The maid, still covering her ears shouts, "Please Axel, calm down and sit!" - "Sit" is a command Axel knows. He immediately sits down. Gathering her courage the maid walks up to him and scratches his ears. This is the first time Axel had ever been given affection. Ever since that day Axel and the maid were friends. She changed shifts so that she always cleaned that room and she always brought him something to eat. He came to love her and she came to love him.

Axel's owner didn't like this situation at all. He felt she was subverting his dog. However, he did think the maid was hot. So, he finally asked her to go out with him and Axel. Interesting, when the Italian guy left the room with Axel, attendant resigned. And who knows… Are they still together? Do they have a good time in Italy?"

Siri wonders, "Nice story, but what's the point?"

Albert makes a move with his shaking hand, "Matt!"

Siri is staring at the black Queen and his white King, "How come?"

Albet is serious now, "The lesson is, that people come to you with stories for a reason… They want to sell you something…At this instance, I did sell you my chess trap, because you were not 100 percent focussed onto the game…"

Siri nods in agreement, "You're goddamn right."

"Remember, everyone is your enemy. The enemy rocks up with their stories… They throw a snowball at you there while they're stabbing you here… The key is total focus. What's your game, Siri?"

"Victory! Always."

"Then focus on one thing and one thing only - the board. Focus to the point where your entire universe converges upon one small point - the board. Next, you'll even stop seeing the board. You'll become the game. Then, when you realize where you are, you'll see that you've won without even knowing."

"Is that why most people lose?"

"Exactly. They keep switching between this and that… They think they're slipping between the cracks, but they aren't. You need to be like the man said "That's the sex that passes the censor, squeezes through between bureaus, because there's always a space between."

"Yeah. The spaces between…"

"Feel that? What you're feeling right now? That's how they get you. You're right, but that kind of right leaves you vulnerable. There are wolves everywhere. One time it is their well elaborated story they sell you on, and the second time - they bring their whole family into the game - THE WOLF PACK…"

"…starving wolves I'm sure."

"Let's play again!"

"ROJO'S DARK SIDE"

At the same time the hotel sommelier spots the next victim of his desires on the corridor. It is a young beautiful Ukrainian housekeeper who works without any permit at the hotel. He threatens her to disclose the fact to the local foreign police. He asks her to go with him to "his" hotel wine cellars… He drags her by her hand.

"THE RED MONK"

The red monk stands on the roof of the hotel Egeria to welcome the first spring midnight rain. The monk is the ghost of the hotel, he does not have a face, but a mirror. The wind blows his long red coat. The bats in the caves woke up and came out in a search for fresh April blood. The sudden strike of the lightning - coming from clean sky - reveals the erratically moving wings of the bats as they encircle the roofs of this expansive building system.

He might exist or he might not. Some hotel staff claim they have seen the ghost in the dark corridors of the hotel - especially around the midnight and then in the very early morning hours. Sometimes the ghost wears red long monk's typical clothes and sometimes he wears a long black coat. When he wears the long black coat, he has a face. When in monk's clothes - there is just the mirror - in which - the one, who is so unfortunate enough to spot the ghost - can see her or his true reflection in that mirror! ...and that is the fresh blood to the ghost! It thrives on the "truth revealed momentum" energy - as the living human sees the true reflection in the mirror. That gives - to the monk - an immense reason to dwell here. That is the passion that keeps this scary entity in this hotel! Many of the guests arrive to this hotel lured by this story inserted smartly into the promotional leaflets across the hotel's concierges, tourist information centers, elsewhere… One never knows what is a smart marketing move or only or partly the truth as well…We do live in a world that is intersected by security cameras, all our actions are being monitored by the monstrous corporations and the very precious data analysed and converted into the marketing strategies and tactics.

Sadly, the only thing I can tell you is that the last person to tell me they saw him was a security guard. A son of someone I liked. One night - as he was patrolling the hotel corridors - he jumped out through a window to an ignominious death. The cuts from the window weren't so much a problem as the sundial that went straight through his heart and out his back. Is the ghost real? How should I know?

This is what happened as per the newspaper articles found in Peter's office:

The security guard walks the corridor and checks the security points with a specially designed device, which monitors the moves of the user and logs them into the security system.

This way the security chief and management make sure the security guy does not sleep somewhere in the boardroom instead of fulfilling the duty. The security guard walks the stairs up to the 4th floor, where the room number 404 is located. The room everyone between the hotel staff is scared off. He listens to the loud music using the ear pieces so he can not hear the window glass rattle under the powerful hits of the winter blizzard. He stops in front of room number 404.

He puts his ear pieces down and places his one ear onto the door. He listens in the attempt to catch some unusual noise…

As the security guard listens and the winter storm shakes the building - he suddenly hears some soft voice whispering some words he does not understand… something like…"al abuablu dublag…al abuablu dublag". The guy stops breathing and then moves fast away from the door hitting something with his back. He turns real fast! It's the statue of the white Greek mythology King - Zeus! Zeus is silent - standing there – he is the witness of many things that happened here…

"Beep…beep…" The security guard is disturbed by the sudden beeps of his mobile phone. He checks it. FB messages! The security guy reads and his face is lit blue, the mortuary blue.

"Turn around! I am behind you!"

The blood in the security guard's veins freezes instantly.

Again a message "Hear me O Zeus! If your ears are closed to me, please, Athena, bless your humble supplicant. Right now, it is midnight, the witching hour! And also the time of the brains!"

A moment of silence.

He turns in two moves back…just to spot his own face…but his face is strange…different…distorted…the face of an ugly mutation of human and horse! One eye of the human and the second of a horse! The teeth are yellow and freakishly huge!!

His own disfigured head makes a creepy noise of a horse!!! The frightened security boy steps back to see the bigger picture of the entity in front of him. It is the monk in the long red coat and with the mirror instead of his face. The monk stretches his very long thin hairy hands towards the poor boy to grasp his throat. The boy starts running across the corridor followed by the flying ghost!! The window at the end of the corridor approaches fast and that's the end of it. The boy jumps through the window down into the white stormy darkness.

The roof of the hotel is abandoned - as the ghost disappeared. The blizzard turns into heavy rain which gradually turns into a waterfall.

The next day policemen examine the outdoor car park, where the body of the security guard was found stuck onto the sharp fence spikes. Under his body - a lake of frozen blood in the white snow. The CSI photographer does his work. The detective looks down from the broken window and searches for some traces that could give some valuable information.

That is what the newspaper wrote, but there is another story about this room, some members of the staff in the hotel try to avoid any contact with this room, some are curious…The reason is - that it is said - the former owner of this hotel - did die in that room in a very peculiar scary way. The housekeeping lady had found him dead on the floor surrounded by broken mirror pieces and with a motorbike helmet on his head. The coroner did state that the cause of the death was the fatal brain injury, caused by a sharp piece of broken mirror that penetrated his eye! The owner did buy a new - special security - helmet which was a bit small for the unusual shape of his head. What most likely happened was the following... The unfortunate man was trying on his new helmet and this helmet did stuck, he could not take it off and tried everything possible. As he did struggle with it he did loose his balance and hit the mirror on the wall, which did break... and as he was falling down - he did fall directly into a sharp piece of the mirror.

"CHESS AT EGERIA"

Guests arrive secretly after midnight to the hotel Egeria. Some in taxis, some by bus, some in their private cars, some come alone, some with their teams. Two come even in two separate helicopters. One comes walking in.

As they enter the reception, Mr. Tea and his assistants help them with their suitcases.

The welcome board at the reception says:

WELCOME TO OUR FIRST KV CHESS TOURNAMENT 2020
HOTEL EGERIA, Ballroom
Official Meeting of
the Best Chess Players in the World
April 10 - April 13, 2020

The posters with a chessboard in the background and information about this venue is omnipresent in the hotel Egeria. The major program consist of the recognition speeches, a workshop for the chess game emerging talents and an official tournament sponsored by German car producer, the winner will get a S cabriolet and 250.000 Euros the runner-up a smaller model and 100.000 Euros. The tournament is to be transmitted by the World's biggest TV stations.

"GOING HOME"

The next morning, it is early, Jane organises her luggages in their hotel apartment whereas James still sleeps. She feels excited and leans over James head and gently speaks, "Jimmy, wake-up baby. I need to talk to you before I go."

James crawls out of the pillows and blankets and stretches his hands and legs, yawning, "What time is it? Come back to bed. Of course I'm listening, what do you need?"

"I'll go now to visit my parents, I miss them so much, would you like to go with me? Wanna change your mind?"

"I'm so busy honey, you know, work is crushing me right now, I'll try to follow you a few days later. I'll take you to the airport…give me a kiss."

"Don't bother, I've already got a taxi…OK dear, I'll miss you."

"I'll miss you too."

Jane kisses James.

"INTERNATIONAL GUESTS"

The hotel Egeria is decorated with the theme of Easter.

The hired hostesses offer chocolate eggs in the Lobby to the kids passing by and distribute the Spa advertisement leaflets luring the guests with generous discounts and attractive packages. The influx of guests from Germany is followed by many visitors of other countries of origin. Today, the reception is swamped and so are the bellboys. Today the hotel Egeria thrives and its staff must push to their maximum and add an extra mile... Even the GM - James Willington arrives at the reception to help Yuki and her colleagues. Many guests arrive to fill the hotel Egeria up to its maximum capacity.

A group of Jews form Brooklyn arrive in a bus, earlier today the World's best chess players arrived, many tourists come for a longer weekend to celebrate the Easter festival. The TV crews arrive from all the corners of the World. In addition a group of rich tourists from Nigeria arrive. They are deafening, they do complaint about everything and are seriously demanding. They did arrive from its former capital Lagos. Many of them wearing their traditional Nigerian clothes. From the moment they enter the hotel, they want everything for free, discounts, VIP service... The head of one family is an extremely overweight woman with a big head. Her name is Tiwa Tawa. The many Nigerian colourful scarfs make her even bigger. Her hands are like the ones of the Arnold Schwarzenegger. James Willington wants to shake her hand as she stretches hers towards him. But she refuses to shake his hand with words, "Kiss!"

James is surprised, "Pordon me, ma'm"

"Kiss it!

James smiles and kisses her hand.

Tiwa is smiling, "Good boy, what's your name?"

"James, James Willington."

"Ok James, my boy, we want one floor - just for us!"

"I'm afraid, we can't accommodate your request."

Tiwa is upset, "What? This is not a request, this is an order. Do you know, who I am?"

"Yes, ma'm?"

Tiwa grabs the tie of James Willington and pulls him towards her and scream, "I want to speak to your manager! Immediately! Now!"

James spots the German group arriving with their bus at the Hotel entrance and closes his eyes and in his mind says, "This just keeps getting better by the minute..."

Mr. Tea observes the worldwide stream of the visitors to their hotel Egeria, whispering, "...and we were complaining, we didn't have enough guests... that's a piece of the pie we simply can't cut...God, please help us all to survive this..."

Another bus arrives...

Mr. Tea, "well...and these, won't be any better..." he is now turning to Mario Brunelli the youngest of the Bellboy team, "Well my friend, that's the beginning of the hotel Egeria...or the E N D..."

One of the family members is also a Nigerian acclaimed chef. Immediately - while checking at the reception - they ask James Willington to call the hotel Chef - as they do have some special dietary requests, they did bring their own foods, spices, ingredients, and they want their own chef to work together with the chef of hotel Egeria.

Sylvester Cavallo arrives at the reception and the fiery discussion begins. Sylvester himself is a hot blooded man from Sicily and he is a kind of macho man too. The Nigerian chef Leonard Sebastian Bongo, a big tall fat guy with tennis balls size eyes and extremely deep voice, looks like a Sumo contestant versus tiny thin Sylvester.

Leonard Sebastian Bongo doesn't like people arguing with him - he is always right. The discussion seems to turn into Sylvester's humiliation in any given moment.

Another member of the Nigerian group holds a cage in her hand - it's a small girl - maybe 5 years old. The scary noises and kind of barking or mumbling comes out of that travel animal cage.

Yuki asks the mother, "Is this a dog in that cage? We have a special policy in this hotel and you did not announce that you are travelling with an animal!"

The small girl – Lara, she has only two front milk teeth growing big starts shouting at Yuki, "Mungala will sleep with us, now way that he will sleep some- where else...!

The groaning sound comes from the cage once again. James Willington enters the conversation and confirms the little animal can stay in the hotel Egeria as long as the family takes all the precautions to keep other guests save. He wants to see also the animal's "Health Passport". The mom of little girl Lara hands it over to James and he checks the stamps and vaccination's dates. James seems to be satisfied with the records, "That is fine,

Ma'm, Mungala can stay with us."

The little monster in the cage whistles as if it knew people talk about it.

Lara speaks to the animal in the cage, "We won Mungala! Our enemy surrendered."

James and Yuki smile at Lara and she shows off her 2 front teeth proudly, "I also have two front teeth, like Mungala."

The Swiss tennis player who is in the top rankings of the ATP arrives as well. He is accompanied by his strength and conditioning coach and by an assistant. They check in at the reception.

Opposite the reception James Willington speaks with the attractive tour leader of the German group. She has the leather trousers on, a massive red belt around her thin waist, white stylish suit with golden buttons, has long black-blue shimmering hair and wears glasses, which make her look sexy. She is of a smaller height and her breasts stand out to say the least. She is an Arabic type of a woman, shiny black eyes, thicker eyebrows, full red lips. She reminds James of Samia from their Sales & Marketing department and even more she reminds him of his wife, just 20 years ago... He feels magnetized by her look and must focus to articulate his words properly as they talk. That young confident woman looks like the devil! It is apparent, that both feel an immediate affiliation to each other, and this fact doesn't escape the attention of James's assistant - Juan Alexandro Polpo.

As Juan passes by, he grins, he starts enjoying working in this hotel. He also spots the sign on the information board at the reception area, welcoming everyone to the KV chess tournament in their property.

"THE DOUBLE ATTACK"

Juan glances back at the sexy tour leader playing nasty with that "poor boy" James Willington. He touches his chin and snickers   "Hmm…" Juan has his plans and he is in his element orchestrating the hotel Egeria dramas.

James Willington glances at Juan suddenly!

Juan smiles back and waves his hand in a friendly manner. Juan in his mind, 'You'll burn my friend, you'll burn…I'll get the furnace for ya…'

James Willington hints to Juan to come to help them at the super busy reception, but Juan deftly pulls out his mobile out of his pocket and pretends to be busy on the call… Juan walks out of the Hotel Egeria's main entrance and sets a cigarette on. He does not care about the fact, his help might be needed. For Juan, the people, guests, hotel staff are just the pawns on the chess board. As he turns back with the cigarette in his mouth, he observes James and the attractive tourleader through the glass door. The idea about a double attack comes to his mind – Juan to himself with an evil smile, "Speak to the devil and he'll come…If the dogs try to hunt you down…use just double back!'

Juan already sees the scenarios of the next few months pretty clearly, 'They won't catch me, I have a reservation in the high speed train!' He holds his breath as he observes the sexy beast doing her deadly moves in slow motion. He has his mobile glued to his ear faking the call and through the smoke rings he enjoys that view for multiple reasons.

"PRAGUE AIRPORT"

At the Vaclav Havel Airport in Prague, Jane Willington arrives with the taxi, she is a bit stressed, as the 110 km drive took them nearly 2 hours due to massive traffic. So she runs to the check-in counter, where a friendly attendant welcomes her, "Hello, ma'm, good morning. Anything to check-in?"

Jane Willington places her 2 huge Louis Vuitton suitcases onto the belt.

He goes on, "I'm afraid the flight is slightly delayed…Please accept our apologies, feel free to use the British Airlines lounge, It's our pleasure to provide you with a complimentary bottle of Champagne and refreshments."

"How long is the delay?"

"Half an hour…"

Jane laughs, "Oh dear…"

"I apologise. May I have your passport. I assume your visas are all in order?"

"Well, I'm an American citizen, I know that big blonde with that fancy hair cut is bit wayward, but I hope I still keep my citizen rights…", handing over her American passport and smiles.

The attendant burst in laughter, "I'm afraid the work occasionally gets the better of me…"

"I know what you mean, my dear."

"Do you have any carry-ons?"

"No, I have only a few books with me, just something to kill the time…"

"All right! What do you read ma'm, if I can ask?"

"You know, mostly romance…"

The attendant and Jane smile at each other.

"MAFIA STRIKES"

It is just before lunch-time when the Swiss tennis player decided to go to the SPA and sits now in the steam bath relaxing after a hard morning training. Two Russian speaking men wearing suit & tie enter. They sit down on both sides of the sportsman.

One of them, who not only looks like a Russian mafia member speaks calm to the player, "We have a deal for you!"

"What kind of deal you mean?"

The Russians laugh and open a suitcase full of money, "The deal with the devil…"

"I get it…but…you got the wrong guy…"

"You can win this by loosing…"

"And if I don't accept…"

"You better take the prize and loose the next game in Munich!"

They close the suitcase and put it onto the legs of the player. The mafia men go out of the steam bath leaving the player sitting there with the suitcase.

"SAMIA AND BUSINESS ADVICE"

Silence.

The candles are lit and Samia performs the Muslim prayer on a small dark green carpet. Then she reads from the Quran. After finishing her duties to Allah, Samia eats her breakfast, which is a healthy food variety. The TV set is installed on the wall just opposite her table and she switches between the channels…

1.   Israel Music Video
2.   The News / The Title."Stock Market Continues to Fall"
3.   The Live Broadcast form the Czech Senate
4.   FC Barcelona again scores
5.   Russian Ballet
6.   The News Weather
7.   The News War in Syria
8.   The News A Car accident on D1 in Czech Republic
9.   Music Video Pop Music
10. The News from Paris People "Yellow Jackets" protest in the streets, break the window shops and set the cars on fire. The police in black armour - protected by the shields – and equipped with sub-machine guns - shoot the plastic bullets at the rascals.
11. CT1 "Cooking with the boss"
12. Interview / The Title "Ancient Jewish Wisdom - Why are Jews Good with Money"

Here Samia stops, as her attention is caught or perhaps she got tired from switching between the channels, but the topic finds her interest, as she wants to make money to return home. She lays the remote control carefully onto a conference table, away from the plates with the food.

She sees a woman in her early 60's and a man in his late 60's - both American Jews - talking about money and psychology.

The man, "Let's imagine that you serve food in a restaurant for an international hotel chain whose name I won't mention, because they aren't advertised on our program…

The woman bursts laughing.

The man continues, "…or let's imagine you are employed by a large car manufacturer - it doesn't matter! You will then, listening to us - talking now, saying to yourself - what do they talk about - I'm not in business, I am not a business owner - I'm just an employee! And what we're saying is, change your mindset, start thinking of yourself as being in business. How does that work?"

"Well, you're an employee of the hotel chain and you serve the dishes, but think about it as you are in the business of supplying the customers with delicious healthy food and that the hotel chain is currently your only customer."

"Think! This will help you to acquire the knowledge and to become a specialist in the field! Expand your usefulness! Let's suppose you work 8 hours 5 days a week or 10 hours 5 days a week, but what stops you to find more customers during your weekend, and some smaller ones in the evenings?"

"Think of yourself as being in business."

"You got to make sure you're delivering value, you want to make customers see, that you're delivering more value. Get accustomed to this idea that you must change who you see yourself as - in order to change your financial fortunes. Don't think of yourself as being controlled by other people. You're in charge of your destiny. You and the Lord who loves you and wants to see you serving human beings - to serve his other children. You mustn't be surprised, when God blesses you with abundance - when you focus - not selfishly on what you need or want - but you focus on serving God's other children. When your service to the others, finding the ways to fulfil the needs of others becomes your obsession, please don't be surprised that God's response to you, is limitless blessing of financial freedom..."

Samia sits in front of a mirror and softly applies make up onto her beautiful face, paints her full lips with the red lips stick, extends the lashes and highlights her eyebrows. She puts her shoes on and grabs a bag and leaves her apartment.

Samia called a taxi to pick her up and now she sits in the backseat and observes the people in the streets - the morning hustle - the fight for life. The taxi driver, "Where to?"

"Hotel Egeria, please"

"Fancy some music?"

"Sure, why not."

The taxi driver turns the radio on.

The taxi departs its spot. Samia stares out of the window. Despite the first green leaves make their way through the hard walls of their buds - prisons, the snow starts falling. The winter does not give up easy. Her eyes catch a super car passing by - it's a luxury brand. A Chinese couple sits in the car, Jonathan and his wife Jenny.

The taxi moves swiftly through the serpentine passing the tennis courts area of the hotel Egeria. The snow immediately melts on the road. The tennis courts are still covered and the Swiss tennis player warms up his body by skipping the jump rope. At first he skips in a fairly leisurely fashion, later he does his jumps at twice the normal speed.

"MISSING NOTEBOOK"

The reception area is full of people, but one gentleman is not to be overheard, Mr. Zenoni, "Yes, as I returned from the rest room to our boardroom, I realised, my notebook is missing!"

The receptionist immediately gets nervous, as she knows, everybody has important information their notebook, private and business ones, "Oh, I'm so sorry Sir for such an inconvenience! Are you sure, you didn't leave it somewhere else?"

"…like where? Do you think I'm stupid?!"

"I do apologise Sir! One quick question, were there some of your colleagues still in the boardroom?" the receptionist tries to investigate a potential support to find the notebook, but Mr. Zenoni is out of his mind already, "Young lady, let me tell you   I'm about to go to the airport as my fucking plane will depart in just 2 hours. This is fucking last time I'm in this damn place of thieves you call a hotel. Is it really so necessary that I call the police?"

"I'm really sorry for what happened…Sir…"

Mr. Zenoni throws the key angrily on the table and with his coat over the shoulder and suitcase in his other hand leaves hastily through the main entrance of the hotel. In the same time the elderly bellboy hints smiling to the beautiful receptionist, meaning he will sort out this situation. He did listen to the conversation… the bellboy swiftly follows the angry customer as he steps into the luxury minibus, "Sir, we will find your notebook and express mail it any place you would like to. If I may ask, where would that be?"

Mr. Zanoni turns back as he is halfway into the bus. He pulls out his business card made of steel and throws it on the older but lively bellboy, as it was the tool of a Ninja. The bellboy catches the card with his hand wearing a pure clean white glove, elegant as if he was a Kung Fu master. Mr. Zanoni freezes in surprise. This bellboy is kind of a cool guy from the action movies… With a soft confident smile the bellboy adds, "You can count on me, Sir!"

"NOT LIKE THIS"

The banqueting department manager assistant - Leos Machalek enters the office, where his boss Aida de Luca is already about to leave. They greet each other with smile.

"How's it going today, Aida?"

"We're swamped, from early this morning... the hotel is booked up... we have many groups...I'll just leave for a few hours, got to go to our restaurant in town...someone broke in! But I'll be right back. Make sure, the guys do the work. OK?"

"Yeah. What happened in your restaurant? Did they steal something?"

"Really don't know... The police is there... I'll be back in a few hours. You know we've got the Jews from Brooklin, and the Germans are eating in the main dining room, but the tour leader booked the small boardroom, then we have that American food company, but they've left now...oh...one of their guys lost his laptop...if you find it guys...let the reception know...ok?"

"OK"

"...oh...and we have that chess tournament going on in the ballroom, make sure they have water, coffee & cookies, that's all they need. They'll have their dinner in the restaurant as well."

Leos is ready to start, "We'll do, no worries."

Aida is about to leave the office, "oh and one more thing - Please...that wine...we got from that band..."

"Yes?"

"That asshole Seb saw you putting the bottles in your bag..."

"Oh shit."

"Don't worry, I'll explain it to him. Just make sure, you do the things out of the cameras sight and after making sure no-one is around...be careful, Leos, ah...? Sometimes it is hard to explain it's a present from the guests...you know?"

"You're right, Aida. I'll be more careful next time."

"Spot on. OK, dear. Ciao."

Aida de Luca finally leaves the office.

Leos Machalek checks the rota, who is in and the schedule of the department, while making notes and setting up priorities. One of the banqueting waiters Petr Frank arrives to the

office with a laptop in his hands... He closes the door and whispers to Leos, "I took it...for us...we can sell it and share the profit...what do you think?"

Leos gets angry, "Are you out of your mind? Give it to me!"

The reception is not so busy at the moment Leos arrives with the missing notebook.

Yuki is wondering, "Oh, is it…?"

"Yes, it is!"

"Oh, where did you find it?"

"It was on the trolley in one of the conference rooms."

"Such a pity, they have left 5 minutes ago…"

"By bus? To the airport?"

"Yep."

"What if I take a taxi and try to catch them?"

Yuki starts laughing, "Well, you can try… Or we can send Mr. Tea…He's superman, batman, whatever…"

"Great idea, because we're very busy upstairs… Thanks, Yuki."

"No worries."

Luckily a taxi was available at the entrance of the hotel, so Mr. Tea jumps into the passenger seat and gives the driver the instruction to chase the bus in direction of the airport. The driver is happy to get such a "special" order and drives like a ralley champion up the narrow Old Prague road. They see the bus and with giving light and horn signals overtake it finally. The taxi stops the bus by going slower and slower until they stand still in the middle of the road so the bus would not be able to pass them.

Mr. Tea steps into the bus shouting, "We've got that notebook…"

He rises his hand with the device. He wears his white gloves on.

The businessman, who claimed it was stolen, emerges - surprised - from the comfort of his leather seat, almost falling down over the extra long cable of his headphones. He is very happy and pulls his wallet out.

Mr. Tea giving clear signs with his hands, "Sir, no!"

But the businessman is stubborn insisting. The battle of the two gentlemen seems to have no end. The businessman finally wins and puts the money bill into the pocket of Mr. Tea. Mr. Tea rises his hands up as if he was giving up.

"CINEMA REVIVAL"

Sebastian Hunter, Mr. Tea, Layla, Peter Willington and Albert Pohadka sit in the old hotel cinema in the evening. They watch the old security tapes from room 404, maybe they find out what the real mystery is with that room…

Albert is an elderly but vigorous man in his mid 80's, who used to work in the hotel as Concierge, some 40 years ago. It was in the communist Czechoslovakia.

The Catalan sommelier, with the help of Hotel electrician, prepares the projector in the projection room. They do their best to connect what can not be connected that easy - the veteran film projector and the VHS Video Recorder. The box full of old hotel security tapes stands on a small sidetable.

Shortly also Sylvester Cavallo and Aida de Luca arrive and they do not come empty handed. They bring a tray with Spanish tapas & pop corn – what else you need for a night at the cinema? They also have prepared a big thermos with coffee.

They watch the first tape with the label on it "CAM 1 - MAIN HALWAY / RECEPTION / Tuesday, May the 7th 1987 / 6 00 AM - 12 00 PM"

Albert is near to tears, his eyes look like wet glass balls, "Once during the communist Czechoslovakia, an American business delegation arrived to the hotel Egeria…the company that was making business with prawns and quail eggs…"

Mr. Tea laughs, "That's some combination…"

Albert continues, "…and with them…one gentleman named Mr. Smith… He was allergic on nuts, by the way…, but let's not interrupt the narrative."

Peter Willington is glancing at Sylvester, "That's a story for you, Sylvester…"

Sylvester winks his eye at Aida.

And Albert continues, "…and that Mr. Smith was an intelligent man… however, even smart men die…I name this story – Dying at the best Moment in Life. Do you want to hear it ladies and gentlemen?" Albert is looking in the round of people in the cinema.

Nearly unisono all say, "Yes Sir, tell us!"

So Albert starts his story about Mr. Smith, "Mr. Smith was a very smart businessman traveling through the world with a silver suitcase full of new gadgets every man would like to have. The only thing he is not aware of, is that his extrovert life-style is not liked by everyone. He was known by all barmen of the hotel bars that he is taking all possible chances to take lonely traveling women to his room to enjoy a great night. So this one day he enters the bar of the hotel and is greeted by the bartender friendly, "Good evening Mr. Smith, how are you today?"

"Fine Nicolay, please be so kind and pour me a double Black Label on the rocks"

"You're welcome, please take a seat at your usual table, I did reserve it for you the moment I got to know you come to the hotel."

"That is very kind of you. Would you happen to know if there are any targets tonight?"

"Mr. Smith, I don't know, whether she fits your taste, but I have the feeling that the lady from 203 may be looking for something of an adventure."

"Do you know if she'll be here tonight?"

"Usually she is here at 10.30 p.m., so that should be any moment she'll arrive."

Suddenly a very attractive blond lady enters the bar.

Mr. Smith, "is that her?"

Nicolay just turns his head with a smile "yes".

"Good evening Mrs. Fowles, how are you tonight? A G&T as usual?"

"Yes Nico, with a lot of ice!" answers the lady taking seat at the bar.

"Welcome, just give me a second." He pours the Gin in the glass filled with ice cubes and a lemon slice, then opens the tonic and pours in a bit of it. He then puts the tonic bottle next to the glass so she can fill up herself.

"Thank you Nico, you made my day."

"Pleasure Madam, do you have a lot of stress?"

"Thanks for asking, but please don't. Meetings, decisions, and many more things I'd rather forget. I'd much rather drown them in that Gin & Tonic."

Meanwhile, Mr. Smith takes his glass and approaches the bar, "Good evening, Madam, hope you're well. May I introduce myself, Michael Smith, I am a frequent guest of the hotel and its bar. How come I did not see you before?"

"Hi Michael, my name is Jolanda Fowles, I'm the first time in town and it's arduous to get acquainted with the people here."

"I've been here at least a hundred times, but the question always is, what are you looking for? Business or partners or a good time? I like to combine the business with a good time, like now."

"Do I have to take it as a compliment? Am I the good time?"

"Well, I do see a beautiful woman, a bit stressed, who is seeking relaxation. This is what I can offer."

"Michael, you're a bit fast, perhaps too fast."

"Did you have your dinner already?"

"No I wanted to have a sandwich here in the bar, they do a fabulous Club Sandwich."

"Indeed, it's outstanding. May I join you, I was just thinking of having a snack too."

"You are welcome, maybe I do forget about my day while having dinner with you."

"I think you just might."

"Nicolay?" Michael turns to the bartender. "Could we have one Club Sandwich and a nice Penne all´arrabiata?"

"For sure Mr. Smith, I'll set up your table for 2, just one second."

Both sit down and having small talk. Food arrives and the communication gets to a hold, as both seem to be starving eating their food fast. Finishing their last bites, Mr. Smith to Jolanda, "having had a great meal with a very beautiful lady inspires me to do more things, maybe it is nasty, but would you like to have another drink in my room?"

"Oh, Michael, that sounds good, though I am feeling a bit dizzy after all the G&T, so a coffee would be fine."

"Ok, I have an Espresso machine in my suite, so that should be no problem." Michael lifts his arm and speaks to Nicolay,"Nicolay, bring the bill all together."

"Sure Mr. Smith, be right with you." Nicolay comes from behind the bar towards the table of Mr. Smith.

"Thank you, Nicolay", Smith says and with giving a 50 USD note, "Your service, as always, was excellent. Please keep the change."

"Thank you very much, always at your disposal Mr. Smith."

Michael and Jolanda leave the bar and go to the hall where they wait for the lift.

"Which floor is your suite, Michael?" Jolanda asks.

"The top floor, I can see the whole town."

"Looking forward to see it."

The lift arrives and Jolanda presses the button on the top. After a short while, Michael presses the stop button and the lift comes to a hold. Michael starts to kiss Jolanda. First being a bit irritated, she starts to enjoy the scene. Until she said, "If we don't get out of here soon, they'll have to call the firefighters and maybe the army!"

Michael presses the stop button again and the lift starts to move upwards. At the top floor, Michael takes Jolanda to his room, the biggest suite in the hotel with a stunning view over the town. With a "Wow" she comments her feeling about it.

Michael turns to the kitchenette and says "I´ll be back with the coffee in no time."

Literally 3 minutes later he comes back with 2 wonderful espressos and a tray of cookies. See what I have here, another dessert for us. They take a seat on the couch and take a sip of the coffee.

"Mhh, exactly how I like it." Jolanda says.

Michael puts his coffee down and starts again to kiss Jolanda. She is ready and supportive, so she keeps on kissing with him also starting to pull off his shirt. They start to undress more quickly. Then, being already prepared to for the loving act, Michael just takes a cookie. And this is a bad decision! The moment he takes the cookie into his mouth and swallows the first bite, his throat begins to swell. He does not get sufficient air and Jolanda gets into panic.

What to do, what happens?

Michael tries to get hold of his jacket, where he thinks to have pills for the reaction of allergies. Unfortunately, there are no pills and his head begins to get blue. Jolanda starts to scream for help, but nobody hears her. She calls 911 and an ambulance is immediately on its way. But too late, Michael is already unconscious. Stops to breathe right after and dies already in the room.

A shock for Jolanda and of course the hotel.

The autopsy is clearly stating that Mr. Smith died on an allergic reaction on nuts, which were in the cookie.

Albert is in good mood as he remembers Mr. Smith very well and the generosity to all staff of the hotel. "Just sorry that he died so soon, he was a very good guest, everyone received tips when one did things in favour to him, eventhough when it was nothing extra…"

"JOZEF"

Meanwhile in the banquet kitchen, the private chef of the Jews from Brooklyn gives Jozef a tip of 2000 Czech Crowns and his business card, "The group was extremely satisfied with your care, Jozef! If you're ever in the States, give us a shout."

When Jozef turns the business card at home, there is a hand written message, "Don't work too hard, be a millionaire instead."

His dog approaches him and puts his leg on Jozef's knee - he wants to play. Jozef is tired, his wife sleeps on the sofa of their only room in their tiny apartment. His brother sleeps in a sleeping bag on the floor. His brother did visit him on his way to the airport in Prague to depart - funny enough - to New York. Jozef sits in the armchair and thinks. His dog observes him with dog eyes you can not refuse.

Jozef's look falls onto the open letters on the table – mostly unpaid bills, he sighs. He checks his wallet - there is his share from the tip by the Jewish private Chef. He stands up and goes to the painting of the shipwreck in the stormy sea on the cracked by mold covered wall. He takes the painting off the wall, goes to the kitchenette and places it onto the desk near the sink. There an envelop is hidden in the frame of the painting. Inside that envelop are banknotes! He does not count them. Jozef spots the wallet of his brother on the small table. He crawls silently to it - not to wake up anyone. He puts the money and business card from the Jewish chef inside his brother's wallet - he hides it there, in order to postpone the unexpected treasure discovery a bit.

Then he takes the box of cigarettes on the table besides the wallet and pulls a cigarette out, grabs the dog leash and calls the dog. Jozef decides to walk the dog after midnight in the park not too far from his micro apartment. He smokes the cigarette just lit in the apartment.

After a few puffs he spots a leaflet on the ground and he picks it up to check it out:

AIKIDO CLUB KV
TRY 1 TRAINING FOR FREE
"MASAKATSU, AGATSU, KOBAYASHI"
True victory is victory over oneself

Jozef throws the cigarette into the shrubs. He walks back home and as he approaches a spacey lit area, he spots a shadow man doing some kind of martial moves. Jozef and his dog observe the scene.

"MOTIVATED TRAINING SESSION"

In the early morning the Swiss tennis star always trains alone. His opponent is a tennis ball machine that throws the balls at him in chosen intervals. The player looks somehow angry hitting the balls with fury. He sharpens his legendary one hand backhand and fierce forehand. He hits the balls so hard, with such a strength, that he releases groaning sounds.

After a short break he trains his serve and the speed meter, attached to a tripod, precisely measures each attempt, well over 150 km/h – all the time.

"THE MATCH IN MUNICH"

In the evening the tennis star plays in Munich – his thoughts are with the 2 Russians, who visited him in the sauna of the hotel. So it does not surprise that during the 2nd set on the Munich tennis court, the player shows some health difficulties. It seems he will scratch the game this evening.

At the same time the Russian mafia men look happy about the game development which they see live on TV in their favourite bar and order a bottle of Vodka.

But the Swiss player continues and stays in the game. At the end – the player beats his opponent after a tough combat. As he hits the winning ball, he drops the rocket and raises his hands above his head. The audience goes crazy as they witness their hero to defeat a biting opponent, despite his health problems… Tonight he had won two battles… He comes to the camera and smiles bright into it. Then he puts his signature on it and adds a "smile" emoticon.

As the Russian mafia men see the result on the screen, they start to get loud and curse in all the languages they know. In the very same moment a police car arrives at the bar entrance. The cops enter the bar and buy just some non alcoholic drinks and coffee to go. The mafia men keep silent and stare into their half empty beer glasses. The two police men observe the rascals, then they pay the barman, pick their paper cups with hot drinks and leave.

"THE FINAL GAME OF THE CHESS TOURNAMENT"

Siri and Bahram gaze at the chess board which is placed in the center of the ballroom. The blond - little girl Siri wears a silver masquerade satin eye mask. In her hand she holds a mascot – a plush pet wolf. Its yellow eyes blink from time to time. Bahram wears a pair of sunglasses, a black winter hat and his long black coat. Siri has the white pawns and Bahram the black ones. This game will decide about the winner of the whole tournament. There are no clocks - no time limit… Siri delays her first move and Bahram patiently waits. There is total silence in the ballroom. But the minds of the two opponents are sucked into the deadly battle. They wait the outcome of the combat of another kind, which takes its place - somewhere else…

The red monk and the wolf fight against each other, way up in the North in the Finnish deep forrest. The Wolf pack encircles them and the Red Monk feels weakened.

At the ballroom of hotel Egeria, Bahram still awaits Siri's first move, she smiles softly, she has a strong sensation she cannot loose tonight. Bahram stands up and approaches Siri, whispering something into her ear…

"HOME SWEET HOME"

Jane Willington arrives to the home of her elderly parents, Julia & Anthony White. They do live in a mansion in Beverly Hills. Jane is exhausted after her long journey, but happy to see her loved ones after those freezing Bohemian months.

Julia hugs Jane welcoming her in front of the house, "Daughter, it's been a long time, we've missed you so much darling, how are you?"

"Oh mom, I miss you too, yes it's been a long time, I'm doing well, what about you mom, how are you?

"What can I say…I'm getting older, but thank God, age has its grace."

Julia and Jane enter the home, welcomed by her small thin father Anthony, they exchange the gifts, all are so happy there.

The family united again, cherish happy precious moments sitting around the table.

Julia has cooked "Beef Wellington" and serves it with pride to her daughter and her husband.

Jane enjoys the mother's food as everyone coming home after a long time, "Oh my favorite dishes, yummy." Julia with a smile, "Thank you, I thought you will like it."

Jane and her mom are in the room talking and talking about all the previous things that happened in the past. Anthony falls asleep in his favourite armchair.

Later Julia and Anthony have a serious talk about one old secret in their bedroom, thinking Jane is already sleeping, but the jetleg kicked in and she is awake.

Julia sighs, "Oh my dear, remember the day when we got Jane from the orphanage? I'm afraid she'll find out that we're not her real parents."

At this time, Jane is on her way from the kitchen, she brings with her a cup of water as she woke up thirsty, but then she stops by the room of her parents, listening to what her mom is saying, suddenly the cup of water falls down of her shaking hands, because of the big shock that the daughter had, she starts crying.

Jane exposes herself and therefore steps into the parent's bedroom. "Oh my God! I'm not your daughter?"

Julia and Anthony look at themselves speechless.

Julia is the first to get out of the tension, "Sit with us baby."

Julia comes to their parents and sits on their bed.

"Dearest Jane, please forgive us, it is a long story honey…We had a happy life when we got married, but we faced a big problem which is sterility, so we decided to get a baby from an orphanage and we did choose you and your brother, but we couldn't take both of you with us."

"Oh, and where's my brother now?"

"We really don't know, he stayed at the orphanage."

"Please, tell me where can I find this orphanage? Do you have an address or contact numbers?"

Jane leaves her parent's house very early in the morning to search for her brother at the orphanage, she is totally broken and so sad. The receptionist at the orphanage welcomes Jane with a smile, "Good morning, how can I help you?"

"Yes, I'am looking for someone who was living here 35 years ago..., I can provide you as much information as you need to find him. It is my brother, who I am looking for."

"That will take some time to look for this information, please take a seat, I'll search for you."

"That is wonderful of you...Thank you."

Jane sits down into a chair in the spacey cold hall of the orphanage, which is painted white. Actually everything in the orphanage is white, cold white...

She feels lost. She did betray her husband with that security Chief Sebastian Hunter, she does not know her real parents and what happened to her brother. Jane stares through the window and tears run down her face as the solitude overwhelms her.

The morning sun shines through the leaves that shake in the soft California breeze.

"DAILY MEETING"

Back in Karlovy Vary at the hotel Egeria in one of the smaller meeting rooms James Willington, his assistant Juan Alexandro Polpo, the head of housekeeping Layla, banqueting manager Aida de Luca and chef Sylvester have their daily morning briefing.

James closes the briefing daily with, "…any other suggestions, guys?"

Juan grins, as he has a plan with James and that attractive German tourleader, "As we have - at the moment - a couple of groups of tourists, it might be a good idea to invite their tour leaders for dinner… Something like a round table… Just to keep them happy…What do you think James?"

James doesn't like Juan and is about to oppose his idea and in his mind, 'I've got to get rid of that ambitious prick!' and then with a cold detached look at Juan, "I think…"

Before he can finish his sentence Aida comes for support to Juan, "I think it's a great idea, Juan! We could arrange one of our boardrooms so they could have some privacy.

Sylvester also wants to give his ideas, "Yeah, we have people from everywhere, maybe a sort of cosmopolitan menu. Something for everyone… What do you say?"

James is overwhelmed by the majority, "Just the tour leaders?"

The two devilish eyes of Juan meet James, when Juan says, "Exactly. The tourleaders only. We'll find out, what's on their mind, maybe if they have any concerns…"

James is back into business and his element, "If you don't mind, I'll prepare everything." He stares at Juan, "OK?" and turns to the rest, "Anything else?"

"YUKI IN DANGER"

At the reception the Nigerian businessman - Prince Dunga flirts with the receptionist Yuki. Prince Dunga smiles bright revealing his big white teeth, "I'm a very rich person back home… If you marry me, you will be a very happy lady."

Yuki laughts, "Really?"

He is in his element to flatter Yuki, "I'll make you very, very happy. Here, have some money…"He gives her some dodgy money bill. "Do you trust me?"

Yuki is laughing, "Of course I trust you, Sir."

"You go with me? Marry me?"

Yuki with compassion, "I'm afraid I won't go with you and won't marry you."

"I have already 4 wives and they are all happy…very, very happy…Are you sure, you don't go with me?"

"I'm one hundred percent sure."

"OK, I'll wait for you here, you - take your suitcase and we go, you are beautiful and we will be very very happy together."

Yuki with laughter, "Have a nice flight, Sir."

The Prince,"Oh, OK. You don't want, you don't want."

The Nigerian business man walks away, but in the door he turns back at Yuki, "Are you sure, you don't go, my beautiful lady?"

"Yes."

Prince Dunga, "Yes? You go?"

"No!"

Prince Dunga is lauging as well, "OK"

The Nigerian business man finally leaves the hotel and Yuki shakes her head in disbelief.

"THE BLACK KNIGHT"

It is the final game of the Karlovy Vary Chess tournament, Siri Susi from Finland versus the Iranian Bahram Zarathustra. The tension is high in the great ball room of hotel Egeria.

Siri moves her black knight in the way she attacks two Bahram's white pawns at the same time. Bahram looks closer to see that even four of his pawns are being under attack of Siri's black knight…That is strange, that is impossible! She must have moved some of his pawns, while he was not looking at the chess board…but the cameras are looking… How come no one has seen it?!…that she is cheating…Bahram wants to scream, but he cannot, because an invisible force holds his throat in its virtual teeth. He feels the breath of the beast…Four of his pawns are under attack and yet she doesn't take any!

Siri makes a strange move with her hand as if she was throwing a spell gluon at Bahram - the charm one…and she rises her innocent but devilish eyes…A hint of a purple dimple showed in one cheek as her lips quirked in amusement. Bahram has never seen such a strategy before. Now not only four pawns are attacked by Siri's black knight, but there is also a triangle cluster of his other pawns being confined by that small devil's two towers!

Now Siri stands up and approaches Bahram having her masquerade silverfish mask on her eyes. She whispers something into his ear smiling. This time we can hear it, "That's a quaternion – a quadruple attack."

Bahram whispers, "You were cheating, you little bitch!"

Siri returns to her seat.

Bahram speaks to himself, "How the hell did she do that? She said "quaternion"…those hypercomplex four-dimensional numbers that describe changes in space. Maybe she wasn't just joking…"

He smiles at her and nods…

"DREAMER"

Peter Willington is in his apartment, four ordinary mechanical ventilators are blowing some breeze to his bed as it is another hot summer night in Karlovy Vary. Peter sleeps on his bed like a baby that somehow got aged. The monotone sound of their propeller's interplay work like a hypnosis. A mosquito enters the room with its thin whistling menacing sound!

Peter dreams and the mosquito is close to his ear. The voice of a female scientist whispers ominously, 'Go back to sleep, Peter! Good boy. Now I'll tell you, how I do it…'

"Hmm…what?" mumbles Peter from his sleep.

'Go back to sleep, Peter! I'm talking to the audience now.'

"All right" is Peter's response as he continues snoring.

'Mosquitos in general use an olfactory sense to track their hosts. To find a human host, mosquitoes face the challenging task of integrating sensory cues that are separated in both space and time. This requires sensory integration, which begins with tracking a plume of CO_2 upwind. Research from the Dickinson lab indicates that mosquitoes are also able to respond to CO_2 by collating it with visual stimuli. This behaviour guides them towards potential hosts, where they also incorporate cues such as heat to identify a potential feeding site.'

Peter opens his eyes, follows the sound of the mosquito, switches the light on and kills the mosquito with a newspaper. He mumbles to himself, "That is what you get, when you want to disturb my night…" Turns of the lights and immediately falls asleep again. After a short while he is again dreaming.

'It's a summer day and the temperatures are higher than ever before. Peter Willington stares out of the window of his apartment in the way only the elderly can do. But, also he observes what is happening outside on the premises of his hotel, as he would be the General, the highest- ranked officer in the military. By some coincidence, he wears only the dark green colours today. Some strange distant sound catches his attention. It comes from the sky, a helicopter is approaching. It becomes bigger and bigger and lands right at the garden of his hotel - the hotel Egeria. Is that an invasion?

All of a sudden he finds himself in an Asian prison being part of an execution. They kill the prisoner shooting him into his head from his back by a firearm of a considerable caliber making his brain sprinkle onto the grey dirty tiles. The brain pieces of grey matter sail the blood river down the wall. The rest of the body falls down with an eerie sound.'

Peter wakes up. Total darkness. He has never witnessed such a black night before. He feels a panic attack coming.

"NIGHT SWIMMING"

The pool in the Spa attracts many guests during the day, but during the night, it is even more attractive, as it is closed…and forbidden to go there…

The major lights are off, just the emergency small green lights illuminate the surface of the water slightly. A group of youngsters sneaked into the pool without permission. It's just them there swimming and playing. Between them there is a couple of lovers. They are like two birds. They hug each other and kiss. The girl is tall and slim with the ideal curves and big breasts. She has long black hair and aquamarine blue eyes. The boy is even taller with a well built musculature, but not too much. He has blonde hair and emerald green eyes.

She whispers in his ear, "Do you still have the shit?"

"Yeah, we've got some left…"

Suddenly the emergency lights go off and total darkness imprisons the girls and boys in its impenetrable black coat. Panic spreads among the youngsters… The majority scream and laugh. The lovers stop hugging and kissing and she asks him, "Hey, what happened?"

"I don't know."

"I can't see!"

"Neither can me."

"What the fuck…"

"It's fun! Let's have a good time!"

Silence – the voices of the other youngster – people laugh as they are drunk and stoned.

She is worried, "Hey, where did we leave off?"

Silence from her lover's side, she hears only the laughter of the rest of the group as they play in the water… She is asking into the dark, "Hey, Simon… Where are you?"

The girl searches for her lover in the water in the total darkness, "Oh…Here he is…My boy… Hey…Aren't they just tits?"

The boy kisses her.

"Hey…" she is annoyed, "Stop! Who are you?"

An ominous deep voice laughter comes in response. A fight in the pool begins.

She is scared, "Hey! Stop it! Asshole! Who the fuck are you? Simon, help!"

The fight in the water continues. The sound of the steps of the security guard coming are getting louder, suddenly the light of a torch illuminates the swimming pool and the people in it. The security guard has just arrived to check the Spa area. He shouts, "Everyone please get out of the pool, and in an orderly fashion."

One of the boys with innocent voice,"What happened?

"There was a power shortage."

The girl wonders, "You mean, the power is out in the whole hotel?"

"No! The power's out in the whole town…"

Simon approaches his girlfriend and sees she is completely naked and to addition she has bruises on her neck and hands,"Who did this to you?"

She is crying,"I don't know…"

The spotlight of the torch falls onto her.

The security guard tries to get the picture of the scene, "Who did this to you, young lady?"

"I really don't know someone attacked me…in the dark…"

"I'll get you a towel…" says the guard to her and to the rest, "Everyone out of the water!

Please!"

"JONATHAN'S STRATEGY"

Jonathan Lee and his guest from Canada Ronald Blacknight talk between four eyes in the back-office of Jonathan's casino. There are newspapers on Jonathan's working desk with the big article standing out, "Canadian sentenced to death in China". There is a mobile phone of the brand "HUAWEI" placed on the newspapers. Two cups of coffee, two bottles of "EGERIA" mineral water. Two serious faces.

Jonathan to Ronald, "So how you gonna do it?"

"Well…I have military connections…high-ranking military connections in fact…"

Jonathan is joking,"What? You're going to invade the hotel Egeria."

Ronald with a short laughter, "No, no, my friend…At least not in the way you mean…"

"Now I'm curious."

"You have a man, in the hotel, you said…correct, Jonathan?"

"Yeah. But he's got some serious problems with the local mafia here…I have to fix his fuck ups…constantly…and I've got a feeling, he doesn't tell me everything…you know…"

"I see. Well…we can put another guy there…Our guy…the specialist…for "clandestine" actions…"

Jonathan is suspicious, "Hm…I like to keep the things under control…"

Ronald smiles, "You don't trust me?"

"Of course, I trust you Ronald. But who's that?"

"Yeah…and that's the part of the game…Even I don't know…"

"All right, you got me, really!...Common, who's that guy?"

Ronald snickers, "It's her! That's all I know…To be honest, I've never seen her…never spoken to her… and here's the good part…"

"You can't be serious…"

"…and here's the good part, Jonathan…You know the only guy who escaped the Chincheng Prison…"

Jonathan's full interest is gained, "Yeah. I read the book about it! Pretty awesome. The only one person who managed to escape from there - in the entire history of the prison's existence…"

"…she handled the logistics…" Ronald smiles.

"OK. How do you get in touch with her?"

"Ehm…I can't tell you that. I can't tell anyone that."

"Email?" Jonathan is investigating.

Ronald bursts in a laughter, "You are out of your fucking mind?"

"You send those fucking pigeons, like in the film "Ghost dog"…like that big fat mother fucking guy…Do you?"

Ronald is re-enacting Darth Vader, "The ability to destroy a planet is insignificant next to the power of the force…"

Ronalds's mobile start's ringing and he turns to Jonathan, "Sorry, my friend, thiswill only take a moment."

Jonathan is making the gestures by his hands as if he was holding the lightsaber from Star Wars, "No worries…"

Ronald Blacknight mirrors Jonathan's moves. And he accepts the call, "Yes, Erick? What? …with Lavinia? OK…oh she came back? Wow, that's unexpected! Just take the medicine with you, all right buddy? Cool. Keep it up! Ciao!"

As Ronald Blacklight finishes the call, his face gets pale and sighs, "What ya gonna do?"

Jonathan taps on Ronald's hand, "All will be good, my friend, all will be good!"

"INVESTIGATIONS"

It starts raining heavily in Karlovy Vary in the morning at some places the wind and the rain produce whirlwinds. In this misty weather a black car arrives to the hotel's main entrance and four men get out of it. One man wears a long black coat, the second one wears a white coat, the other two wear police uniforms. The men try not to get wet by holding leather folders above their heads, but it does not help. They hastily enter the reception area. One of the policemen approaches the male receptionist, "We're here to speak to the girl and her friends…the girl who was attacked in the swimming pool…"

The receptionist awaited them already, "I'll call the owner, Mr. Peter Willington and he will accompany you to the boardroom… Everyone is waiting there…"

The receptionist calls the security using the walkie talkie. A security guard arrives swiftly and escorts the group.

In the boardroom, the group of investigators and the young hotel guests sit around the table and discuss, what happened in that pool during the black out last night.

The man in the black coat is the detective in charge of the investigation, the man in the white coat is a doctor, who will examine the bruises and other injuries of the victim. The two police officers stand outside of the boardroom, securing the door.

The detective asks into the round, "…so nobody saw anything…"

The group of youngsters all shaking their head, "No, it was completely black…"

"Interesting…Hmm", he proceeds and asks the girl who was hurt, "Are you sure, it wasn't your boyfriend?"

Her boyfriend gets angry, "Why the hell I would do that, detective?" And the girl adds nervous, "I am absolutely sure!"

The detective continues, "OK, there were eight of you…in the swimming pool. I don't see the reason, why something like this would happen amongst friends. But, of course, we'll have to take you all to the hospital…for DNA, and other, forensic testing… Just to be sure…so we can cross you off our list of suspects… of course, it's purely a formality…"

"UNTIL HE WALKS IN"

The first summer rain falls down on the roofs of hotel Egeria and an old man walks slowly up to the hotel using a walking stick. Mr. Tea swipes the leaves off the entry road. He looks up – and freezes in his action. Mr. Tea cannot believe his eyes - he knows that guy! But can this be true? He shakes his head. He continues his work. The mysterious man approaches him. Mr. Tea looks up. The man wears a long black coat with high collar. It must be him! That man holds a suitcase in his hand. Mr. Tea comes closer, "May I help you with the suitcase, Sir? Mr. …"

The man replies, "Is this the hotel Egeria?"

Mr. Tea friendly, "It is, indeed! How may I help you? Will you be needing a room?"

The man answers with broken voice, "No, thanks, just coming for a look. Lunch…perhaps…That's all."

"May I help you with the suitcase?"

"Sure. Thanks!"

Mr. Tea grabs the suitcase with smile and words, "I think I may have seen you somewhere…"

While he says this, the mysterious man bites his tongue. They both have their hands on that suitcase.

The man shakes his head slightly and blinks an eye, "People have seen things…"and releases the suitcase into the temporary ownership of Mr. Tea. He notices - the bellboy wears white gloves cleaner than snow. Mr. Tea is surprised - as he looks at the suitcase and tests once again its weight.

Mr. Tea grins, "So light…It is empty…?"

The mysterious man laughs shortly as he follows the bell boy to the hotel using his walking stick as a support.

Mr. Tea laughs shortly as he did recall the case of the two Chinese ladies and their suitcases heavy loaded by stolen "Four Trees" cutlery and stuff. Yes, I have seen things…"

The man stops and hits the suitcase with his walking stick violently, "What do you mean?"

Mr. Tea turns back and winks his eyes, "Why would one carry an empty suitcase?"

"How do you know it's empty?"

"I don't know…You know…What's in there…"

The man now with a bright smile, "…the stuff to fill the bullet holes?"

Mr. Tea laughs from happiness, "I knew it! I just knew it!"

"TWO MONTHS LATER"

The summer knocks on the door and a fresh smell of myriads of flowers turn our world into the hypnotic dream. The black train - historical steam train - departs the Munich main station, heading over the border to the city of Karlovy Vary.

The steam train dives deep into the black forrest. Its windows emit yellow light creating a picturesque view of the fast moving tree branches.

Between its few passengers sits a Jewish man in his mid 30's. His name is Shefatyah Immanuel Meir and he is a mathematician scientist teaching at Munich University. He loves God and he loves his name. Every Hebrew name has some meaning - Shefatyah means "God is the Judge", Immanuel means "God is with us" and Meir means "to give light". He is on his way to meet his fellow scientist from the Charles University in Prague - Johan Steiner, they will meet at the hotel Egeria in Karlovy Vary. Shefatyah sits on his own in the coupe.

And as he is in a very good mood he sings a Hebrew song,"**Im Hashem Lo Yivneh Bayis,** Im HaShem lo yivneh vayit shav amlu vonav bo im HaShem lo yishmar ir shav shakad shomer Hineh Hineh lo yanum lo yanum ve lo yishan lo yanum ve lo yishan Shomer Yisra'el

The lyrics of this beautiful song "Im Hashem Lo Yivneh Bayis"contain two soaring passages,

"Unless the Lord builds the house, its builders labor in vain on it; unless the Lord watches over the city, the watchman keeps vigil in vain" (Psalm 127   1) and "Behold the Guardian of Israel neither slumbers nor sleeps!" (Psalm 121   4).
Im Hashem Lo Yinve Bayis (Psalm 127   1, 121   4) ולמע אוש תיב הנבי אל הוהי סא
וב וינוב

Im Hashem lo yivneh bayis, shav amlu vonav bo - Unless the Lord builds the house, the builders' labor is in vain.

רמוש דקש אוש ריע רמשי אל הוהי סא

Im Hashem lo yishmar ir, shav shaked shomer - Unless the Lord watches over the city, the guards stand watch in vain.

לארשי רמוש ןשיי אלו םוני אלו הנה

Hine lo yanum velo yishan shomer Yisrael - He who watches over Israel will never slumber nor sleep.

"MYSTERY MAN"

The mysterious man sits in the hotel restaurant with his hat on his head and black "Ray Ban" sunglass on. He observes what is happening around and makes some notes. He has his suitcase right next to his leg and the walking stick is leaning against the table. He also types notes into his notebook. The young Maître d'hôtel keeps serving him drinks and food across the whole morning and day and he wonder's who that man could be, what could be his profession, but he can't find the answer…

"HIGH TECH CRIME"

The back of the black van is equipped with the latest technologies. One driver and two specialists sitting in the back. They have a video conference on the go with their boss Ronald Blacknight.

The specialists wait for their boss to join the conference call. After some moment the music announces that their boss is coming live. Ronald with his German accent, "How are you doing guys? Where are you about right now?"

Greg Robson is leading the partners, "Hi Boss! We're en route from Munich to Karlovy Vary. We just crossed the Czech border."

His partner Leonard Respect is more reserved, "Hello Boss! How are you doing, Boss?"

"Great! What is the plan?"

Greg sounds uncertain, "Well, we suspect, the location might be compromised, it's their security Chief… They recently installed a state of the art security system. Apparently, it's to detect wild animals at night."

"What? What the hell for?"

"You're not going to believe this, I didn't…they had a deer running around on one of the upper floors. Really. They had to shoot it. We might have to come up with another idea…"

Ronald is joking and impersonating his loved Star Wars figure, Darth Vader, "I find your lack of faith disturbing!", and adds seriously, "We stick to the plan, Greg."

"As you say, Boss!"and to Leonard, "We've got those new detectors, we'll analyse the premises, find a way to set up the machine… securely…"

"Good. Our man is in the hotel?"

"Yes Boss, our man is in the hotel."

"Good. If something goes wrong, then we'll do what?"

Both specialist answer unisono, "We'll just make it happen!"

In the evening the men are in the forrest to install the machine. Greg Robson opens the black steel suitcase and pulls out the machine.

Leonard, "What does it actually do?"

Greg is educating him, "It is a machine called "USW-NAUSEA101X". It's a real ear drum breaker. This is a compelling and very precise weapon. Using only sound it can incapacitate, injure, or even kill an adversary…

Leonard curious, "How is that possible Greg?

"It's capable of releasing high-power sound waves that can cause humans nausea, or more discomfort."

"No, shit!"

Greg opens another black suitcase and pull another smaller machine, "But wait, there's more. This one is even creepier…"

"Tell me…," Leonard is getting more and more curious.

Greg is in his element to talk about the latest secret technology, "This baby is the "INFRARED-ELEPHANT-Z22" It's a lot smaller than the "USW-NAUSEA101X", but it'll make your eyeballs vibrate in their sockets - from a good distance…"

"No way!"

"…when your adversary can't see, they aren't much of threat anymore…" Greg is continuing as if he was telling a horror story to kids, "…These babies employ infrasound, sound below 20 Hz, lower than humans can hear. But just because we can't hear it, that doesn't mean we don't feel it; in certain individuals, infrasound can induce feelings of fear, dread, depression, or even kill. Elephants, in particular, produce infrasound waves that travel through solid ground and are sensed by other herds using their feet, although they may be separated by hundreds of kilometres. They can do this by stomping on the ground. Up close they can even do it with their trunks. Makes the phrase "elephant gun" take on a whole new meaning eh? So, amigo, let's rattle some eyeballs and penetrate their ear drums, let's give 'em some nightmares they'll never forget!"

Both men stand in the middle of the forrest and look up into the crowns of the trees. High in the tree tops the two machines are attached and pointed in direction of the hotel. The sun disappeares below the horizon.

The sky is red, for sure illuminated by the light from the hell.

"JONATHAN'S ADVICE"

A small black private plane flies above the hotel Egeria. It flies as if it was hungry to catch the sun rays escaping to China. Inside the small plane sit Jonathan Lee, his wife Jenny, Ronald Blacknight, his wife Karen and son Erick, Bony Eins and their pet, the black panther. They sit around the table and a young valet keeps bringing foods and drinks. The black panther sleeps - as usual - on the sofa and observes, by one slightly opened eye, what is happening around him.

Jonathan, "We've got to stop these bullshit espionage accusations about our mobiles."

Ronald without emotion, "The espionage or the witch hunt?"

"Both. We don't do anything everyone else isn't already doing. When are you going to talk to the president?"

Staring at his Rolex watch Ronald answers, "Monday..."

Jonathan is pushing, "I spoke with the president Friday...You know, how it is in our country...family is everything...If she won't be released anytime soon, people die in prisons...but I think, you love your family...and as a fellow patriotic citizen, I think you love your country ...don't you?"

"We're quiet capable of defending our citizens. Just google Global Firepower, Jonathan..."

Jonathan smiles with confidence, "Well...GOOGLE is for the masses...we know the real numbers...and they are on our side..."

"You're right. Well...we're both businessmen, after all citizens of the world... It really doesn't matter, where we actually live..."

"Yep. We'll just keep moving, following opportunities our ancestors started to generate..., let the politicians clean up the shit..."

Ronald smiles, "Potatoes or rice," and now unisono with Jonathan, "we'll be rich twice!"

The both men laugh like the two devils and cheer to each other with glasses filled by wine - red like blood.

Ronald as if he did buy a loaf of bread at the bakery, "Oh, by the way, I bought a castle in Scotland..."

Jonathan's red alarm triggers off in the back of his head, though still calm, "How dare you?!"

"...you and Jenny are invited!"

Jenny also seeing the focus of Ronald in Scotland and not at their plan, directly ask to Ronald, "You promised to get us the hotel Egeria..."

"He will," Jonathan calm to his wife.

"Rest assured, that even if something can't be done, I get it done," Ronald says to Jenny and then changing his voice impersonating Darth Vader again, "I find your lack of faith disturbing!" and stretches his hand towards her throat.

"Enough of this, Ronald, release her!" Karen insisting.

Out of the blue Erick says, "Tomorrow I'm going to meet with Lavinia Angel…"

"Where?" Jonathan sounds astonished.

"The park in Tsim Tsa Tsui."

"That's a lovely place, my son!" Jonathan as if he knows that park as well.

Erick starts shaking little as if he was getting his seizure…Karen and Ronald look at their son worried. Jonathan taps the young man's arm, "I'll recommend a decent restaurant, where they serve best black tea you and Lavinia have ever drunk and the best Peking duck with Jasmine Rice and steamed green vegetables you'll ever find!"

"But, first we have to meet up in the park…"

"Yes, it's a beautiful park, Erick. My favourite one."

"Really?"

"There are beautiful flowers, trees…and dragonflies…"

Erick stops shaking and finally starts eating.

Jonathan continues like a teacher, "…the dragonfly normally lives most of its life as a nymph or not quiet mature…It knows flying for a mere fraction of its life and usually not more than a few months. The adult dragonfly has only few few months to fulfil a lifetime of desire. If we understand, this symbolises and exemplifies the virtue of living the moment and living life to the fullest. By living in the moment you are aware of who you are, where you are, what you are doing and what you want, on a momentby-moment basis. The dragonfly has no regrets. If you can truly understand the dragonfly, neither will you.

Jonathan rises his glass and so does Erick, who did listen carefully while cherishing the food.

With the toast "We're Dragonflies!" Jonathan finishes his speech.

The red emergency lights of the small plane keep blinking until it disappears in the darkness of the black night.

"BUSINESS AS USUAL"

Sylvester Cavallo supervises some hotel school students in the main kitchen and he is in his element to educate the future generation of hoteliers. Between them there is one beautiful and little nasty girl. As Aida passes through the kitchen she witness the teenage girl student flirting with "her" Sylvester! She leans against him and Sylvester doesn't protest…she can see a soft happy smile under his thick black mustache! Aida doesn't say anything and flies through the kitchen like a fury.

At the same time, the sexy charismatic tour leader arrives to the hotel with another German group of tourists. James Willington expects her arrival and waits in the reception back-office. As she arrives to check-in, he hastily comes to help to the busy reception staff.

The mysterious man with the hat and black sunglass still sits at his place from the early morning and doesn't seem to be leaving anytime soon. He keeps observing and writing his notes - both into the notepad and notebook. He doesn't talk and if he has to…he keeps it to the possible minimum. He sees a woman running out of the kitchen, furious, red in face, angry… its Aida. Then he observes waiters talking, having fun, boys flirting with girls… The mysterious man smiles softly. He contemplates for himself, "There on the other side of the restaurant, the sommelier serves the wine with panache. The Maître d' hotel…the handsome young man isn't his usual dashing self. What's wrong with him? He must be in love…But with whom? That's the question…Perhaps with the Asian receptionist…Yuki…who else or…maybe the Arabic manager…Samia…who can tell…?"

The mysterious man with the hat, with his suitcase and his walking stick became the icon of the hotel - as he had spent the last two months here in the hotel Egeria. And yet, no one had recognized him…only that smart bellboy… maybe the owner…too…He even changed his voice, cut down his typical UFO haircut, changed his gestures…changed everything…He is getting ready for the role of his life…He has enough of himself…He is someone else now…but, his former himself keeps chasing him…it waits behind any give corner…the stalker!

There they come…the Management of the hotel, together with a group of tourleaders…and that sexy beast between them…They sit down as the seats are marked by names…There he comes as well…the white hair snake - "Richelieu" of the hotel…Mr. Polpo…the Octopus…Mr. Poison…the devil in the Paradise… with the fresh delicious apple in his pocket…

The mysterious man observes James Willington sitting right next to the attractive tour leader woman devil…Something is about to happen…According to someone's plan…He sees Juan Alexandro Polpo observing the couple with the devilish grin…He is James's assistant…he does the jobs for him…he's the organiser…the orchestrator…Peter Willington - the owner of the Hotel is missing… Why? Lately he looked ill… His face was without life, his face was pale…the last time he has seen him… The mysterious man makes his notes…

The detective arrives back to the hotel in the afternoon to do some more searches and interrogations regarding that "Black Out Night" and the girl that was hurt. He meets Sebastian in his office and they observe the CCTV footage. As they observe the footage they do not find anything specific. But, Sebastian shows him the footage from the Chess tournament finals. Something happened there… like two parallel worlds intersecting, two pictures over each other - translucent…Some kind of heat wave making the air swirl and the world twist…

"INDIA LOVE"

The temperature outdoor is deadly hitting almost 40 degrees at the Mumbai airport, even well after midnight. A young man leaves the bus and enters the airport. He passes one Indian soldier who uses his machine gun as the walking stick. The man to himself, "Shit, it's hot as hell in here."

He enters the confinements of air-conditioned hall. The young man is Karel Kunkal, the hotel Egeria security guard is on his way to return from his holidays in India back to Karlovy Vary in the Czech Republic. In the very fact it were not so much holidays as it was a meeting with the girl he did meet online and it seems Karel is in a good mood…He chats with the girl on his mobile device and a lot of hearts, hugs and kiss emoticons are exchanged. He walks across the airport departures area like a lunatic and observes the glittering stuff in the shops. He sees two Indian soldiers patrolling the lounge. They wear the typical Indian uniforms and hold machine guns in their hands. Then he spots a restaurant with Indian food and the visuals and smells drag Karel in that direction. He approaches the buffet and his stomach screams, "Karel, please, feed me!"

Karel taps on his stomach, "Don't worry, we'll get you something."

A Danish tourist, who stands right behind Karel, turns to him with the words, "You should try that one." He points at the meal.

"Wow, what's that?"

"It's Chana dal - Bengali receipt, delicious, this one is super spicy…but for those who love chilli…an unbeatable dish…"

Karel laughs, "I'll have that then, I love spicy food and I'm a champion when it comes to eating chillies!"

"Yeah…and get some of those pancakes, they are called Chapati, you'll love it, my friend. Just put a little bit on one of those and you'll remain champion. Then "kill the devil"."

"You're funny guy. My name is Karel by the way…" He stretches his hand towards the Danish tourist.

"Kill the Devil - means Rum in Sailor's lingo…" He shakes Karel's hand, "My name is Edward Hansen and I'm from Denmark and you?"

"Wow, I heard that name for Rum, I'm from Czech Republic, we have excellent and cheap Rum, which - because of EU rules - we call it, tuzemak, but it's good my friend."

Both men smile.

Travelling is great. Meeting people, sharing stories and testing food is the best thing in the world. On the TV screen above the tills an Indian music video plays - adding another spice to the space's ambience. It's a romantic song.

Edward says, "Let's go to the bar. We can get a proper drink."

"Cool, let's go"

Both men sit at the bar, enjoy the delicious food and drink Rum.

Karel with his mouth ful, "…what about you, what do you do for living?"

Edward in contemplating mode, "I do business. Swim wear. I have a shop in Hong Kong. One back in Denmark, and I own a small factory, where it's all made, packaged, shipped. I also have an online shop and also normal shops in bricks as we say in Denmark. But, business is slowing down… Too much of cheap stuff from Asia… they can make it almost for free there…know what I mean…I provide quality…,but people just don't care… maybe I should find a different product, something more in demand…"

"I see…"

"Have you ever been to Hong Kong?"

"Never."

"You should go, my friend. You'll love it. I'd bet my boots on it."

"How is it?"

"When you'll be there, you must visit two places. The first is the bar "Felix" in the hotel "Peninsula" in Kowloon, at Tsim Tsa Tsui. When you piss, you can see all of Hong Kong through the floor to ceiling window. The toilet attendant will hand you a towel… In the restaurant - you eat right off the marble table. Foods you have never eaten, delicassies you have never seen, and the waitresses can kill you by their appearance… The bar has a view of the entire Hong Kong Island skyline.

The second place is Lantau Island, one of the most peaceful places on Earth. Go there, take the ferry, amazing abandoned beaches, walk through the jungle behind your hotel, enjoy strong black tea, Peking style duck with Jasmine rice and steamed green vegetables. You won't think of anything else at all."

Karel listens with his mouth open, "I wanna go there. You know, my grand father's name was Edward as well…"

Edward gives a new order to the bartender, "Two glasses of the "SEA DOG" please!"

The beautiful Indian girl smiles at Edward, "Here you go, my charming sailor!"

Edward pulls out his business card and hands it over to the bartender, "My swim wear will make you look even more beautiful…"

The girl laughs, "Oh, really?"

Both men blush with their glasses and smile, the bartender polishes the glasses and observes the two handsome gentlemen.

"To your success my friend, and here's my business card…" Edward throws it onto the bar table in front of Karel, "…you never know, what tomorrow may bring…"

"Thanks a lot, Edward. Should you come to Czech Republic, visit Karlovy Vary, I'm with the stunning hotel Egeria, a beautiful landmark in a beautiful region."

Both men drink to the bottom.

"ABOVE THE CLOUDS"

It is Czech Airlines flight 104 and Karel sits in his seat right next to an Indian gentleman. Karel observes from the small window the shimmering Mumbai city down below after the take-off. Karel chats with his Indian girlfriend again and tells her about the encounter with Edward. Especially that his swimwear would suit her very much.

After a while on the plane the stranger wakes up and murmurs, "Oh, where are we?"

Karel also wakes up, but only from his day dreaming, "Don't know, maybe somewhere above the Iran…"

He checks the real time map on the small LCD touch screen realising they are right above the capital city Tehran. "We're over Tehran, right now."

As the plane now flies low and as the city is situated in high altitude in a mountainous area, it is possible to see more…Both men look out of the window and observe a glittering sleeping city…

"Amazing…"

"Wow, yeah…" confirms Karel.

"Are you from Prague?"

"No, Karlovy Vary, which is…two hours drive from Prague."

"Wow, actually, Karlovy Vary is my final destination…"

"TWO MONTHS BACK IN TIME"

It is in the ballroom of hotel Egeria, when Siri stands up and approaches Bahram having her masquerade silverfish mask on her eyes. She whispers something into his ear smiling. This time we can hear it, "That's a quaternion - the quadruple attack."

Bahram whispers, "You were cheating, you little bitch!"

Siri returns to her seat.

And to himself he wonders, "How the hell did she do it?"

He smiles at her and nods…Bahram stares at the chess board and cannot see the way he could overturn this game, he plays in his mind many scenarios one by one…

Bahram plays in his mind more and more scenarios with the many moves ahead.

Siri smiles.

Bahram gets into trance and hears a sound of a plane and two male voices speaking to each other,

"Is that Tehran?"

"According to the map, that should be Tehran."

"Isn't it beautiful?"

"Yes it is…"

"Going to Prague?"

"No, to Karlovy Vary…the hotel Egeria…"

"What do you do for living, if I may ask…I've got the feeling I've seen you somewhere before…"

"I'm a singer."

"Wow…but you have a day job…no? To pay the bills…"

"I used to… not anymore…"

"How'd you manage that?"

"I risked everything! Never stopped believing…slept on the streets…went hungry…but never stopped believing, that I win in the end…"

"How'd you get so confident?"

"I knew a girl…"

Bahram returns to previous reality, back to the ballroom in the hotel Egeria.

Siri whispers under her nose, victory ahead, "It's over…"

Bahram observes Siri and realises she is beautiful, his beautiful enemy… Such a young smart girl… He spots the chance finally! He can make the draw, two moves and it's the put situation…But he does something else…he folds his king…the strategy she did use was too beautiful…too unique…Respect to that. He stands up and goes to her to shake her tiny hand leading to the power brain. The audience applauds and the photographers shoot the flashes at the main protagonists of this magic night. They shake their hands with smile…above all… it's just a game… She smiles from happiness and whispers to his ear, "Next time… I'll let you win…"

"SING ALONG"

The head of the Sales & Marketing department - Samia Sahar strolls the corridor and looks sad. Suddenly she hears music and someone singing. She comes to the room no. 215 and stops there, listening. A miraculous smile arrives to her face right from her heart. She knows the song - the song is sang by famous Indian male and female singers - she used to work many years in Mumbai and as she loves singing, she knows even the words…She sings softly the woman's part and dances a little…In this precious moment she looks even more beautiful.

The young man in his mid 30's stands in front of the bathroom mirror and sings. The famous Indian singer sings his own song, the music goes out of the room speaker system, his mobile is connected to the TV. There is him singing in the music video playing on the TV. Just the female singer is missing…Or maybe not… The face of the singer freezes and focuses, sharpens his hearing. He hears some woman singing - so beautiful sound…he smiles…fades the volume little down and keeps singing his part and when the woman sings…yes…he can hear someone really singing the female's part and she sings it really well… The famous Indian singer - staring at himself into the mirror - realises his face got little red… He feels some kind of excitement…like in those times…back in the childhood… like in one of his first relationships… His soul switches into the innocent kid's mode.

He has a flashback and remembers the first time he had seen the girl's breasts as the God graciously created them… It was in her room in the house of her grandparents… He did put the thin, but most expensive golden necklace he could possibly afford around her snow-white neck tiding her long blonde hair. He did save a big portion of his salary to buy this present for her as, at that time, he worked in a construction company. They did chat and kiss each other softly and then she did something he would expect the least since those were the first days of their relationship. She did take his head and put it under her T-shirt… The external world ceased to exist for him… They were immortal…and the flashback ends abruptly.

The famous Indian singer, listening the anonymous and yet familiar voice, says to himself, "She has the exact same voice!"

Suddenly tears sprinkle from his eyes and he cannot explain why… Perhaps he realises what everything he had lost to win in this world and that it wasn't worth a single milligram of his love, not a single smile of the loved one…

Now is his part to sing again,
Shining in the setting sun
Like a pearl upon the ocean
Come and feel me
Oh feel me
Shining in the setting sun
Like a pearl upon the ocean
Come and heal me
Oh heal me"

And as he finishes his part he goes out of the bathroom following the direction - source of the woman's voice. He is lead to the room's door, but he hesitates to open them. The woman on the other side stopped singing…He breathes fast and then he decides to open the door… He looks out…but the corridor is already empty.

"NOTHING TO SAY"

Maître d' hotel stands in the hotel room in front of the mirror and he trains his speech, the speech to the receptionist Yuki. He wants to invite her to a date, "Hey Yuki, how 'bout dinner. Something great. Me and you? no…Yuki, shit, that's not good…don't know what to say…"

"VIBRATIONS"

The mysterious man with suitcase and walking stick strolls the hotel corridors apparently having no final destination…This time he wears the big square shaped sun glasses with thick black frames. He walks slowly and pays attention to the smallest details, observing the painting of Egeria, the statue of Zeus, the spring in the marble wall…he tries the mineral water from it and frowns in a disgust… The man spots the hotel cat, who approaches him carefully. The mysterious man squats and lets the cat rubbing freely against his legs. Then he spots something on the red carpet at the end of the corridor… He stands up and walks in that direction. It's a small green translucent ball… As he wants to pick it up, the small ball starts to roll. He jumps in an attempt to grab it fast… but the ball rolls faster and faster…The man tries to follow it to catch it and the cat with him…but they are not successful…The ground below their feet shakes little as if they were on the boat on the sea…It lasted just for a short moment, but it was unexpected and therefore left the man and cat slightly in shock and disoriented…the mysterious man takes off his sunglass and tries to sharpen his eyesight… He has a strange feeling the world he sees keeps splitting twice… He feels dizzy and there are some sharp needles penetrating his ear drums!

The mysterious man to himself, "Oh this feels familiar…"

He has to squat again, because he doesn't feel well, he touches the wall supporting his balance. As he stands up slowly again, he sees the hotel Egeria owner Peter Willington approaching him. "Are you all right, Sir?"

"Yes, I do, now. Thank you."

Someone starts to play piano downstairs…

The mysterious man still holding his sunglasses in his hand looks to Peter, "Did you feel it?"

"Feel what?"

"The ground was shaking!"

"Yes, it happens sometimes. Our hotel is located directly above a large spring…" shaking his head in disbelief, "This time it was quite a bit stronger, stronger than ever before in fact…"

"I've seen most of the world at least twice…" adds the mysterious man.

"Oh really? I thought maybe it was just me, you know…yesterday we had a Rum tasting… I thought it was just me… something with my eyes…Did you feel the pain in the ears as well?"

"So it wasn't just me." The mysterious man wonders.

"No, I felt the same thing…Well, it's over now and I hope you are now well Sir?"

"Yes, I'm fine, just fine."

Peter smiles and stretches his right hand to the man, "Well, my name is Peter, I'm the owner of this hotel. And you are…?"

The mysterious man smiles as well and shakes Peter's hand but does not answer the question.

"You do not have to say your name, Sir. I know who you are…but I didn't see your name among the reservations…"

"Peter, do you always make it a point to know all your guests?"

"I'm a very diligent man, that's the only way…to change the world…"

The mysterious man shakes his head, "You're goddamn right, you know… sometimes…I have the feeling…that just maybe, angels are guiding my actions."

"I've heard them speaking to me now…They said, "CHANGE THE WORLD"…but, anyway…I know who you are…and it's a real honour to speak with you…to have you as our guest…"

"We're all guests, no? It's an honour to visit…"

"Would you mind taking my hand and telling me, what you see?"

The mysterious man laughs, touches Peter's hand and closes his eyes.

"I see…the Earth shaking…a charming man from China throwing colourful gluons…the hotel set afire…an explosion…An assassination of the president… the wall…the prison…full of slaves…."

The both men laugh heartily.

"OBSERVERS"

The sun goes down fast leaving the teared clouds red hanging up on the sky. Something flies above the hotel and it looks like a hawk waiting in the air to attack in the sun set. But it's not a bird, it's a drone monitoring the hotel area. A little high definition camera attached to its belly moves its all seeing eye to do the surveillance, to capture the data. The drone flies also close to the two sonic and infrared sound gun - machines, attached to the trees high above the ground.

The black van - with its windows blinded - sits parked in the side street. People walk by - returning from their daily jobs – not knowing about the other layers of our reality. The specialists observe the moving images, captured by the drone, on the screen of a notebook. They drink coffee and eat Chinese noodles from the paper boxes, using chop sticks.

The underground world is like an underwater part of the iceberg, what we normally see is just its small peak…and often its better this way…

"BAD NEWS"

Peter Willington sits on the edge of his bed with his hands falling down between his legs, he is motionless and his eyes seem to be dead… The hotel cat sits on the window rim observing what is happening outside. The weather worsened lately and it's about to get rainy anytime soon. The dark red clouds gather together to do the summer storm congregation. Down in front of Peter there are open suitcases and mess all over the room… The empty dirty plates and cups with black dried coffee grounds in their bottoms are dispersed across the space… Finally the door opens. James Mc Dermott - his only son enters the room and after a short look around, "Oh good God, it looks terrible here. You look terrible, dad. What's up?"

"Have a seat, son."

James sits down on the chair next to his dad.

"I have to tell you something…"

James has the feeling of an invisible force grabbing him by his throat, "What is it, dad?"

"I just got back from the doctor…" Peter continues with a sad voice.

James is uttering, "…and?"

For some reason tears try to make their way out of James's eyes…but James fights hard to suppress the feeling that is about to overwhelm him…"

A black raven lands on the window rim of Peter's apartment and observes the two men inside. They do some moves and gestures, the two shadows… The raven doesn't understand, he doesn't have any urge to understand…he is just the observer… the witness…

What attracts the eye of the raven is the cat… and the cat spots the black bird as well and rises its one leg tapping onto the window glass. The soft rain drops sprinkle the window.

Peter is motionless staring at the raven behind the window, "…I have 2 maybe 3 months left…" and bites his tongue.

James shakes his head, "No! That's not possible! There has to be a cure! Experimental treatments, ancient wisdoms, traditional Chinese medicine…We'll figure out something, dad! Never ever give up! I'll never give up on you!"

Peter is looking sad, "Sooner or later we'll all have to go, James…The metastasis spread all over my internal organs, liver, stomach…it is fourth stage, James. There isn't a fifth…Look at me…I'm hitting 80 soon…I won't be here forever…

James has his mouth open softly and is still holding back the tears, "But…"

Peter is casting down his tired eyes, "I know…little Jimmy…I don't want to go." Then by rising his eyes and looking directly and firmly into the eyes of his dear son, "Listen… I made my will…"

"But…why…?" James emotionally.

"Everything goes to you, James. The hotel, you know…everything…"

James shakes his head in his resolute disagreement, "I don't want anything! I don't…"

"Our lawyer has it…"

Peter stands up and walks to reproduction of the Mona Lisa, he puts the painting down and opens the safe, pulls out a big thick yellow envelope…and comes back to his bed, "Here…" He hands the heavy envelope to his son. "Here's the money I saved for you and Jane… "

"I don't want it!", James is rising his finger making the negation gesture, "I swear we'll find a way…"

James Willington's mobile starts ringing. He switches the phone off angrily and throws it against the wall, the phone breaks into thousands of pieces.

Silence.

The other of his phones starts ringing. He hesitates and then he picks it up, "Yes! No! …I said No! …Which part of "NO" don't you fucking understand? It's one fucking syllable."

He disconnects.

Peter now serious, "James, you shouldn't talk to people like that…"

"I know, dad…You're right…like always…" holding back his tears fiercely, "…about everything…"

James stands up…his father also stands up…there are no more words left…everything has been communicated…they hug each other intensively.

James Willington leaves his father's apartment and strolls the hotel corridors without any final destination. Then he arrives to the bust of the Zeus…He stares at it and his tears find their way out finally…He stands there and cries like a small boy. Everything is falling on him, like the remnants of the heavy massive pillars of the ancient Greek monastery on the abandoned mountain.

"TALENT IS AVAILABLE"

In the other wing of the hotel Samia Sahar, the head of Sales & Marketing department, walks through an empty corridor and sings to her self. "Her working hours are pretty much free and she doesn't run anywhere…She wears a white elegant costume greatly contrasting with her long shiny black hair…She has the black leather comfortable leasure shoes with the tiny high heels on…"

At the same time the Indian singer steps out of his room and walks through the spacy empty hotel corridor with his suitcase and leather hand bag. He wears a blue shirt and red tie, his suit over his arm, it is a hot summer in Karlovy Vary. He realises the lift doesn't work… There is a notice directing the hotel guests to use the lift for the staff… but he can't see the second lift at first… As he looks around like in the famous John Travolta's GIFs, his ears notice singing… Then he spots Samia Sahar approaching from the opposite direction singing to herself – is it her? His heart almost stops as he is overwhelmed by her natural beauty.

"Hello, Madame…"

"Yes, Sir?"

Singer in his mind 'It is her, that's the voice he did hear the other day!' and to Samia, "I'm…I'm looking for…"

Samia smiles, "…the lift?"

"…actually yes…"

Samia turns and points her finger, "It is right behind you…Turn around…"

The singer turns around and back to Samia, "Oh, I'm stupid…Thank you."

"Are you checking out now?"

"Sorry?"

She is calling the lift, "Will you be leaving our hotel?"

"Oh yes…yes…", His eyes meet with those of Samia…and they connect immediately, "unfortunately!"

Samia is a bit suspicious and has the feeling, that she had seen the handsome gentleman somewhere, "Oh? You didn't enjoy your stay? I hope that's not the case."

"Yes, definitely, everything was great, the food, the bed…ah…I mean the room…comfortable…everyone so kind…like you…"

Samia laughs, "Really?" and looking at him closer, "Are you from Bharat?"

"Yes, indeed."

"From Mumbai?"

"Yep."

"Oh, that's awesome. I lived and worked in Mumbai for many years…"

The eyes of the singer smile, "That's wonderful! It's a small world…"

"Yes"

"Did you like Mumbai?"

"Honestly… It was a great experience, but I hate the heat & humidity, I'm glad I escaped, but of course…I've a lot of good memories."

He feels that he does not have much time left to get more information about Sami, "Well, should you find yourself back in Mumbai sometime…"

The lift arrives and the singer opens the door for Samia like the true gentleman.

The door closes and lift goes down. Now the proximity between Samia and singer shortened greatly and both feel kind of uneasy…Samia observes the singer and he observes her - just the brief side looks… Silence. Tension in the air between those two. Suddenly the lift shakes, the light blink, few more metres and the lift stops in between the floors. Samia and the singer touch their ears with the painful grimaces in their faces. The world splits in two and the vision gets blurry. It lasts just for a few seconds, but it's very unpleasant for both of them. The singer touches Samia's arm, "Are you all right?"

"Yes, but, did your ears hurt too?

"They did…and my eyes got blurry…"

Samia touches the hand of the singer, "How about you, are you OK? It's the second time today!"

"Really? What was it?"

"I don't know, I really don't know…"

"Did it ever happen here before? Was that an earthquake?"

"Not sure…The Czech Republic doesn't have earthquakes…definitely not that strong…"

"Well, it looks like we're stuck here…"

"I'll call security." Samia grabs to the walkie talkie she carries with her, when on duty.

"If I have to be stuck in an elevator, it's great to be stuck in one with a beautiful woman like you!"

Samia is getting nervous, "I'll make that call…"

Samia tries to call the security but without success, she says to the singer, "The line's dead…"

Silence.

"Sir, don't worry. Someone will come soon…Though I hope you won't miss your plane…"

"No…Even if I do, I won't mind…"

"OK" as she glances at the singer, "I think I've seen you somewhere before…"

"Anything's possible…"

Samia is shaking her head, "Yeah"

Silence.

Samia is trying to fill the silent vacuum, "Where are they…?"

"Well, I guess that's it. We'll have to live the rest of our lives here. Just the two of us. Like a couple of Robinson Crusoes...on a small island...lost and forgotten forever..." the singer with a firm voice.

"That's a lovely dream...far from civilisation..."

"Away from people..."

"Just nature, the sea, sunshine..."

Silence.

The singer glances at Samia and starts singing quietly,

> "Shining in the setting sun
> Like a pearl upon the ocean
> Come and feel me
> O feel me"

Samia smiles and gets little red in her beautiful face.

He continues,

> "Shining in the setting sun
> Like a pearl upon the ocean
> Come and heal me
> O heal me"

Samia looks into the singer's eyes and smiles softly, he smiles back and sings further,

> "Thinking about the love we were making
> And a life we were sharing
> Come and feel me
> O feel me
> Shining in the setting sun
> Like a pearl upon the ocean
> Come and feel me
> Come on heal me"

The singer hints to Samia to continue her part and she starts with slight hesitation,

> "Hua yo tu bhi
> Mera mera
> Tera yo ikraar hua
> Toh kyun na
> Main bhi

Keh doon
Keh doon
Hua muyhe bhi
Pyaar hua"

Samia and the singer both burst in a laughter and clap their hands, "Well donee…we make a great duo…"

But then they realise they are not a couple… The melancholic smiles on both faces follow…

Silence.

Samia, "Maybe we should press the button again?" and saying this she does so and the lift starts moving down again. "I told you…"

The singer acts sad, "I didn't want to do it…"

Samia casting her eyes down on the singer and gets to his shoes, "Hey, there is something on your shoe…" she pulls a papernapking out of the pocket and wants to clean the dirty spot on the shoe, but the singer is a true gentleman and stops her halfway through, grabbing her hand softly, rising it towards his lips. "Please don't" and he kisses her hand softly.

The lift doors open suddenly revealing the lift couple to the audience at the reception… The newly arrived guests witness the singer kissing the hand of Samia…and they freeze in whatever action they were merged into… The hotel cat suddenly runs down the stair directly towards the lift couple and the singer grabs the cat into his hands and rises it in front of Samia's eyes. They feel a little bit caught in doing something, that they shouldn't have been doing…Them three walk out of the lift. The singer wants to ask Samia something, but the GM's assistant Juan Alexandro Polpo hastily arrives at the reception asking Samia to go for the monthly meeting, which she completely forgot about…

"Yes, I'll be there in just a moment…" She turns back to the singer, who wanted to tell her something… but in the same time the receptionist Yuki with the phone in her hand shouts at the Indian famous singer… unknown in Europe, "Sir, your taxi is here…waiting…YOUR FLIGHT…".

Juan addresses Samia, "It's urgent, Samia, we have to go now. Right now!"

Juan grabs Samia's hand and drags her away… Samia turns back for the last time to see the Indian singer waving his hand at her… He smiles but his smile is kind of sad… He observes Samia disappearing behind the corner…The Indian singer to himself, "I didn't even get her name!"

Juan is angry with Samia, "You always forget meetings. It's like you're not even here…".

They take the stairs up hastily.

The famous Indian singer approaches the receptionist Yuki, "Could you please tell me the name of that woman, please…"

"I'm afraid we can't give out such an information… about our staff or guests sir.

"Please…" he pulls out some money and hands it over to Yuki, but she shakes her head, "I'm sorry, Sir, but no."

The angry taxi driver pops into the reception area shouting, "How long will you let me wait? Tell me!"

The singer knows, that the driver meant him, "I do apologise."

Then he turns back to Yuki making dog's eyes, "Please…just her first name…"

Yuki shakes her head, "I'm really sorry, but it's against our policy. The only hint I can give you, check the hotel's website and you will find her. She is there for sure…" Yuki twinkles with her eye.

"Ok, thank you so much, I will search for her on my way to the airport already."

The taxi driver comes close to the singer, "Sir, let's go. You don't want to miss your plane and I don't want to miss any more fares."

The singer smiles and follows the taxi driver out.

"SURPRISE, SURPRISE"

Mr. Tea stands lonely at the door, outside of the hotel, looking sad. He observes through the glass door what is happening in the reception area. A young man arrives to the reception. He doesn't have any suitcases, he is empty handed, his face looks pale, he wears glasses, has brown hair and a thin small body. He speaks with the receptionist Yuki and asks her to arrange for James Willington as he needs to speak with him. Yuki tells him to sit down, that she will call him. Yuki tries to call James's mobile, but without success, there is no response.

By coincidence James arrives to the reception himself and wants to go out pulling the box of the cigarettes out of his pocket and the lighter. James passes the reception and is stopped by Yuki. She points at the young man sitting in the leather sofa in the reception area. James Willington walks towards the visitor and greets him asking what is it so important he needs to tell him…

"I'm afraid, I don't know you… Should I?"

The young man with erratic behaviour, "Could we perhaps talk somewhere private?"

"To be honest, I don't have much time…and I don't see the need for confidentiality, much less privacy"

"I have something important to tell you…"

"I have more pressing concerns…"

The young man feels abused and conters determined, "Perhaps I should talk to your father then…?…to tell my story to him…?…or maybe your current wife…?"

"What's your name, young man? What it is so important, you want to tell me? Tell me now!"

The young man laughs shortly, "It's not so much about what my name is…, but rather who my father is…"

James spots Mr. Tea outside as he observes them, then he realises that Yuki might be listening, she seems to be diving into some administrative work…, but her ears are certainly ready to catch the sounds, "Let's go to my office!" The both men head into the James's office being followed by Yuki's and Mr. Tea's eyes. On their way the conversation continues.

The young man asks nasty, "Could you send for some dinner please. I'm hungry…"

James just now realises the young man's hair are ginger… and his two frontal teeth are like the ones of a rabbit, or rather a rat. "Well, you can certainly select something from our menu…but I have to warn you…we're not cheap…"

"I'm in the mood for something like my mom's cooking…I want to feel like being at home, here…dad…"

James stops on the spot as if he was just hit by a North American truck delivering trees from Alaska.

The young man smiles, "…but you can call me Frank…or Frankie…mom calls me Frankie…little Frankie…"

James with a deadly cold look, "What's your mom's name?"

Little Frankie nasty, "Let's go to the restaurant first! Dad!

"The fuck you say! Prove it!" James has the devil in his eyes.

Little Frankie is sucking the air and mouth water back inside through the crevice between his two rat teeth. "I got the paperwork on me, dad…"

James thinks, then grins and even smiles, "Maybe we should eat something first, then you can tell me more."

"I think this is the beginning of a beautiful relationship…"

"WALK OUT OF THE MYSTERY"

The mysterious man with suitcase and walking stick walks out of the hotel. Mr. Tea stands there alone, and as the mysterious man assesses the posture of the bellboy, he seems to be feeling lonely too.

The wind, snow, rain, darkness of the night, weight of the day…life… bombard the bellboy's hat without mercy! The mysterious man approaches carefully Mr. Tea.

Mr. Tea sadly, "Good evening Sir, how was your lunch?"

The mysterious man pulls up the cigar and hands it over to Mr. Tea who accepts it - surprised - with a smile. The mysterious man pulls another one for himself.

They both smoke in silence. There is no need for words as both men observe taxis arriving slowly with new guests.

"I am sorry Sir, I must return to work! Thank you so much for the exquisite cigar, more delicious, because I could smoke it together with a great man like yourself!"

The mysterious man nods, "I must go as well."

"Let me please organise a taxi for you…"

"No! I'll walk…"

"Please allow me to walk with you. It might be dangerous to walk alone here in the night…"

"…I only walk alone…ALWAYS!"

The mysterious man grabs his suitcase and walking stick and moves off the entrance. His long black coat with high collar looks now ominously in the summer darkness. Mr. Tea walks towards the arriving taxis and glances in the direction of the departing mysterious man. Mr. Tea then shouts at that mysterious man, "Hey, would you dance for me? Could you please do your dance?"

The man in the distance turns towards Mr. Tea, drops his suitcase down and throws away the walking stick. Then he starts his worldwide famous dancing!

Mr. Tea smiles from happiness and feels warm suddenly and he says to himself, "It is him! I knew it!"

He raises his hand and greets the mysterious man in the far distance - already disappearing - as the bellboy shifts his focus onto the heavy suitcases of the fresh new guests. He opens the door of the taxi with smile, talks with the people with smile and walks them through the reception to the lifts with smile. The guests appreciate Mr. Tea's friendly and gentleman approach very much. They talk to him as if he was their long time friend. Mr. Tea smiles, because he knows, he is not alone…

"HIKING IS DANGEROUS"

James Willington and his "son" Frank left the hotel Egeria early in the morning to drive up to the close mountains near the German border. They want to get to know each other better and James thought a trip with Frank would help him to receive more information about his "son" and his mother, but he also has a plan no one would expect.

They are on the way from the parking lot below to the entrance of an abyss and James is walking up a steep path ahead of Frank.

James turns back to Frank, "C'mon son, I wanna show you something!"

Frank is breathing heavily, "Yeah, coming…"

James Willington and his bastard son Frankie walk towards the edge of a massive abyss.

James grins, "You don't get much exercise, do you Frank?"

"We go bowling every Sunday…"

James with a laugh, "I meant something like jogging, biking, swimming or…"

James arrives first at the edge of the super deep abyss and his face gets rather serious and eyes gain a cold deadly look whispering, "…flying…"

Frank arrives to the edge as well and taps on the arm of James Willington, as if he was searching for some support. They both enjoy the amazing and eerie view while the wind combs their hair. An eagle is circling in the blue sky. It's getting warmer as the sun rises above the horizon.

"This is an amazing view, little Frankie! I'm ovenoyed to have a child after all, and really glad you found me, my son…" James sounds friendly.

"Thanks for taking me here. Sure, it was a long trip. A hard trip. And, even sometimes…an adventurous trip…I'm getting hungry, dad…"

"We'll get you something…"

Frank out of the context, "Are you wealthy, dad?"

As if he expected this question one day, James lies, "to be honest, our hotel doesn't do too well…"

Frank is sucking the mouth water through the crevice between his two front teeth, "…and when will we go to California? Mom said you have a big villa in Beverly Hills. "White and stunning" I think she said."

James is annoyed or better to say disgusted, "She said what?" and in his mind 'How the fuck does she know that?'

"She saw it on Facebook…Can I go there?" and Frank continues, "I'd rather live with you. Mom always tries to tell me what to do."

"Did she also tell you to find and get ahold of me?" James is really getting pissed off.

"No, no…It was my idea."

"You just said, she saw the villa on Facebook…" James is investigating the situation further.

Frank gets nervous, "It doesn't matter."

Just now James Willington spots the picture on Frank's T-shirt. There is an alien poster from the film "Covenant". The alien stares at James from the darkness, acid liquid dropping down of his ugly scary double mouth with long thin quick-silver teeth. What a coincidence, the similar T-shirt wears their hotel Spanish sommelier…

James can not breathe. He doesn't smoke but suddenly asks Frank, "Any chance you have a cigarette Frankie?"

"Sure, dad!"

He pulls out a box of cigarettes and offers one to James. He lights the ciga-rette. Then he pulls one for himself and lights it too. Frank goes closer to the edge and glances down…

James observes his bastard son monster with his mouth slightly open, "You know, I always wanted to have a son…" and he puffs a blueish smoke out of his mouth.

James makes a silent step crawling behind Frank.

"And I always wanted to have a dad. A dad whose legacy I could carry on. A dad whose secrets I could keep. I really wanted to be a good son. You know, the kind of son who'd be worthy of a large inheritance…"

James steps back silently biting his tongue angrily…Frank turns back towards his dad James Willington…"oh, my Lawyer awaits my call…"

Both men lock their eyes for a moment as a group of mountain bikers arrive to the scene, greet the two men and disappear between the trees again.

James pushes Frank further through the forrest until they come to the ruins of a castle. Frank is exhausted and the tension in the air can be cut. All of a sudden James takes all his power, turns saying, "…and I have doubt you could afford a decent lawyer…" and stabs Frankie with a big steak knife into the stomach, again and again and as he mutilates the ginger boy, he starts smiling - realising - that he likes it, "…you know what…Frankie… maybe I should do this more often!"

"Please…let me go…I'll stop chasing you…" whispers Frank.

"It's too late for that Frankie. Would you like a Nat Sherman?"

"No! Please. I fucked up. I know." Frank is sobbing.

"Well, now you know…you were dead before you started your bullshit…but, I'll make it short. Call me sentimental."

James sticks another - bigger kitchen knife - right through the neck of Frank and the blood bursts out as he hits Frank's artery. James smiles and cuts his head off. "It goes smoother than I thought…my boy…Thanks a million, Sylvester, for keeping your tools sharp! And I know who is next…! Now, I'll clean the mess and then I have another pleasure meeting, my boy…"

The eyes of Frank gaze at James from their sockets in the head right below the decapitated body.

"BARCELONA - GUINARDO"

The sun raises above the easel. The man in his late 50's paints in the streets - the motif: The narrow street falling deep down and raising again up towards the sea, which surface shines like gold. As the painter stares down into the abyss of the concrete jungle he gets dizzy and feels some kind of vertigo. He is afraid of heights and even this view makes him uneasy. And this is what fascinates him.

The sea level appears to be above the buildings and shines really like pure polished gold in the spotlight. The view is unreal, magic and dream alike. It reminds him of one of his childhood frequent dreams, "he walks the beach and approaches the cloth with tiny holes in the shape of hexagonal bee wax cells. The cloth hangs from the wooden trunk erected from sand in the middle of the beach. He attaches his eye onto the cloth and observes the world through the tiny hole. The world shines like an orange-yellow honey. The greyish cloth smells of Argan oil. He sees a girl…She has a long black hair that shimmer blueish. He knows, this is the eternal paradise. Sometimes he falls asleep and has a nightmare, that he has a face he can touch, the hands that can kill and a heart that can painfully blow-up…sprinkling the mirror in front of him with a red viscose liquid. But here, in the yellow-orange paradise, they are happy with the girl, immortal, beautiful and calm… He doesn't remember when they had met and where…for the first time… Perhaps they were always like this…since the eternity…since the beginning of everything…but there is no time here…no…just an omnipresent strong desire of two burning hearts…that's the immortal fire…the love…God… ALL IN ONE!

The sea waves lazily fall over each other like the honey waterfalls. There is total silence - in the terms of human - over here, but somewhere inside - he and the girl can hear a soft beautiful melody that underlines tranquility of this space. The melody is produced by an angels' orchestra making the hidden crystal gems vibrate in the massive mountains – with their peaks travelling through the clouds to the stars. Him and the girl played "seek and hide" game ever since…stalking each other through the multi-universe - over the space and time…despite all possible and impossible physical laws made up by the observers who were never comfortable with the wonderful mystery…who were always calculating in order to expand their comfort zone…Now he found her here on this abandoned island. She is so close. Now, he can catch her! But something happens…The devil's eye rises above the sea and throws the spotlight onto the boy, who covers his eyes as the rays are causing unexpected pain…The girl runs away laughing…That is the end of the paradise.

"STREET ARTISTS"

The painter protects his eyes from the rising sun. The world around went black. He can hear girl's laughter, he turns around to see two small girls chasing each other, enjoying themselves. An elderly man with a white mustache passes the painter on his motorbike stopping right in front of a small bar on the corner. The name of the bar is "MORENO" (which means "brown" in Spanish). The regulart guests of this bar are local pensionaires. All they do is enjoying morning coffee and a cigarette, occasional chat and most of all – the view. With such a view, there is no need for words… Everything is mutually understood. The painter covers his unfinished painting by a grey cloth. He picks his stuff, the easel, bag with the oil paints and other things and walks to the bar. He finds a seat under a big white umbrella, where he sips his "cortado" from a small glass. He also enjoys his cigar and observes the morning city. The escalators transport people up to this small plateau as the Guinardo hilly area is really steep. It looks here - in this part of Barcelona - like in the city of San Francisco. Down there, below the plateau, the cars, busses and taxis move impatiently to their today morning's destinations.

"E.R.A."

The man is in his late 50's and sleeps deep covered by many heavy blankets. He is one of the famous Spanish painters and originally from Zaragoza. The man sits on his bed and opens the bulletin describing his upcoming paintings exhibition in the hotel Egeria in Karlovy Vary, Czech Republic. There is also his photograph and name Enrique Romero Aleman. He signs his paintings with E.R.A. only, but everyone knows who is behind these three letters.

E.R.A. crawls - being exhausted of life - to an old gramophone, selects one of the gramophone records, it is an old Pink Floyd title, "Shine on you crazy diamond". As he walks back he passes many of the canvas with his paintings leaning against the wall. From the drawer of the bedside table he pulls out a bottle, opens it and thinks…finally he closes the bottle again and puts it back. Then he opens a plastic box with the pills, he picks a portion of medicine from the section "THURSDAY", stands up and goes to the kitchen.

E.R.A. speaks to himself, "Far too cliché to take the medicine with spirits, hehe, and it could be dangerous as well…"

When he enters the kitchen, he doesn't bother switching the light on. A soft greenish light of the street lamps give enough of illumination to the space. In fact the street lights here in Barcelona have rather yellow colour, but the kitchen light green window blinds turn the incoming light into the greenish one. Again, there are many E.R.A.'s paintings on the walls, paintings leaning against the walls, paintings in the drawers appointed to the cutlery, plates… He approaches the fridge. There is a photograph of younger version of himself holding a small baby. On another photograph there is a beautiful young girl with long black hair, she smiles softly, not too much.

E.R.A. is getting a flashback when watching the photo.

"The painter and the girl from the photograph make love in the bed covered in white translucent veils shaking softly in the summer breeze. The bed stands in the black sand at the beach and both lovers can see the turquoise blue sea waves approaching them closer and closer with the upcoming high-tide. Many green parrots scream in the emerald green crowns of the palms crawling like snakes above the black ground. A volcano - the landmark of the Island - erupts and churns out lava and dust. As they make love, a shadow emerges from behind the shrubs - a man with a pistol. The shots tear the dream apart and the satin translucent white veils colour red.

The painter holds the head of his lover in his hands sprinkled by blood and cries. Her eyes gaze at him, but there is no life in them anymore… Not the life as we know it…"

E.R.A.'s mind gets back to reality standing in front of the fridge.

The photographs and notes on the papers are attached to the fridge by the magnets, those souvenir magnets from all over the world… The man opens the fridge, there are canvases with his paintings too, the small tubes with oil colours, colourful wax sticks, a bottle of outdated milk, meat in plastic boxes, olives, one apple, cheese, a pistol…the bullets to it in a box… He takes the milk and the gun.

E.R.A. packs a few things into a mid size leather bag, he goes to the bathroom, stands in front of the mirror with the pistol pointed at his head.

Silence.

The neon light keeps noisily blinking.

Then he spots the red notice on the porcelain tiles written by the bloody red lipstick   "We are all just a dream!" The man sighs and gazes at himself from the mirror. Spontaneously he starts laughing mad and drops the pistol into the sink. He can not stop. The neon light keeps blinking. The door behind him opens slightly with a crackling noise…But no one enters the room… The painter opens a small wardrobe with a mirror and touches a small bottle with the sign   "FLUOXETINE", "for depression, panic attacks and obsessive compulsive disorder" With his hands shaking he manages to open the bottle, takes one pill and swallows it. He closes the bottle and puts it into his pocket. The reddish tears run down his face and the world around him vibrates. It feels like thousands of sharp needles penetrate his head skin, a lean bone, brain cells. He touches his stomach with pain and slouches. Then he washes his face with a cold water making the sighs of pain.

He drops his airticket to Karlovy Vary into the bag. The bulletin informing about his own paintings exhibition at hotel Egeria follows.

"Enrique Romero Aleman"
"Hotel Egeria Exhibition of Paintings"
"Encaustic and Oil"
"THE SPIRAL ESCAPES TO THE DREAMS"

He grabs the bag and the canvas in the grey cloth, walks out and the spiral stairs down. The man looks up and stops walking…there…on the floor above him…he did spot a hand wearing a purple glove touching the wooden banisters…or was that just a dream…?

Silence.

The painter continues walking but another pair of shoes above him add to the sound of his steps…He stops again and leans over the railing looking up searching the source of the steps.

Silence.

As he moves back he spots a deep abyss below him – the beautiful spiral pattern – and gets the vertigo, making him almost falling down! But he keeps his balance at last and wins his life. A panic attack overwhelms him and he crawls backwards away from the low height banisters…He leans with his sweating back against the wall. His heart is beating fast and erratic. Now he has to wait to calm down and gather his strength to continue walking down the steps.

Some person with the face masked by many black scarfs, with black sunglasses, a hood over the head, hands hidden in the pockets of the long black rain coat, black army leather shoes… approaches him, passes him and continues walking down… The painter doesn't make a single move. He stopped breathing as if there was no more air left. The sound of the steps fades down as the mysterious person disappears in the spiral stairs abyss. The painter breathes out in relief and decides to continue walking down.

E.R.A. walks through the narrow street falling deep down and sometimes there are escalators too, since the streets are too steep… The painter has a strong feeling his body will stop resisting the gravity and totally loose its control falling down directly to the down town. He is afraid to use escalators, he was always afraid to use them. But here he fights his fear and uses the escalators, because the vertigo is too strong. He holds the railings of the escalator by his both hands and his legs shake…

As he arrives down he jumps out of the ever-moving escalator deadly machine. There, in the corner, under the palms - again that mysterious person in black sits on the bench! The painter gets aggressive and in his mind he prepares the speech, 'Why the hell are you following me? I'll fight! I'll call the police!'

But he just passes the person sitting on the bench holding his breath. Then, as he takes another outdoor escalator down, he keeps turning - double checking the person in black. The mysterious night walker still sits there, and as the painter is taken by the second escalator down, the person on the bench disappears. The painter walks faster frequently turning back. He walks through the narrow streets, dark corners, back streets, small eerie parks, viaducts, crossing the bridges. When he walks the narrow bridge with very low railings, again he gets that strong vertigo and crouches low to the ground, because he is afraid that a sudden attack of the strong wind could blow him down. This part of Barcelona is chilling. One could get lost here easily - especially in the night - but E.R.A. uses his mobile and a navigation app. There is not much of crime over here in Guinardo, but it's about the rather invisible forces and dark energetic streams flowing up and down the super steeps streets - like the flying of Chinese dragons. It's the "Witch" hill in the middle of the labyrinth like city. Something one can hardly describe unless having personal experience strolling the area after midnight. The painter arrives to the viewpoint from which one can see the whole Barcelona with a 360 degrees stunning view. The city lights shimmer in the night. The thousands of streets fall down into a dark sea. The sharks are waiting down there…He wants to lean against the rail, but it shakes greatly as it is quiet loose…The painter gets into panic as he feels he might fall down now and fly......fly above the town......fly until he realises he can't fly...and then fall down...into the concrete jungle...breaking his bones, head, tearing his internal organs, bleeding out, being paralysed...merging with this nightmare...for ever...maybe the invisible "Guinardo Witch" wanted to push himdown! The man steps back from the edge feeling the witches' bony cold fingers around his neck. The night city lights hypnotise him and he knows he is trapped here.

He runs down the street fast as if he was on the escape! He comes to Plaza Catalunya, the massive spacy square and searches for the bus to the airport.

There are thousands of abandoned black - yellow taxis dispersed all over the place...Their drivers disappeared somewhere... as if some force took sucked them into another dimension... This place is alive - however - even at this time of the night. The African black salesmen sell the fake branded bags, the watches, shoes, having their dodgy goods displayed on the grey clothes down on the ground... and they sell drugs too...The prostitutes are selling their bodies...

Drunk tourists, aggressive gays walking with their small dogs in hands wearing pink shirts, short tight trousers, the men kissing each other...a group of young drunk girls whose voices are rather too deep...in their search for another night adventure...frequently get the hard cash from the rich visitors of the city... two drunk men fight there...a lake of dried blood on the ground...the homeless sleep here, in sleeping bags, one with a cardboards in front of him on the dirty ground saying,

"NO TENGO CASA, SOY PADRE DE QUATRO HIJOS, NECESITAMOS COMER, POR FAVOR AYUDA"

A big wooden cross with Jesus Christ guards the safe sleep of the poor man. At least that is his hope...Very often they get robbed, beaten or even killed...No one cares...The policemen sitting in the comfort of their car just care about the cash bribes, named here "allowance fees", from the street sellers and pimps.

E.R.A. comes closer and drops a few coins into the paper coffee cup. But over there - in the corner of two luxury brand shops - where the watch costs 20,000 EUR and bags 2,000 EUR sleeps another one covered by many blankets. The card board sign says.

"WHY LIE? I NEED A BEER"

The painter first passes the guy, but then he returns and with an annoyed face drops him a few coins as well...but just a small amount...he puts the bigger value coins back into his pocket...Then he types into the mobile app "Airport - bus station near me."

The two drunk fighters approach him dangerously shouting and kicking, hitting each other's faces. The navigation shows him the direction. The painter better speeds up his walk crossing the square in the hinted direction. He realises that the bus stop for the direct airport transfer is temporarily closed and has to continue walking to the open one at the "Plaza Espagna". The mobile app shows him it is 1.6 km more to walk. E.R.A. just hast one word to explain his emotion in this very moment,"Shit!"

He must keep walking as there is no taxi working, but the place seems not to be too safe…

The painter mumbles under his mustache, "Next time I take a taxi, next time I take out my gun"

After the ride with the comfortable bus, E.R.A. arrives finally at the Barcelona Airport. The painter strolls the airport departure lounge waiting for the number of his gate to appear on the LCD screens. Then, suddenly he stops walking - frozen to the spot. The person in black – the stalker - walks from the opposite direction - approaching the painter! The painter looks around in his search for some airport security officers…then he chooses one random direction and walks that way…occasionally turning back…The person in black follows him!

E.R.A. in his mind, "Now - it can't be a coincidence!" He speeds up and gains some lead.

Now - as he turns back to double check - there is some anonymous crowd between him and the stalker. He gets an idea as he passes a shop with newspapers and refreshments. The painter enters the shop and hides in between the shelves gazing out through the souvenirs. He randomly picks one of the magazines and puts it in front of his face and waits peeking from behind it carefully. The people pass the shop. Then, the stalker turns up! Looking around as if he had lost something…or someone…E.R.A.!

The painter doesn't breathe hiding behind the magazine. He peeks out a little by his one eye just in the worst possible moment! The person in black stares directly at him. Their eyes - well the painter's eye and the sun glasses of the stalker - lock for a considerably long eerie time…The world around them slows down and so the heart beat of the painter does. The mysterious person turns away and keeps searching in the anonymous crowd…

E.R.A. breathes out in relief and in his mind, 'Perhaps he didn't see me…'

The stalker walks away and the painter follows that mysterious person with his gaze. Then, E.R.A. shifts his look to the opened magazine's page in front of his face…there is a beautiful female model…she wears only sexy underwear and the angel's white wings…also she wears the pair of purple leather gloves…The title of the article says,

"SOONER OR LATER, I'LL CATCH YOU!"

E.R.A. starts to daydream imagining what might happen next.

The pages of the opened fashion magazine is suddenly sprinkled by blood! The model has long black hair that glimmer indigo blue in the stage spotlights. She looks like the woman from the picture on his fridge back home… The shadow rises from the backseats along the stage and pulls out a gun, he starts shooting at the model - the angel with the snow-white wings! She falls down… The page of the magazine turns completely red. The painter turns the page just to reveal another one and there on that page - there's a man with the black mask laughing directly into his face.

In his shock he gets back to reality.

The painter walks with the fashion magazine towards the counters and along the way he grabs a bottle of water. The price tag says, 4.95 EUR.

E.R.A. in his mind, 'This is ridiculous! Fucking ridiculous!'

As he waits in the queue, he pulls out his mobile and makes a call, "Hey, is this hotel Egeria? Cool. Did you manage to change my room? You know for one on the first floor… I told you I have a bad vertigo and cannot stand upper floors… OK, please change it then and confirm it's…done? oh thank so much… no I'm not angry…no…sorry what's your name again?…Samia? …oh yes now I remember…you handle the all details of my paintings exhibition at your hotel… yes now I remember…really?…that's wonderful…yes…yes I'm all right…now?… at the airport…no..in Barcelona…well…something just happened… not angry with you…what happened?…oh…just someone was following me the whole night…or maybe it was just my imagination…hehe…yeah…well…thanks so much Samia…and I'll see you soon…bye, bye."

The person in black stands at the airport and the wind shakes the long coat making sounds. The stalker observes the security red lights blinking on the roofs of the airport buildings. The world slows down…The rain starts falling and a thick white haze swirls towards the lonely person in black…The radar monitoring the flights keeps turning. The mysterious person disappears…The plane moves on the runway faster and faster and finally it takes off the ground. The plane then disappears in the darkness. The haze gets even thicker. An airport worker in his transparent yellow vest drives a small cart with the luggages which can be hardly followed.

At the arrival hall a cleaner drives the machine wiping&cleaning the floor. The people who wait their planes sleep on the floor, in the seats, on the large window rims, in the closed cafés… The Chinese family, parents and two girls push a steel trolley with a huge pile of luggages ahead of them. A lonely bird who managed to get into the hall enjoys the rests from the bin.

One of the airport attendants approaches the bin and the small bird lifts off with a piece of sandwich in its tiny beak…

"FLYING TO THE MOON"

At hotel Egeria - its owner Peter Willington, his son James as GM and their staff meet extraordinary, extravagant, eccentric and sometimes out of mind people. So one day there is the request of a very wealthy client to have an adventure of his life-time organised. The reception and the concierge consult, what to offer the client and searched the internet for something special.

Today are in charge of the reception - a handsome Czech slim young man in his early 20's – Jiri Mlady and a smaller full bodied Italian man in his mid 40's Francesco Roma. They are two funny guys who are constantly on a lookout for doing some jokes and pranks. The Maître d' hotel - Thomas Koenig enters the reception asking, "…and where is Yuki today?"

Francesco promptly answers, "She's on vacation."

Jiri smirks at Francesco, but he addresses his greetings to Thomas, "Hello, Romeo…"

Francesco with serious voice, "We thought you went with her…"

"Yeah. She told us she really fancies you, but…" Jiri adds.

Thomas confident, "But…?"

Jiri glances at Francesco winking his eye, "…oh…we can't tell him this… can we?"

Francesco still serious, "But we're all friends here…no secrets between us… tell him, Jirka!"

Jiri with resistance, "No…you tell him, Francesco, I can't…"

Thomas starts to be curious and smiles not believing those two jokers a word, "Know what you can do with your secret…you can suck it out of my…"

"Yes! That's exactly what we were talking about…" Francesco with serious face and Jiri adds, "Exactly. More importantly, that's what Yuki was talking about…"

Thomas starts laughing in anticipation, "Ok ok ok. What'd she say? Something about me?"

Francesco bursts into a laughter, "Not about you per se…more like your little friend down there…"

"Fuck right off!" Thomas getting stressed.

Jiri Mlady laughs.

Francesco is in his element, digging deeper, " She said you could come with her. Well, if you were bigger."

All three men laugh.

Thomas goes swiftly into the counterattack, pulls out the keys from his Audi 6 and drops them noisily onto the reception table, "If you two pansies can't stop jerking off into your mom's panties for a second, maybe I'll take you somewhere you can meet some real women. Hell, where I'll take a couple of pussies like you, you might even be able to get laid".

Three guests - wearing the same Ray Ban sun glasses approach the receptionists. A business man trading with oil & gas Amir Abd Al-Aziz from Qatar, an owner of a Chinese Telco company Adam Cheung and an American businessman dealing with real estates – Rich Turner. As they approach the reception they are in the middle of a talk.

Amir kindly, "Please. Allow me to take you there in my plane."

Rich adds serious, "…or we can use my plane…"

Adam smiles, "…oh, between you two I feel very poor indeed…"

Rich smiles back, "Why?"

Adam joking, "I don't have a private plane like you two."

Amir, "So buy, one."

Rich laughs, "We're not exclusive, Adam. All you need is a good pair of sunglasses and a plane. Maybe one day you feel like working in a call center, maybe the next day driving a cab, maybe the next day rolling sushi in Okinawa. It's all the same to us. Really. We're not exclusive. Well, not completely exclusive."

Adam friendly, "That's a hell of a dream, Amir."

Amir says, "A wish can be deadly…I once dreamed of being married and having children…Now I have 4 wives and 12 children…all girls…Imagine - me one man in the house and 16 women…?

All three men laugh as they approach the reception table.

Rich now serious, "I'm guessing you're either very happy or…well…you get the idea…What you desire is what you want, what you have is what Allah wants. Nouman Ali Khan said this. He's an American Muslim speaker."

Adam turns to the receptionists and Thomas Koenig, "Really? I thought that was Nusrat Fateh Ali Khan. At any rate, I like his music. But maybe a little help?"

Franceso is professional and very polite to the guests, "Anything, gentlemen"

Adam starts, "We would like to have a once in a lifetime adventure…just us three…"

Francesco sees that the Chinese wants to impress the other two and introduces his idea of a lifetime adventure, "We have here avery special offer. The offer is an adventure trip by plane to the Alps, walking up to the Montblanc and have a diner served on the top of the mountain. Then taking the helicopter down to a 5 star hotel overnight and in the morning flight back. Total cost is about 45000 EUR per person."

Adam is grinning, "Thank you, but I'm afraid that is nothing special, because I own a chalet in Zermatt and we could do this trip any day as my friends own their private planes…"

Thomas Koenig grabs his car keys off the table, apologises to all and leaves to the restaurant. Francesco Roma calls the girl from the Concierge desk and she arrives immediately - her name - Natalia Alexandra Kirkorova - a beautiful young blonde woman with indigo blue eyes. Natalia introduces herself and the important question follows immediately, "What is the budget, if I may ask?"

Adam politely, "For the right thing - unlimited."

Natalia is thinking hard and then suddenly comes up with, "We might have something… „Flying to the Moon" – it's not public yet, but to get the feeling, we offer a rather remarkable flight, where you feel no gravity at all – it's an astronaut trainer. Something we affectionately call the "Vomit Comet". Would that be something you might enjoy, gentlemen?"

Amir gets shining eyes, "Inshallah. How much?"

"That all depends - from 25K USD. For an exclusive individual experience 150,000 USD."

Rich is also excited, "OK, We'll share the joy."

"ONS WITH THE TOURLEADER"

As GM one has long working hours, rarely weekends off but still, there are times, when the GM is no longer on duty, though still in the hotel enjoying the beautiful property. So this time, James sits on a bench in the park and sees a group of tourist arriving by bus. With the tourists, a tall, black haired woman exits the bus and she holds a notebook in her hands – she is the tourleader.

Being impressed by her appearance, James stands up and goes to her.

„May I help you, Madam?"

„Oh just with the luggage, I have to check-in my group"she replies smiling.

„I'm the GM, but I'll make sure your luggage is brought to your room!" James tells her.

"I'm very sorry, I didn't realise. I'm out of my mind with those other guests. They are so demanding and yet no tips…" she complains softly.

"Would you give me your name please?" James asks her, "To identify your suitcases."

"Of course Tamara White, one black, one orange both Samsonite"she responds.

"If you need anything else at all, please contact me" James says, "Perhaps dinner together tonight? If only to forget the difficulties of earlier today."

"That sounds great"Tamara answers "Where and when?"

"7 p.m. at the reception desk." James says.

"Will be there" and with moving to the entrance "Looking forward to it!" she agrees.

James is happy about the development, as he has no plans for the evening - and the tour leader is really a top shot…

At 7 p.m. James is waiting at the reception and when he sees her coming out of the lift a little "WOW" came over his lips. He hopes nobody had heard that.

There she is, Tamara in a tight leather outfit supporting her outstanding figure. 15 cm heels and she is walking with them as it she was born with them on her feet.

"Hi GM, where are we going? I'm starving."

"Hello Tamara, you're looking gorgeous, right to our restaurant then, please follow me."

Both are having a nice dinner and several glasses of wine with it, so Tamara feels a bit dizzy already. Tamara giggles after the last dish, "Hey GM, I think it's time to go to bed!"

"Well, Tamara, I'll show you up to your room."

"Such a gentleman you are, thank you."

Arriving at the door, Tamara changes her behaviour from drunken lady to very fit power girl.

"So GM, are you coming in? I'll show you your borders…"

"The pleasure is all mine." Anwers James, not knowing what to expect, but he loves curiosity and quick changing, spontaneous moments.

The room was prepared for this situation, Tamara planned all and every moment, so she has a pair of hand cuffs ready to apply and James is happy about it – this will give him the extra kick. Tamara then takes out a rope and fixes James to the bed. He is ready for the life time experience and Tamara as well. But when Tamara puts her pants down…surprise…surprise… the long fat magic stick hangs down…James just opens his mouth, but is speechless…

Tamara switches her voice into her natural deep voice and this time nasty, "So…?"

James is nervous and badly surprised, "Hey, this might be a bad idea!"

Tamara is smiling, "We'll have some fun together…I promise."

James gets angry, "Hey, bitch, untie me! Now."

"Or…?"

"Untie me!"

"Oh, where disappeared your courage?"

Tamara goes to her branded leather bag…she turns around to James, "fancy some toys first?"…and she pulls out a small tripod, sets it onto the conference table and attaches her mobile to it…

Tamara turns to James, "It's already recording…"

"Bitch!"

"GM! You will do exactly what I say, otherwise I'll post it on Facebook… send it to your wife…and anyone else I can think of".

James Willington sighs and his eyes gain a cold but submissive look.

Tamara makes a sexy grin and with a woman's voice says, "Wanna be daddy…?" then she switches her voice into her natural male deep one, "Oh…or…?"

She laughs heartily and James closes his eyes.

James is giving up, "We only have half an hour."

Tamara snickers and continues with her deep voice, "But I have changed my mind, sweetie, we have all night!"

James makes a sigh, "Go to hell!"

Tamara comes to the bed and jumps on James, he fights, kicks, but Tamara shows unexpected portion of strength. She even punches him into his face so the blood comes out of his nose.

James is surprised by her strength and violence, "Shit, you just broke my nose!"

She licks the blood of his face.

Tamara grins, "Hey, don't be such a pussy! Just be my bitch now."

Then Tamara pulls out a knife and touches his neck with its blade, "I knew you want me…"

"SOUND EFFECT"

E.R.A.wakes up in his bed by some noise! It's coming from the adjacent room. A couple makes love there and they are deafening, sighing, screaming and yelling. The sounds coming from that room would colour all ears red. To his surprise he only hears male voices…

E.R.A. to himself "All right sweethearts."

E.R.A. hides his head under the pillows, but it doesn't help much. He stays like this for a moment, but the fiery lovers don't seem to stop any time soon. He crawls out of the blankets and gets ready to snap on the wall, but he freezes halfway and an unexpected smile enters his face…saying to himself, "Oh good God, they must be killing each other over there." Laughing, shaking his head… and mumbling to himself, "sex is for kids".

E.R.A. sits behind the conference table, headphones on his ears - attached to his mobile, listening to some music, he makes small sketches into his notebook. All of a sudden he stops and thinks. He throws his headphones out and switches the mobile off. He listens.

Silence.

Amazingly, the neighbours stopped yelling and screaming.

Silence.

He opens a drawer of the conference table and pulls out the fashion magazine he purchased at the airport. He finds that page with the beautiful model who looks like the girl on the picture on the fridge back at his home. He stares at the angel. Then he scrolls through the rest of the pages and stops on some article about a successful business start up – with the title,

"FROM ZERO TO HERO"

Below the title is a quote from T.S. Eliot "Sometimes things become possible, if we want them bad enough."

E.R.A. to himself "Do not conform to the pattern of this world, but be transformed by the renewing of your mind. Then you will be able to test and approve what God's will is – his good, pleasing and perfect will, "*Romans 12 2*"

The painter returns to the page with the fashion model with angel's wings and devil's smile…and gets another flashback:

The colours of the flowers are hypnotic. Anna is outside with her son, they pick up flowers in her parents' castle garden at the Alhambra Castle in Granada, Andalusia, Spain. They smell to them.

E.R.A. enters the garden and comes directly to Anna. She is very surprised, can't believe her eyes. They start hugging each other and crying.

"Anna!"

"Where have you been? All these years?"

"I must have lost my mind…I was in a mental institution…at the behest of my family…I don't remember much…"

"…but…I got married…"

"What?"

"Enrique, what did you expect? …you disappeared for such a long time…I thought you left me…I was searching for you…"

"But I love you, Anna!"

"I missed you my dear, I had such bad moments without you, I'm living with a bad man, I don't love him and the only thing that keeps me alive is our son…"

She touches the head of her small boy and the boy looks up at the painter. The painter smiles at him, but his smile is sad.

"Anna, my love, I'm so sorry for making your life worse. I swear I'll do anything so we can be together, forever…"

"Dad won't let us, if he knows that you're still alive he'll try to break us again… He never accepted you, because you were always poor."

"Please come with me, we can leave the country tonight. I became a famous painter, I'm rich now. My paintings sell all over the world."

"Oh, I'm so scared."

"Don't worry my love, I'll take care of everything, us and your son, we'll start a brand new life all together, no more suffering."

With a reserved smile he remembers the time, but then gets back to life.

E.R.A. stands behind the canvas and paints with an enormous obsession in his eyes, his face, in his gestures. There is a fiery aura around him. The darkness in the background. The hotel Egeria room no. 101 is lit by many candles. It looks like an occult ceremony and the face of Enrique, illuminated by the erratic light of the candles, looks like the face of devil or wizard.

There is nothing more important - here on Earth - in this reality called "Life" - than to capture the signals from her…the plan…how to escape…back to dreams…to perceive them and throw them onto the canvas…people keep telling him about the importance of daily ordinary things in life…about the practicality and pragmatism…but as long as he is connected with Anna…he can remain to be disconnected with this life…anyway…sooner or later…we're all dead…

The maestro uses wax colours to finalise his final and very last encaustic painting.

He looks like the devil conducting his hellish orchestra, the musicians are in trance and the audience in silent awe.

The sky above the hotel Egeria is red for some reason. Very rarely something like this happens, but this is already the second time in a short period, something is going on in the sky of Karlovy Vary…

All the windows are black as all the guests returned to their real themselves and balance on the verge of reve, perhaps dreaming dreams which might be more real than the world they see, when they're awake. There's a light only in one of the windows and the light is red.

E.R.A. paints there his masterpiece that will complement the encaustic & oil thematic series he named,

"THE SPIRAL ESCAPES TO THE DREAMS"

"MEETING THE WILD"

A black car drives through the deep forrest, the red light of this night gives it a special atmosphere. James Willington drives the car and the scary black branches of crawling trees welcome him to their arms. Occasionally the tree demons hit his car windows. The engine mumbles a demonic mantra and the heart feels like stone suddenly…cold…dead…The forehead of James is sprinkled by the streams of sweat. From the back mirror, on a golden chain, hangs a photograph of his wife Jenny and a small tiny bear. Both smile at him.

Bang!

He just hit something hard with his car… James breaks on the spot and the engine stops its mantra. James Mc Dermott sneaks out of the car to have a look. It's a boar - wild pig!

James swears, "Shit!"

The left light is broken, blood all over the place. James looks around, the forrest is silent, in a creepy way…Only the wind, in its episodic gusts, rattles the tree branches and rustles the leaves. The bony fingers of the morning frost crawl through the shrubs and together with a soft haze adds to the forrest's eerie ambience.

James opens the trunk and pulls out - breathing heavily – a big black plastic bag. He drags it away off the road deeper into the forrest and walks until he can still see something in the light of his car. He drops it there in between the shrubs and walks back to the car. James takes a spade and returns to the dead. He finishes digging and wipes the sweat off his forehead. Then he drags and pushes the black bag down into the hole. A soft smile enters his pale sweaty face.

"Nice one, Jamie!" whispers James to himself. He breathes heavily and his hands shake, he is nervous. He squats down the hole and tears the black bag open…there is a decapitated body…he searches in the pockets…and finally he finds what he was looking for - the box of cigarettes and matches…

James drags the wild pig to the hole and pushes the dead animal down to join Frankie and with a short laughter, "Here, some company, son…"

Then he lights the cigarette red and takes a rest. Looking to the grave, he makes a devilish grimace, "Sleep well, swine!" and throws the burning cigarette down on them.

"RAUL RENDERMAN"

The sun rises fast above the horizon and the hotel. The fresh green leaves dance and rustle in the soft morning breeze reflecting the sun light, as if they were tiny mirrors. The trees in the garden shake a little, they are silent witnesses of what's happening here around the Hotel Egeria. They don't judge, they just observe, but they do feel the emotions…like us…people…

A rented car is moving on D6 from Prague Airport to Karlovy Vary, the driver is a big over-weight man in his early 40's. The type of Freddie Mercury, just the XXL size. He wears a mustache, thick short black hair tided by brilliantine, perfectly fitting T-shirt with the pictures of palms, beach, sea, police car and sign,

"FEEL SAFE AT NIGHT,
SLEEP WITH A COP"

His name is Raul Renderman. He likes to throw dirty jokes and friendly educational punches. He is all people's friend right away from the moment they interact with him. Raul is someone who helps to anyone without asking. Sometimes a bit pushy, but he knows when to pull off. And he loves puzzles and he is damn good in solving them. Raul doesn't ask many questions as he prefers to observe carefully every detail and awaits the criminals to reveal themselves. When he asks - the question usually equals to conclusion…then it is too late… But it can happen, on some specific occasions that he looses his temper and bursts into a manic violence to get the confession from the suspect. Then even an innocent tells the truth. On the seat beside him sits a woman - Jane Willington. She observes the countryside, the nature, which seem to be now much friendlier, than in the winter, which she escaped from to sunny California. Now is here everything in flowers and warm. She thinks about hotel Egeria's security chief Sebastian Hunter… and here, for the first time she thinks about the possibility of divorce… Her face gains the killer's grimace switching from an angel to a devil.

Jane in her mind, "…maybe I should tell him…"

Jane looks now even better, fresh, relaxed and happy. She has found her brother! And she invited him to go with her and visit the hotel Egeria, to introduce him to her husband she is not in love with anymore…

Raul turns his head to Jane, "Jane only 40 kilometres left, we'll arrive soon. Time to make the call…"

Jane picks energetically her phone and dials James's number.

"Hi James!"

"Hi Jane…"

"How are you? Where are you?"

"I'm good. In our apartment…How are your parents? How's California?"

"Full of surprises…"

"Tell me…"

"No…"

"Tell me, I hate surprises…"

"We'll be in 20 minutes with you…"

"Oh…" James wonders, "What do you mean by "WE"?"

"See you soon…"

"Jane…"

Jane finishes the call, she and her brother Raul look at themselves. Raul is having soft devilish smile running across his sun tanned face.

Jane like a mother to his child, "Behave, ok?"

"You know me…"

"Yes…I know you…"

Her mobile starts ringing and the picture of James appears on its screen.

Raul hints, "Him?"

Jane frowning, "Yeah…" and lets her mobile ring further until it stops.

On the other end James is in the apartment on the property of hotel Egeria and he gets into panic. He throws his mobile onto the kitchen desk. Then he spots the knives in the sink! Blood! James opens his eyes wide, "Shit!" and pours plenty of washing liquid on them and hot water, he starts washing them thoroughly… As he washes the knives, in their reflection he sees his neck and something red on his neck…a red spot… He lets the hot water flowing onto the knives and runs to the bathroom "Fuck, I have to return the knives back to the hotel kitchen!" he tells to himself in his mind.

James stares at his neck in the mirror. There is an imprint of red lips…

James shouts, "Tamara! Bitch!"

He cleans it off hastily but thoroughly, "Damn! Towel…not good…" The towel is red from the lipstick. James grabs a black plastic bag and throws the towel inside it. He glances at his platinum watch, nevertheless it is a rare edition from Omega - the time runs fast now!

James shakes his head, "No time…" Then he spots the soil he brought from the forrest on his shoe treads on the floor…and as he steps out of the bathroom…not only into the bathroom… James looks back at his watch to calculate the time and divide it into the tasks as per their priorities. Then he spots something on his watch…he observes the clock hands speeding up… …there's something inside…some dark red spots…it's the dried blood…it got somehow inside… James touches the glass covering the face of his watch and it sticks to his finger glued by more of semi dried blood…The glass stays attached to his finger.

James yells, "How the hell is that possible?"

And as he gets angry - the glass cover from his watch falls down and flies jumping under the sofa…James follows it, pulls the sofa away, but nothing…it must have slipped through the crevice behind the inbuilt wardrobe wall!

"OK!" He stands up, pulls off his watch throws it into the bag. He throws the knives into the bag as well, but then he pulls them out again and says in his mind, "Sylvester might miss those…" he washes them quickly again and hides them in the drawer.

James mops swiftly the floor in the whole apartment. He wants to throw the black bag into the bin but then he shakes his head. He leaves the apartment in one hand the bag in the other the spade into the garden. James digs a small hole in the soil between the shrubs and buries the black plastic bag there.

Back in the apartment, James throws all of his clothes into a washing machine, adds plenty of washing powder, sets it up and runs to the bedroom. He opens one of the inbuilt wardrobes and selects swiftly something to wear, and as he wears the trousers, shirt and clean sweater, he observes himself in the mirror and a smile spreads all over his face.

James confident, "It's been an adventure." But then his smile shifts into a fearful grimace… He freezes.

James whispers, "Car…broken light…"

The silence in the room is broken by his phone ringing, he sees it is Jane and keeps it ringing. He knows Jane and company is somewhere near the hotel already. James puts on socks and clean shoes. From another drawer he picks another watch from his collection – a "TAG Heuer", he puts them on. He smells something…

James in his mind, 'Fucking sweet perfume! Fucking Tamara!'

KNOCK KNOCK!

James turns his head towards the door and shouts from the walk-in wardrobe "Comiiiing!"

But then he hears the sound of the electronic lock in the door!

"Fuck!" He opens another drawer, pulls out a random perfume and sprays the room with it, then runs into the hall keeping spraying everything counting himself too. And as he stands in front of the door and they open to reveal his wife Jane smiling with some big tall heavyweight stranger right behind her…He realises - smelling the air - that he made a mistake after all…

Jane frowning, "Gosh! What's that? Oh, James, my parfume? Why?"

Raul sarcastic, "Maybe he missed you…Check his pants too…" and starts laughing wild with his deep voice.

Jane glances at Raul with the silent sign, "Stop it!" and then turning back at James, "James, this is Raul, my brother,…the one I was searching for…The one I told you about."

They enter and James steps back nervously.

James reaching his hand, "Nice to meet you, Raul, I'm James."

Both men shake their hands. Raul's fist grasp is like the one of the pneumatic clamp. James wants to release his hand with a painful grimace, but Raul keeps holding his hand firmly applying rising pressure.

Raul smiles heartily, "I'm so glad to meet you, James. Your wife, my sister, Jane told me lots of good things about you…Yeah, Jamie, only good things…"

Raul holds the hand of James and glances at his watch, "Nice piece, expensive?"

"No big deal…" James tries to release his hand from the Raul's grasp, but without any success… Raul pulls his wrist closer to his eyes, then he moves the watch a little lower down James's wrist to reveal a reddish imprint around his wrist…

Raul glances seriously at James, "I see…" and he finally releases James's hand.

James shakes his hand and sighs in a relief.

"You wear a lot of different watches, right, James?"

James in alert, "So?"

Raul turns his head as the chameleons do, mourning his eyes, "Hm…just curious…Why did you change your watch very recently?"

James is first speechless but then, "How'd you know…?"

"It's obvious, there is a much larger imprint from the watch on the skin of your wrist than the current watch would do…"

Jane shakes her head, "Raul, I think I told you something…"

Raul bursts in a laughter, "Please forgive me, James!" and approaches James and gives him a big heartily hug, "Hey, you smell like a bitch."

Jane apologetic to her husband, "Please forgive him, he doesn't mean it."

James smiles as Raul releases him from the bear's hug, "That's fine, Jane. How have you been? Where did you find find this asshole?"

Jane serious "At the police station in L.A."

Raul nods smiling.

James is curious, "So, Raul, what do you do for living?"

Raul smiling, the time of cruel revelation, "I'm a detective…"

James is speechless, thinks 'it could not be better…' and then says controlled and as if he needed the confirmation for himself, "…detective…"

"Yeah…LAPD…you know…I just show the B A D G E…"

James feels his heart will stop and he will loose his self-control.

"Hey James, come on, I'm just a normal guy the boy next door…wanna hear some joke? … Listen to this: I wasn't planning on going for a run today, but those cops came out of nowhere! What you say Jamie! We're going to have a lot of fun together, I promise!"

Jane and her brother laugh, but James doesn't know what to say…

James in his mind, 'Gets better by the minute…'

Raul gets serious, "Last question…just for today…Why the hell did you put handcuffs on your hands? Tell me. Tell us!"

James in shock, "Handcuffs?"

Raul is laughing, "You know the answer…before we'll find out…"

"Hey, stop humiliating my dear husband, will you!" interferes Jane.

"You know…", Raul pulls out a pair of handcuffs out of the blue, "see these?…Jane, stretch your hands!", she does so and Raul attaches the handcuffs onto her hands - gazing at James, "When you wear them for a while, your wrists will get red and on some occasions even blue…You see?" and continues, "So the final question of today is - why the hell did you wear the handcuffs?"

"Hey, your imagination, Raul, is unspeakable, you're a funny guy. Aren't you hungry? Let's get something to eat!"

"You wanna bribe the LAPD? Well you can do that, you're my brother-in-law after all…"

Jane nods, "I'm hungry! Let's go!"

"Please forgive me, brother. Let's get a dinner then or lunch or whatever…these timezones…they still have that Zankou on Colorado and Verdugo?"

James puts a smile on though being mentally tired, "Yeah, they do. Right in Glendale."

"But I hope you'll tell us sooner rather than later. Even Glendale is dangerous".

Raul grabs James and Jane under his both arms and says, "We'll make things right and we'll have a lot of fun!"

"FEELING EXCEPTIONAL"

The three Billionaires approach the reception with happy faces. Each of the gentlemen pulls out one hundred dollar bill and give it to Jirka, Francesco and Natalia. Then, Rich Turner pulls out of his wallet another two hundred dollar bills and gives them to Natalia with words, "For your beautiful eyes, my dear." Natalia smiles and thanks for the gentlemen's generosity.

Francesco is curious, "So, how was it?"

Amir is smiling, "It was only for a couple of seconds, but living without gravitation is for us human beings on earth impossible. Great experience, thank you!"

"EXHIBITION"

In the ballroom of the hotel Egeria paintings on snow white panels await their observers and sophisticated thoughts. The energy is cumulating in the open space in between. The visitors enjoy their welcome drinks at the reception just outside the ballroom. The young elegant hostesses make sure there is no dry throat. There is our famous painter making his way hastily through the crowd, he holds a painting under his arm covered by grey cloth.

Some guests already recognise him and try to exchange few polite phrases.

The ballroom is still empty and E.R.A. uncovers the painting and hangs it onto a panel in the corner of the spacy room. The painting motif is not visible as the painter attaches the piece of grey cloth onto it then pulls out a transparent red marker and writes something directly onto the panel, "Your Eyes Only, Beautiful Stalker".

Then he attaches a notice written with big letters, to the panel below the painting, covered by grey cloth,

"DO NOT TOUCH!"

E.R.A. leaves the ballroom and mingles with the visitors until the exhibition is opened. The first visitors enjoy the art, between them a silhouette of a tall slim woman moves in an elegant way. The waiter offers a welcome drink from his silver tray. He wears white gloves and looks down to the ground as he is daydreaming. At some moment a purple glove grabs a flute glass with Champagne.

The waiter wakes up from his daydreaming to trace the owner of that purple glove as he was hit by a mesmerisingly hypnotic mixture of the perfume and woman's body smell! But it's too late…all he sees is just an anonymous crowd…

The waiter follows the scent of that mysterious woman. But very soon he gives up as his tray fills by empty glasses and the guests demand more of the Champagne, orange juice or water. And what is more important, he passes the hot station with Sylvester Cavallo doing his magic tricks with the food this time with the help of Japanese chefs. They prepare teriyaki on demand. They are very busy and it seems they gained the hearts of the visitors more than the paintings of the famous Spanish painter. Sylvester Cavallo sends the waiter to the kitchen to get him some more meat, vegetables and mushrooms.

It is near to the end of the exhibition and E.R.A. still is in the ballroom, answering questions of visitors, but also the press.

The waitress Sophie, a blonde young girl with a pony tale and devilish grin, approaches the painter, "Are you the amazing artist?"

She offers him a drink. E.R.A. picks it from the tray with thanks and sips a little. He forces a smile into his tired face, "Yes, I am."

Sophie innocent, "Hey man, I like you so much, I mean your paintings…, can I ask you something?"

"Sure, babe."

"Who's that woman who is in almost all of your paintings?"

E.R.A. is overwhelmed by the innocence and beauty of the waitress, "She was…someone like you…beautiful…innocent…"

The band on the stage starts playing one of the songs from George Michael.

E.R.A. "What's your name, if I may ask?"

"I'm Sophie."

"Lovely to meet you, Sophie, call me Enrique."

"You're from Spain?"

"Yeah, from Zaragoza, and you, Sophie?"

"From Denmark. My boyfriend is a musician…"

The lights in E.R.A.'s eyes die, "…oh, you have a boyfriend…"

Sophie hastily adds, "…but it's no big deal…he's a bit crazy…I'm not that into him…you know…"

E.R.A.'s eyes shine again and he bursts in a kind laughter, "Got it."

He is now in his element to cry on someone's arm once again as he needs a new angel to take care of him, "You know, her name was Anna…"

The band on the stage changes the song playing now the one from Sade.

E.R.A. continues, "…Anna was so kind, she had a pure heart, we were deeply in love, her family was rich, they lived in a castle in Granada in Andalusia, her parents didn't want us to be together, because I was a poor young artist from the outskirts of Zaragoza…" The painter stops talking as he feels the tears entering his eyes. He fights back hard and surpasses his emotions. He breathes heavily.

"Are you all right?" Sophie is worried.

"Yes, just need to take my pills…"

"What happened next?"

E.R.A. is annoyed, "Next? God showed me how deep love can be!" and continues, "I ended up in a mental institution, because…I had seizures…Ten years…"

"…and ten years after? I'm sorry I'm so nosy, man…What happened to Anna?"

E.R.A. glances at Sophie with the cold eyes, "Anna is dead, she's dead, my dear…"

Two scientists stand in front of an encaustic painting, which is painted by wax and have a discussion about the motif and the title of it:

"A MURDER IN MOJACAR"

'Men on horses with their guns pointed up to the sky. There is a typical Andalusian house - a mixture of Arabic and Spanish architecture. There is a beautiful woman with long black hair shimmering indigo blue in the light of the Mojacar desert sun. She holds a bamboo basket with cakes.'

Right behind the scientists, the brother of Jane Willington - LA detective - Raul Renderman stands and listens with great interest. He has a sickness from his profession and has got sharp open eyes and sensitive big ears. Excellent observer himself…everything is interesting…he fully lives in the present moment… obsessed by the smallest details…he is a materialist.

One of the scientists is a Jewish man in his mid 30's, short, thin, bolded - his name Sheffatyah Immanuel Meir. He is from Munich, Germany. The second one is an Austrian from Graz, living and working in Prague, teaching at Charles University. He is a tall vital man in his late 70's.

Sheffatyah has great knowledge about painters, dead and living ones, he studied art in Tel Aviv and finished as best of his class at the young age of 23, specializing in modern art. From that day he travels around the globe to see new artists and their exhibitions and of course is at home in all museums of modern art. He is one of Sotheby's experts, who taxes the paintings for collectors.

But the Austrian starts with his impression, "The technique, the painter uses, is really unique. For example, this painting "A murder in Mojacar", the longer I watch it, the more I have a sensation, that it changes, transforms… That woman, with long black hair glimmering indigo blue…she appears almost in all of his paintings…I have a strong feeling, I know her, that I have seen her somewhere…these paintings aren't just ordinary ones…it feels like they are real, that she is real, more real, than we are, as if we were the part of some painting together with this ballroom as our background…all these guests… might be just painted…by…Johan Steiner…her? It's possible…If the multiverse theory is correct and there is a never ending number of parallel universes… in which we exist as well, just in different timelines and with different destinies…and when we die…the consciousness or our spirit just jumps to a different version of ourselves into the one of the parallel universes and merge… then not only we're immortal and we talk the quantum immortality, but we can exist simultaneously in many other universes, and if we take it to the extreme, basically everything is possible, the paradise, time travel, God, hell, you name it…You know, I have one of his paintings in my studio flat, back in my home town - Graz. The motif is as following, there is just a box, a card board box."

"Just a box?" Sheffatyah is wondering.

Johan goes on, "Well, not exactly. As the title of the painting states,

"IS THE CAT IN THE BOX DEAD OR ALIVE?"

There should be some cat inside the box…"

"You don't see the cat inside…"

"But it's not a proof the cat is not inside…is it?!"

"Yes, and if it is inside, we can't know whether the cat is dead or alive…Yes I know, that's the "Schrödinger's Cat" theory. The observer decides whether the cat is dead or alive – it cannot be both…"

Johan smiles and is happy about the young gentleman's knowledge,"Yes! And the observer is always right, until he opens the box! As it is with the particles, they do change their behaviour, according to their observer!"

Raul Renderman comes closer to the painting and to both scientists, stares at the piece of art and starts laughing. He turns to the scientists, "I beg your pardon, for my intrusion, I couldn't help but overhear your discussion, well, if I do understand the dilemma correctly, and from my point of view as of being a cop, I'd say it's like this,

A cop is doing standard patrol when he notices a car swerving all over the road. He quickly turns on his siren and pulls the guy over. "All right," says the cop, when the man gets out of the car. "Walk in a straight line!"

"I'd be happy to," says the drunk "just stop moving the stupid line."

The two scientist don't react, don't laugh, gazing at Raul through their glasses with many dioptrics…

Raul stands there and then he points at some painting in the far corner, "All right…there's something interesting…" He walks away.

E.R.A. returns to his room in the early morning or better to say late night hours. He sits tired behind his conference table.

Silence - The neighbours are quiet tonight.

He opens the drawer and pulls out the fashion magazine, opens it on the page with his angel wearing nothing but extremely sexy swim wear, the white angel's wings and purple gloves.

Tears come out of the E.R.A.'s eyes and they are red. They keep dropping - one by one - onto the picture. His face is white pale. With every drop of his tears he gets older by a decade…His white hair and mustache grow longer and his yellowish finger nails stretch…

Enrique whispers, "I'll see you soon, Anna, my dear angel…"

The Anna's voice, "But you didn't take it with you…"

"I thought I didn't…but this morning…I found it between my socks…you must have put it there…Anna…didn't you?"

"Nothing can separate us, Enrique, we were always together…I'm waiting for you…"

Enrique opens his bag and pulls out a pistol… He whispers, "I'm coming…"

The ballroom drowns in the darkness of the night. There is absolute silence.

Across the wooden floor the translucent small green ball rolls chased by the hotel cat.

Silence.

Then steps… Some shadow crawls erratically across the walls and panels…

The hand in the purple glove takes the grey cloth off the painting to reveal the following motif, there are two people levitating in the air above a long road ending in the sea. The road falls deep down and raises again up towards the sea, which surface shines like a gold. There is a silhouette of a gentleman pointing with a pistol…

The silent satin translucent indigo veil of the hotel Egeria is painfully teared by an unexpected noisy gun shot. Boom!

…and in front of him a stunningly beautiful naked woman – the femme fatale with snow white angel wings covering one of the gentleman's eye by her body …There is a note on the panel signed by the maestro.

"For Your Eyes Only, My Beautiful Stalker"

"ARCANE CIPHER"

Hotel Egeria with a blossoming garden in the front await its new guests, ready for joy and challenges.

A Chinese family arrives at the reception. The parents Archibald and Maria Chu and their two small kids, daughter Bao and son Mao. They complain about the room number they received - 404!

Archibald is annoyed but smiling, "I'm afraid we cannot accept the room 404."

Francesco Roma is at the reception desk and is wondering, "Why would that be? The room is amazing, roomy, fits perfect for a family."

Bao repeats after Francesco, "Dad, why would that be? Why would that be?"

Archibald kindly explains to Bao, "…because, in China, the number four is a symbol of death."

"Oh, I don't want to die, dad!"

"Don't worry, sweetheart, I'm here to protect you."

Francesco smiles, "I see, where the problem is, what numbers would make you happy, Sir?"

"Numbers like…eight…nine…"

Francesco searches in the computer, "Let's have a look, what we have here…"

"I want the room number 525!" comes from Mao and he laughs, so all start to laugh and smile Francesco polite, "We have 658 available. Will that do?"

Archibald happy, "That's fine."

After a while the family has accommodated themselves in room No. 658, which means, there is a big mess in the room. It seems the lucky numbers make everyone so happy there. The kids move erratically across the spacy room with VR Googles on their eyes and cubes in their hands. They wear pyjama completes and look like two animals. The boy is a brown whitehead owl and the girl a purple black panda bear.

They jump everywhere wearing the VR glasses, playing virtual reality games. They scream and yell as they play. The more mess they make, the happier they are. Their father watching them, returns to his childhood and his mind switches into an innocent rebel mode. The kids are allowed to do anything they want unless their lives are on stake.

Archibald is dancing in front of the large LCD screen TV and Maria is the only one who stays cool and does something rational. Mom prepares boiled rice in the rice steamer they had brought with them in the small adjoining kitchenette. On the pan she prepares slightly spicy chilli sweet vegetables with tofu and soya sauce. For a drink she prepares an avocado soya milk shake. The kids - animals – owl & panda - occasionally bump into her as they don't see her, since they live now in the different - virtual world.

Archibald stops dancing for a moment and looks at his wife, "Why don't we just go down to the restaurant Maria?"

"The kids prefer the rice I make…we'll go next time…"

"OK"

"They need healthy tasty food."

"OK" he continues dancing, "It's a lovely room though, isn't it Maria?"

"It was a lovely room…"

Father Archibald keeps dancing as he approaches his wife Maria from her back…Then he catches by her breasts and makes a sensual dance…

Maria smiling, "Hey, stop it, not in front of the kids!"

Archibald moves his hands away and dances away back – smiling - to the living room, "All the simulated world's stage, and all the men and women, merely players. That includes our children, who also happen to be playing. So let's play."

Maria heard what he was saying and shouts to him, "They may be just players but they're still playing here. So calm down. Calm them down too while you're at it."

Archibald shouts back, "The director of this stage has stepped away for a smoke break. By the time he gets back a few thousand years will have passed for us."

The kids - Mao and Bao keep playing. Their father moves from dancing into a different activity - building a castle from wooden pieces they have brought for the kids to play with during the travel.

Bao and Mao from time to time bump into their father as well. Finally they kick into the - by their father almost built castle - and the wooden colourful pieces fly across the room in slow motion.

Bao now walks carefully as if she was focusing on something crucial or as if she appeared to be in some kind of dangerous situation.

Bao sees as if she walks through ab obscure corridor in some industrial building from the rusty iron and bloody red bricks with a machine gun, the monsters pop out from dark corners and she shoots them dead. When she kills the king of scary creatures, an animated picture of pizza in the box pops out of the blue accompanied by the messages, "You Won the Pizza of Your Choice! Please Select your Toppings!"

Back to reality, mom Maria turns her head to see Bao raising her hands with the black cube and yelling, "Yeah! I won!!"

Maria smiles.

Mao sees as if he wears the clothes like Indiana Jones from the film "The Raiders of the Lost Arch". He strolls through the Aztec pyramid ruins deep in the jungle and when he finds a treasure, golden mask, a picture of two cinema tickets pop out from the mouth of scull, "You have won 2 tickets to movies of your choice!"…"Please select your movie!"

"AIKIDO"

A waiter brings some refreshments into the old cinema of hotel Egeria, it is in the lower floor and not many people know about it as it was closed for many years. Peter as a lover of films and supporter of the film industry did buy the hotel only because of having its unique private cinema, which can not be found in any other modern property. The films shown in the hotel cinema are very specific and for sure not to be seen in the regular cinemas anymore.

There is a sign on the cinema main door,

"AIKIDO FOUNDER MORIHEI UESHIBA"
"Asahi News Film (1935)"
"*International Aikido Federation*"
Welcome to the 16th
CONGRESS in KARLOVY VARY 2020
HOTEL EGERIA

The waiter reads more,

"HEAVEN IS RIGHT WHERE YOU ARE STANDING, AND
THAT IS THE PLACE TO TRAIN"
"Morihei Ueshiba"

The waiter enters the cinema to refresh the coffee station. The film is about to begin and one could hear a needle dropping down on the floor despite the room is crowded. People even stand in the corners or sit on the stairs.

Silence.

The waiter hesitates to leave the cinema as he is curious about the show. A black and white old film accompanied by minimalistic music played by Japanese traditional instruments begins.

There are Sensei and his disciples in Dojo sitting on the ground. They sit in "Seiza" style and meditate.

"DANGEROUS NIGHT"

It's another hot summer dream at the hotel Egeria in Karlovy Vary and the starry night hypnotise the lunatics to walk out of the hotel with their pillows and blankets. A shooting star flies down the night sky painted by the "Milky Way". Another one appears, but before it can burn in the atmosphere, it explodes releasing a considerable amount of light and energy. The black windows of the sleeping hotel Egeria shake vibrating, but do not break.

It is night and in room 658 the Chinese family finally sleeps, but it lasts only for a moment and yet it manages to call some souls from their OBE (Out of Body Experience) back to earthly "Life Game". One of them is the little Chinese girl called Bao (meaning "treasure"). She crawls over her snorting parents and brother down out of the bed. Bao comes closer to the window and disappears behind the curtain falling heavy down to the ground touching its cooling marble tiles. As her small cute naked feet touch the tiles, when she stares out of the window at the shooting stars, she doesn't realise a big hairy spider approaches carefully her tiny pinky toes.

It's such a silence, that a well trained ear can hear even the spider's legs tapping ominously onto the marble tiles. TAP…TAP…TAP…

Some noise scares Bao to turn towards it's source. It is her younger brother Mao who walks, covered in blanket and holding a small pillow, out of the room. The door opens and he gets lost in the vast spacey never ending corridors. The small boy walks out of the hotel and continues to the forrest… He has with him a mobile and he sends messages in numbers…As he wakes up, he gets scared, he switches the flashlight on and points it into the direction where the scary sounds come from… There is a pack of wolves! The boy screams, turns back and runs towards the hotel.

Then he falls into some hole…under a massive tree root system. A dreadful sound - groaning crawls following the crying boy - he turns back to see a scary monster with long rotten teeth and bony long fingers with yellow-black sharp nails – the forrest witch! Her hair is long and has the colour of rat's fur, only one greenish eye…The green eye releases soft hazy green light. She screams, "Give me back my eye! Give me back my eye! Or I'll claw both your eyes right out of your skull! I'll suck your brain out through your ears! I'll tear out your tongue and strangle you with it. Then, just before you're dead I'll stop so I can eat you alive!"

The little boy cries and yells loud. But here down under the trees, in between the sneaking roots to medieval times, no one hears it.

"You've stolen my green eye, I know, and I get back what's mine, one way or the other."

The scary monster hunts unfortunate Mao trying to catch his little legs. The tunnel is long, Mao crawls forward and catches some unusual shape - stone. Mao puts on his VR glasses, inserts his mobile into it and using the GPS app, he can clearly see in the narrow tunnel. It's a meteorite ... cube with numbers... the cube is petite and leaden perhaps a small pyramid but with more faces...a strange shape... He turns back but there is no one behind him... At the end of the tunnel he spots a tiny light spot...

In the meantime one security guard searches, together with the parents, the hotel and its area. Even Sebastian is called, because of such emergency.

A group of people is involved in the search of Mao also outside of the hotel as his sister claims she had seen him walking out of the building with the blankets and pillow. Bao said he does this often as he is a frequent lunatic. Peter Willington and Mr. Tea help them in their search as well.

Peter to Sebastian, "Will the police be here anytime soon?"

"Yes…By the way, did you hear or see tonight's explosion?"

Peter opens his eyes wide, "Oh, you saw that too?"

Mr. Tea informed as always, "It was a Russian rocket, it was carrying an extremely rich passenger and exploded shortly after lift-off."

"Wow, and I had the strangest dream…"

"Dream? Tell me. I'm curious."

"You won't believe it, but I was there, seeing it…I saw the explosion there in Siberia…and I saw a murder…wolves in the terrifying forrest old trees and huge creepy roots…swamps…"

Jonathan Lee observes the TV set at his casino and learns about the explosion of the Russian rocket and about the murder of the "Baikonur" technician.

"BACK IN TIME"

The night club of the hotel Egeria is often the place where the owner's family meets, have a drink together or just enjoy being together, as they are living and working together. Of course guests are always invited to join. Sebastian Hunter sits on the high chair and plays his songs, which again triggers the feelings of desire in Jane Willington. All are present, Jane, James, Raul, Peter…Layla does some flamenco dance and taps her hands like the Andalusians do.

There is a painting of Enrique Romeo Aleman, who gave it to Peter Willington, hanging behind Sebastian Hunter on the stage. The motif of the encaustic painting is the "Last Supper" of Jesus and his disciples, just instead of Jesus, a mysterious woman with long black hair sits there in the middle – she wears an eye mask and the purple gloves. The disciples are Berber fighters with guns.

Layla finishes her dance, the guests applaud and one of them comes to the stage and whispers something into Seb's ear. He nods in agreement. Sebastian hints to the sound technician and he comes to the stage. They discuss something in Spanish as the guest is a Spaniard. Another two guests come to the stage - one with a guitar and second one is a woman.

The group accompanies Sebastian Hunter to perform the song of the Gypsy Kings "un amor" on stage. They all have fun.

"OSAKA"

At the same time Yuki arrives back from her holidays and drags many suitcases. Thomas Koenig talks with her colleagues at the reception and immediately - as he spots her - he hastes to offer his help. Yuki lives in one of the hotel rooms. Yuki and Thomas walk towards the lift designated to hotel staff and the male receptionists follow them with a jealous gaze.

Thomas is breaking the silence, "So how was it? Did you get a lot of R&R?"

"Yes, it was good. Short, but good."

"How was the flight? For sure long…"

"Very…15 hours, 1 stop…I had a layover in Helsinki, so I was travelling like 30 hours or so…"

"Wow. You must be pretty tired then…"

"Yeah."

"What city did you actually go to?"

"Osaka."

"Nice. I've never been…"

"Next time we can go together…"

"Wow that would be awesome!"

"It's amazing, you'd love it, Thomas."

"Big?"

"Well…not that big…About 2 and a half Million people live there…but in the metropolitan area…12 Million…"

"Oh, I'd get lost there on my own…So you'll have to be my tour guide…"

"Sure…I was born there and I still get lost if I don't use GPS…haha…today you can only get lost in Antarctica…where is not mobile phone connection."

Thomas laughs, "Yep."

The lift arrives and the two colleagues enter it. Yuki and Thomas stay in the lift that moves swiftly up.

The silence is claustrophobic. Both try to avoid their eyes to lock. The proximity is really dense and both feel some kind of magnetism between them. Should the lift journey take considerably long enough time, there would be a decent chance of very close contact…But…the lift stops abruptly at the 7ᵗʰ floor, where Yuki has a small staff apartment. They approach number 770, Yuki's place and stay in front of the door - as if they were afraid to open it. Many things go through their minds…Yuki points at the number, "This is my lucky number…"

"I wish it was my lucky number too…" Thomas says looking with flirting eyes at Yuki.

"In Japanese folklore there are the "Shichifukuin" (the Seven Gods of Luck) and "Tanabata" (Evening of the Seventh) - an important summer-time holiday that's celebrated on July 7th (7/7). The number seven also shows up in pachinko parlours and lottery tickets. Yuki opens the door turns to Thomas, "I guess…"

Thomas makes a small step in, "Yes…"

"…it's time for me to take shower and go to sleep…" she glances at Thomas and their eyes lock for a moment, leaving the questions in the air…

"Thomas, wait here! I'll be back in a moment…" Yuki drags her suitcase inside. Thomas waits until Yuki comes back and hands a small cute present precisely wrapped in a red paper.

Yuki smiles, "Thank you for your help, Tom! It's a Pon Pon. A traditional rice confection from Osaka. This one is strawberry! My favourite…Good night, Tom."

"Good night, Yuki."

Yuki smiles, nervously waves her hand and closes the door. Thomas stands there and stares at the magic door numbered "770" and says to himself, "Magic number…right…"

Yuki stands on the other side of the door and thinks about something. Then she decides, takes the handle and wants to open the door, but she freezes…

On the corridor Thomas decides to knock the door…but he freezes…he lowers his head down, bites his tongue, steps back…and walks slowly away.

"STAND-UP COMEDY"

It is late evening in the à la carte Restaurant of hotel Egeria, where Maître d'hôtel Thomas Koenig serves the finest wine to Japanese guests. He smiles at them and they smile at him.

Chef Sylvester Cavallo finalises the dishes at the kitchen line as all chefs do, they check and arrange the food on the plates to perfection.

Thomas serves the dishes. One small Japanese boy plays with a toy plane.

At the nightclub, the brother of Jane Willington – Raul Renderman does a "Stand-up" and tells the following joke…and to finish my embarrassing "One Man Show" I have a couple of "Pilot Jokes" for you,

"Q: What do you call a black pilot? A: A pilot, you damn racist."

The audience doesn't laugh.

"Q: Where can you find Tom Cruise on a flight? A: Risky Business Class…"

Embarrassing silence.

James Willington is happy about the situation Raul is in…Juan Alexandro Polpo spots it… Raul feels the audience has 2 match balls… But Raul doesn't give up, takes a deep breath and throws another one,

"Q: A plane crashed and every single person died except two, why? A: Because they were a couple for fuck's sake!"

The audience laughs a little. Raul turned off the first match ball…

Raul continues,

"…and here is the last one…years ago, I was into skydiving, and my skydiving instructor was kind of a straightforward guy… he'd always take the time to answer any of my stupid first-timer's questions. I asked "If our chute doesn't open and the reserve doesn't open, how long do we have until we hit the ground?" My jump master looked at me and deadpanned, "The rest of your life."

The audience laughs. Raul is back in game.

James Willington frowns.

Juan Alexandro Polpo laughs out loud.

Meanwhile at the reception a famous actor and Aikido master arrives to the hotel. He checks in.

"ATOMUS"

Back in the nightclub the magician Atomus and his beautiful assistant Rachel X are about to start their show for the audience. They perform many tricks, between them, walking through the wall. The audience greatly enjoys the show and applaud after each piece of magic art. Peter Willington and Mr. Tea sit together at the fireplace. Both enjoy cold alcohol free beer as the summer temperatures rise high with no mercy. A big portion of the audience doesn't care that much about the magician's tricks as the people are focused rather on the beautiful sexy body of Rachel X who wears a seducing outfit consisting of very few & minimalistic parts.

Mr. Tea says to Peter, "OMG, this is for kids! Walking through the wall? It's a bullshit! I've seen how they do this on YouTube!"

"How do they do it?"

"It's really a basic trick."

"THE ROOM 525"

The Russian magician Atomus walks through the corridors accompanied by Peter Willington and Mr. Tea. Atomus wears, as usual, his black sunglasses…

Mr. Tea looks at Atomus and thinks of the things he has read about him, to be informed about the guest, '…he really does see, what others don't…sometimes he tells others what he sees…well, if they buy a ticket to see his show. But, he never tells anyone how the hell he sees what he sees… That's not the only magic he's capable of though. He actually can walk through walls. But what's most important, the real magic is that he can hear the sounds that only come from the silence. Nevertheless, the biggest and most treasured power Atomus possesses is the power to heal. His philosophy is "First learn to heal, it's easy to hurt someone, but to master yourself and your destiny, learn to heal first." His stage name is Atomus. People across the globe speculate, about his real name, but nobody knows. Atomus claims he was born in Siberia in some small forgotten village on the shores of Baykal Lake where the people chose him to be their shaman. He was healing, but he was also hurting… One day, his master appeared to him with the message that it was time to pay for his services. The master gave him a commercial name "Atomus" and sent him on a journey of 369 weeks across the globe to perform Magic for paying audiences. Atomus and his master share the profits equally. Atomus travels with a quite charming, beautiful young girl, who assists him during his shows. Some have said that the girl is actually his Master…But who would ever have thought that Atomus had a Master in the first place? But there is a hidden truth about real magicians… the ones that can perform the most impenetrable illusions…the ones that no one can ever differentiate from reality…the ones that make anyone doubt the veracity of their senses… for each of those…the very few…those real magicians have all sold their souls to the Master and such sales are forever.

Atomus, when being a very young man back in time before he became the village Shaman, was approached by a geological expedition of Russian scientists led by the charismatic engineer Leonid Blavatsky, who gave to the young boy a mysterious suitcase. A few years later, the young boy learned, that Leonid Blavatsky died under rather peculiar circumstances. He disappeared in his own Moscow apartment during the birthday party of his wife Tatiana. Gossip was flying that Tatiana had indulged in witchcraft…that perhaps she was a fearsome witch herself! A few days later, Blavatsky's apartment burned to the ground. Afterwards, the young boy became his villages' Shaman. As he grew older, he started to hear voices of angels. The voices of angels and two that belonged to demons. One sultry summer night, a beautiful girl with long black hair arrived in the village. She represented an association of Russian scientists, numerologists, and "inward explorers" that wanted to exploit his supernatural skills. Atomus refused at first, but the Association kept sending the charming girl and he fell in love with her. The girl was the daughter of Leonid and Tatiana Blavatsky. Atomus had always a suspicion, that some of the voices he hears belong to her parents…'

"OK, Atomus, show us the real magic now!" Peter in the direction of the magician and Mr. Tea ads, "Please show us how you walk through the wall."

"You mean my illusion from my performance tonight?"

Peter begs, "Yes, please."

Mr. Tea interferes, "Oh not that one, I know how you did it!"

"How did I do it?"

Mr. Tea explains that he has seen the video on YouTube.

Atomus admits, "You're right, it was just a trick!"

Peter, "So you just do tricks…?"

"OK, I don't usually keep aces up my sleeve. But as I'm really interested to see room 525, the one you keep hidden…'thing is, when people see the real shit, the quite often go crazy, permanently… It's like seeing your long dead grandmother walk into your bedroom with a knife in her hand while you're casually reading a book…Imagine that…wouldn't you go crazy? Performing real magic is psychologically dangerous. Extremely psychologically dangerous. For you…and for me. Because when it's real it hits you hard I mean real hard…well, you asked for it… But first get a big mirror."

Peter friendly, "Mr. Tea, can you please go and find one somewhere?"

Mr. Tea is thinking hard, "Let me see…I'll be right back. Bear with me."

Mr. Tea walks away and in a couple of minutes returns carrying a big mirror.

Atomus starts, "Now gentlemen, I'm going to walk right through this wall…" he taps onto the wall, just to see what's on the other side…" then he gets serious, "but, you two, I'm warning you… don't look directly at me…take the mirror and walk away at least 90 steps…then, position the mirror in such a way you can see me in its reflection. That's the only way I can see my way clear to show you magic. Real magic. It really isn't a trick. But by doing it this way, with the mirror and whatnot, you might still be able to convince yourself that what you're seeing isn't actually real. Maybe it's all just a trick."

Mr. Tea with sarcasm, "Why don't you just walk through the wall right in front of our eyes? We can bear the shock." turning to Peter, "Right, boss?"

Peter is more reserved, "Let's do it as Atomus says."

The guys walk away from the magician and then point the mirror in the way it reflects Atomus.

"Is this alright, Sir?" Peter calls.

"Now turn around and watch me in the mirror! No peeking." Atomus says.

"No peeking…ehh…Isn't that just what you'd expect to hear a magician say?" Mr. Tea is looking at Peter who says, "OK we can see you and we're ready."

"OK, hold onto your pants and don't break the mirror, otherwise…it means seven years bad luck." comes from Atomus.

Peter and Mr. Tea grin at each other and observe the magician in the mirror reflection. Atomus makes a few steps back from the mirror, makes an eerie side look at Peter and Mr. Tea. His eyes change for just a split of the second into yellowish balls with black dots.

Silence.

Atomus stands there like a statue for a moment staring at the wall. This moment feels like an eternity to Peter and Mr. Tea. The lights in the corridor turn red and start blinking erratically. A soft haze crawls through the corridor. The mirror in their hands becomes hot, but they don't want to let it go down to break, remembering the words of the magician. Then it happens…

Atomus walks towards the wall, then he touches it by his body, but doesn't stop there, he merges with the wall and then he is sucked by it fully!

Silence.

The lights stop blinking red and the haze disappears.

Peter and Mr. Tea stare into the mirror and then turn back. The corridor is empty, Atomus disappeared at once! They lean the mirror against the wall carefully and hastily approach the place Atomus did stand just a few seconds ago. They touch the wall in the search for some kind of secret door or something but everything looks perfectly normal. They look in their eyes in great disbelief.

Peter Willington approaches his home passing some guests and hotel general staff. Right at the door, on the fence, sits a big brown owl with white head… Peter stops not believing his eyes, such a wonderful bird with yellow eyes and black dots in their centers. Peter comes a bit closer, but the bird is not afraid. It just wings its eyelids and opens its beak slightly. Some members of the general staff standing nearby say to Peter, "Don't worry, boss, it's a nice bird, it won't hurt you."

Peter comes even closer, stretches his finger towards the owl. The owl bites him softly into that finger first… Peter cannot make a single move as if he was paralysed…The owl takes off and starts flying like crazy around Peter's head! The surprised old man feels the warmth of the bird's body and softly spoken feathers hitting kindly his pale face…It lasts for some time until…Peter wakes up in his apartment.

It was such a vivid dream, it really felt like real! How come he felt the warmth, he heard the sounds and he could touch - while asleep? Peter to himself, "This dream was vivid enough to be reality…maybe a different one…"

It wasn't a nightmare, no, on contrary, Peter feels as if someone had spilled over him an elixir of life. He wants to continue his sleep, but then it happens… the thin voices of two angels whisper into his ear, "Don't pick 666, you're stronger than that, pick 525…"

Peter sits on his bed terrified and perhaps concerned about his own health… his mental state…he whispers to himself, "Why the hell did that magician walk through that wall? Why going into room 525?"

Peter Willington and Mr. Tea did not see the magician again that night.

"WHERE IS ATOMUS?"

Peter Willington arrives at the reception in the morning just to see Mr. Tea and Yuki dipped into a discussion, he greets them, "Hey guys, have you seen Atomus today?"

Yuki and Mr. Tea turn their eyes towards Peter.

Yuki takes the initiative to answer, "They checked out this morning, both Atomus and his assistant Rachel X."

Mr. Tea shakes his head and mumbles, "Who are these people? Atomus & Rachel X…"

"So, you've seen Mr. Atomus this morning, Yuki?"

"Well, I just saw his assistant, Miss Rachel X…"

"And Atomus?" wonders Mr. Tea.

"I must have missed him somehow…"

Peter finally decides, "Yuki, please call 911, we need the fire department, now."

"OK. I will do." Yuki picks the phone and dials.

The fire station is not far from the hotel Egeria, so it takes only a couple of minutes for the arrival of the fire brigade. Their chief asks Peter what to do and gets the instruction to find a missing guest, the magician Atomus, who disappeared last night into the closed room 525 and did not come out again.

The firemen finally break the wall open. They have to bring a powerful light inside as the windows were walled as well. When they enter the room 525, on the dusty conference table they find a small yellowish paper, burdened by a paper weight from brown agate, with the following message,

"I was in here, but you shouldn't have opened this room,

You don't know what you're playing with…

Atomus."

Peter Willington and Mr. Tea gaze at themselves totally speechless. Security chief Sebastian Hunter sniffs around. And there, in the corner! There he is, crying, the small boy of the Chinese family, who got missing!

Sebastian comes carefully closer to him and squats, "Come on, little boy, how did you get in here?"

The terrified boy just keeps on crying.

Sebastian takes off his jacket and puts it over the half frozen body of the little shaking boy wearing only the owl pyjamas. Sebastian puts the hood shaped into the owl's head kindly onto the small boy's head and to him, "Everything will be fine, your parents will be here shortly."

With these words, Sebastian glances at Peter, who sees the small boy - owl, suddenly recalls his dream… The parents arrive soon after the mysterious discovery of their beloved son, crying from happiness and relief. The small boy holds an unusual small greyish three dimensional shape with 8 faces. On the each of the faces there is a runic number. The small boy hands the strange shape over to Peter with smile. Peter examines it, but cannot understand the mysterious signs.

Mr. Tea taps on Peter's arm, "Give it to me!"

Mr. Tea takes a closer look. Then just nods, "Each of the signs is a number - written in Runes."

"Interesting…what are the numbers…what does it mean?"

Mr. Tea turning the shape in his hands, "0…5…2…5…1…9…9…1…"

"Thank God we opened that room! But how the heck did that little Chinese boy get in there? Tell me…how?"

"That magician Atomus might be the key to all this…"

Peter nods, "We need to see the security videos!"

The ambulance personnel arrives to the scene examining the state of the little boy. Shortly after them the police arrive to the premises as they have been searching for the boy in the hotel surroundings anyway. They are joined also by the LA detective Raul Renderman who was helping them to search.

Sebastian to himself, "There must be some way that boy got in here…"

In the CCTV room Sebastian, Peter, Mr. Tea, Raul and one police officer check the footage, but the only people they see in the corridor are Peter and Mr. Tea with the mirror…Atomus is missing…They rewind back to see that Peter and Mr. Tea talk to someone, of course to Atomus, but the magician is not there…

It is lunch time already and the Chinese family invites Peter for lunch. Peter asks Mr. Tea to join them and so they sit around the round shaped table. They talk heartily about many things, regular smalltalk nobody is interested to hear. After a while Mr. Tea walks away to continue his duties but the rest stays.

Archibald Chu says to Peter, "You should do yourself a favour and escape this hectic life once and for all…"

They talk about the current politic situation and frictions between two world super powers USA and China. But the tone of their voices is kind, it's a rational discussion. They use the allegory with so-called "Thucydides trap".

"GUAYABA PEOPLE"

Jane Willington and Raul Henderson sit in the Café Vienna.

A mid age female artist plays the harp and a young Mexican guitarist does some background to it. The music is rather joyful, but not too much…letting the guests digest the lunch in peace and harmony. It's siesta time. She wears long red costume like the one the artists wear at the opera and plays with her long thin fingers on the golden strings.

Jane enjoys hot black coffee, no milk, no sugar and Raul sips a chocolate milkshake with plenty of crushed ice through a thick straw, "Yeah, that's awesome Jane!"

"You like it?"

"I love cold drinks. It's just missing something…"

"…something?"

"Something strong."

The waiter passes by and Jane makes a "stop & come over"hint to him.

Jane looks at Raul, "What do you want?"

"Hmm…do you have some good Tequilla…I mean some of the finest Mexican elixirs? Not the piss sold in local shops."

Jane to the waiter, "What we got there, Joe?"

Joe, "We have one bottle of "Partida Reposado"…if I may suggest, Sir."

Raul grins, "Cool…and get us some Guayaba juice, plenty of ice, and I mean plenty, thanks."

"I'm afraid we don't have that juice, Sir."

Raul is disappointed, "Oh you gotta be kidding me man and you need to order some. I love the stuff, you know."

"We'll order some for you, Raul." interferes Jane.

"Ok, then, Guava?"

Joe offers, "White- or Yellow, Sir?"

"Whatever…"

The waiter bows and leaves to get the drinks prepared.

Jane turns to her brother, "Tell me again about our family. Our real parents."

Raul smiles, "We were born in Zamora Michoacan Mexico and spent the first years of our life on a "Guayaba"farm. Our family owned that farm and their whole life turned around the fruit of Guayaba."

Raul pulls out an old yellowish photograph with some of its parts partly burned. He places it in front of Jane. She observes the photograph without touching it. There is an old man on the photograph. He sits in the window and smokes a cigar.

Jane,"Who's that, Raul?"

"Our grandfather. That's what our neighbours in the village told me."

The artists - the harpist & the guitarist change their happy tune into the melancholic one.

"And what happened to our family?" Jane asks.

"They're dead."

"There must be an uncle or aunt or cousin left…"

"No."

"Really…?"

Raul adds, "It happened on a dry summer night. The fire raged across the entire countryside. Our farm burned to the ground. The villagers could only save you and me. We were the lucky ones…unlike the rest of our family…They're all dead, Jane. All dead."

"Very sad."

Jane and Raul stare at the photograph on the table, the man from the past, their grandfather sits there on the chair gazing at them through the open window. His face is sun tanned and bearing many wrinkles. His eyes are black and shimmer like the coffee liquid surface in the morning sun. He smokes a cigar and smiles at them.

The artists - the harpist & the guitarist change their melancholic tune into the more cheering one. The waiter brings the tequila, juice and the big bucket of ice cubes…so frozen…that the soft vapour swirls up to the ceiling. He places the drinks onto the table, "Anything else…?"

Raul happy, "No, that's it. Thanks."

The Joe wants to serve the drinks, but Raul stops him, "It's fine, I'll do it."

The waiter leaves. Jane takes the photograph of their grandfather into her hands. She thinks her grandfather smiles even more and Jane gets a feeling he revived and the smoke from his cigar dances out of the photograph.

Raul smiles sadly, "This photograph, is the only thing that survived that hellish blaze…well …and the two of us…".

The brother and sister rise their glasses with Tequila cocktail and their eyes lock smiling but also a little sad.

"BOARDROOM MEETING"

The waitresses and waiters of the Restaurant serve the guests digestif, they are having happy faces as they have had a great lunch. The kitchen is now almost empty, only two birds kiss each other there…It's the hotel chef Sylvester Cavallo and his fiancée banqueting manager Aida de Luca.

Mr. Tea almost enters the kitchen, but as he spots the two in action…he steps back and closes the door with soft smile on his face.

The management has been called for a meeting to the boardroom, as tourleaders complain about the strange annoying sounds in the hotel.

Peter is angry, "I tell you something, when the elevator stops between floors, there's a fire in the building and you have a solid chance to escape because of how they built the elevator, what you gonna do?"

People in the room exchange concerned looks, "What the hell is Peter talking about?"

Juan Alexandro Polpo brings is to the point, "We'll need you, Peter, to find us a specialist who can figure out where those annoying sounds are coming from."

Sebastian Hunter adds, "…now that you mention fire, we also need a better fire alarm system."

Peter stands up and walks away angrily smashing the door behind him being damn upset about the tourleaders, the hotel management, about his whole life.

Juan runs following him, "Peter, wait, where're you going?"

Peter doesn't respond, he just walks out of the hotel Egeria, leaving the eyes of the Yuki gazing at his back with two question marks.

He can still hear Juan shouting behind him, "Where are you going…?"

"GETTING OUT OF TOWN"

Peter walks the road down to Karlovy Vary downtown. Hot summer rain falls down, not leaving a dry thread on Peter. A police car stops and Peter jumps in. The cop, who drives is silent, he knows Peter from various occasions at the hotel and just wanted to give Peter a lift. Peter likes to be driven and the attitude of the police officer, he stares out of the window merged with his thoughts and asks to stop at the fountain near the colonnades. Peter strolls the city and observes people, for example a young couple - lovers, who walk before him hugging each other and kissing occasionally. This underlines Peter's feelings of solitude. He walks through a pedestrian tunnel and passes an Asian street-artist playing an instrument he had never seen before. It has two strings only held vertically and the bow hair passes in between. He stops and listens with high curiosity, because the melody is oriental and that man is a true virtuoso.

The man is very old, perhaps a decade older than Peter, or at least he looks like it. A long greyish beard, bolded, but the face...looks like the one of a young person... As Peter listens to the melody he heads towards unexpected tranquility, he observes the messages, posters and graffiti on the grey concrete walls:

THE MESSAGE
Life is your eyes.
Life turns around.
Life is a love.
Life is a bet.

THE POSTER
Red pictures and signs on the yellow background.
"LEMONADE JOE"
1964
A GUN
THE BULLETS
A BOTTLE OF "KOLALOKA" LEMONADE
(*on the wooden table*)
DIRECTED BY OLDRICH LIPSKY

THE FILM QUOTE
SHERRIFF "HOGO FOGO...?"
HOGO FOGO "YES, HOGO FOGO, WITH TWELVE NOTCHES

ON THE HANDLE OF MY SIX GUN!"

THE GRAFFITI

There's a monster, a mutant, part animal part human making a face eyeless
a pale zombie on a black background saying

"FUCK KARMA"

"What do you call this instrument?" Peter asks the artist.

"It's a BANHU."

"Ban…"

The artist again, "BANHU."

Peter nods, "Very interesting, nice…"and pulls a couple of coins out of his pocket and drops them into a custom made nylon carry case lined with a dark red velvet. The golden coins shimmer in it reflecting an artificial light. The street-artist smiles and bows with sincere thanks. Peter bows back and walks away. A little later he passes a fashion boutique. There are colourful T-shirts with a variety of signs, on one of them, there is a picture of a well known City Sky Line accompanied by the following message,

"COME HERE!"

Peter knows what to do and goes straight to a travel agency, he sits in front of the travel agent, a lady with a red satin scarf, wearing a light blue costume. There is a big map of the world on the wall behind her. The clocks showing the times in different timezones - different cities. There are various travel magazines on the table in front of Peter.

Peter friendly, "…yes, I want the first flight to Hong Kong!"

The lady with a smile, "Tonight, or early tomorrow morning?"

"Yes, tomorrow morning."

"What about accommodation?"

"No need. Just the ticket"

The lady asks further, "Car rental…?"

"No thank you, just the ticket."

With his purchase in his pocket and a bag of groceries he goes to the Café Elephant, a famous place in Karlovy Vary. The café is full of people, crowded, people enjoy here the time after work, the time of shopping, the time together… Only Peter is alone and looks lonely. Music sneaks softly out of the speakers.

Peter sits at a table for two. He drinks cappuccino and chews an old croissant. He stares out of the window and observes people. Then he glances at the empty seat in front of him where sits only the plastic bag with some foods and stuff…

Peter daydreams,

'His wife sits opposite Peter and drinks hot tea. She stares at him over the cup and smiles, "Hey, darling, you really need to visit a hairdresser…"

"Haha…for my three hairs? I'm like Homer Simpson over here" showing with his finger at his head.

"You haven't been taking care of yourself lately…have a shot of whisky… cheer up my man…".

"You're telling me this? You, the one who told me to stop drinking in the first place?"

"You can have one shot…just one!"

"Hmmm…is it our anniversary or what?"

Peter wakes up and raises his hand as the waitress passes by. "Yes, Sir?" with a smile.

"A whisky…Irish Jameson preferably…if you have it…"

Suddenly Peter's wife materialises again before Peter's eyes, "Hey…I was just testing you! Your willpower…"

The waitress is about to leave.

Peter bites his tongue, "Actually, young lady, I've changed my mind… the bill please…"

"So no whisky?"

"No whisky, just the bill."

Peter's wife smiles heartily and disappears.

This dream is influencing Peter to go to the barber's shop and so he sits in the chair covered in towels and the barber does his miracles for Peter's revival. After cutting his hair he also shaves his face with a razor blade. Peter observes the posters on the wall. There is only one man on all of those - Elvis Presley.

"THE NIGHT OF POWER"

It is the 27th day of Ramadan and Samia does her prayers, reads in the Quran, all the night, this night is called the power of night "Laylat al-Qadr". The candles are lit in the living room of her apartment creating a calming ambience. Samia sits in her favourite armchair and reads out loud from the Quran.

Quran S2 V102
(*Surah 2 Verse 102*)
"And indeed they knew that he who buys it has no share in the hereafter. And, indeed, vile is the thing for which they sold themselves away. If only they knew!"

Something hits the window! It sounds as if someone just threw a stone at it. Samia feels scared but hastes to the window to see what causes that disruptive sound. There is a man standing down on the road. He smiles and waves his hand. It's Samir Smith, the young man she had met yesterday. She opens the window letting the warm summer air sneak through in.

Samia is surprised and in the same time slightly annoyed, "You again, what do you want from me?"

Samir smiles friendly to her, "Hey, Samia, sorry if I'm disturbing you, would you come down for a chat?"

"Ok, just wait!"

When Samia opens the door, she wears her "Djallaba" and a scarf and looks georgious. As she walks out from the house and looks around, she can't find Samir. She turns around, but no one is there in the summer silence of the night street. The orchestra of the grasshoppers perform the "night of power" score. The light of the street lamp seems to be today somehow greenish. Samia is about to return to the house, when Samir jumps out of the dark corner, "I'm hereeeeeeeheeeee…"

Samia is shocked and puts her hand on her chest, "You're crazy, you scared me! How dare you!"

Samir is laughing like a small happy boy, "Samia, forgive me please, it was a bad joke. I'm sorry."

"You scared me, Samir. I do not like these kind of pranks, it is behaviour of kids in the kindergarten, not from real men."

Samia and Samir stroll the abandoned streets passing the sleeping shops in the downtown. Samir talks a lot, Samia listens carefully. He lives alone in the city of Prague, his parents live in Morocco.

Samia opens her eyes wide, "Wow, you're Moroccan??"

"Yes, I am, my mom is from the city of Fes, and dad comes from here, the Czech Republic."

"I'm so glad, I met you, man, I've lived here for some time and before that I lived and worked in Mumbai for many lonesome years."

"Do you miss Morocco?"

"A lot! I do miss a lot about my country   the people, the food…and when I meet someone from my homeland, I feel very glad."

"Hmm…me too…despite of my mixed background I feel a strong affiliation to Maghreb! The spirit of community is strong there, living together as one. Green boys!"

"Oh, you're a "Raja" man…"

"Yep."

"I follow football too!"

"Amazing."

"How will you spend your "Power of Night", Samir?"

"Well, I've got some friends from Morocco here, and we'll go to pray in the Mosque and read the Quran, It's a crucial night."

"Yes, It commemorates the day when the Quran was revealed to Mohammed, peace be upon him."

"Inshallah."

"Perhaps it's time to go back, Samir, but we'll talk again soon, right?"

"Inshallah."

Samir walks Samia safely back home. They encounter some stranger in a long black coat, collar raised up, sun glasses, a baseball hat, suitcase rolling noisily. The stranger stops, Samia & Samir continue.

The stranger observes the couple, he puts his sun glasses down, he is Peter Willington…He is on his way to the airport. Peter stares at the couple - which is getting smaller and smaller, disappearing in the early morning haze - far at the end of the narrow street rising upwards. Peter turns back and continues walking slowly.

"FINAL DESTINATION HONG KONG"

After a short flight to London Heathrow, Peter walks through the airport and passes the electronics shop with many TV's. On their displays runs the following program,

"Atomus Magician"
Assisted by Jinns

Peter stops at the wall of the TVs being hypnotised by the devilish Atomus's gaze, he stares at everyone through the screen with his intense blue eyes.

The program starts. The stage in a TV studio is set-up like for a talkshow where, the magician Atomus sits on the sofa and responds to the questions of young blonde female reporter, Elsa Hogpen.

Elsa is smiling, "What do you say to people who think there's something else behind your magic, not just the usual "prestidigitation"…isn't that what you call it…but something far beyond human skill. Something…darker, more mysterious…that helps you…to create these illusions?"

Atomus is taking a cool posture to impress the reporter, "Maybe there is…"

The airport announcement interrupts the interview, "Final boarding call and final call for VIRGIN ATLANTIC flight X1991 passengers to Hong Kong via Mumbai…please come to gate number 9."

"This is the final call for Mr. Peter Willington, Mr. Peter Willington this is the final call for flight X1991 to Hong Kong, please immediately come to the gate…"

Peter wakes up from the hypnosis and looks around searching for the gate number 9. Finally he catches an airport attendant and asks, where to find the gate number 9. Peter is panicking, "Please, which way to gate number 9?"

Airport attendant answers calm, maybe too calm, "Well Sir, you're in the wrong terminal, Sir."

Peter shocked, "What?"

"Don't worry, it's just only a twenty-minute walk…"

Peter has to find words, "20 minutes…?"

"20 minutes, Sir." The airport attendant seems not to understand that Peter was already called by the PA system, so Peter turns with a short, "Thank you!" and he runs across the airport hall - passes the security check - walks fast through the lounge towards the gate number 9.

They are already closing the glass door, but as the attendants spot running Peter, they make a walkie-talkie call to the crew inside the plane asking them to wait a little bit more.

Peter enters the plane and a Chinese beautiful stewardess with a baby face welcomes the sweating old man on board.

The door closes behind him. It's exactly 05.25 a.m. and the plane begins to move to the runway.

"THE FLIGHT NUMBER X1991 AT 0525"

There's a seriously overweight Pakistani gentleman sitting right next to unfortunate Peter. He holds a golden bag in his hands as if it was concealing some big treasure. Both men fight for the space on the armrests. Peter gives up the fight but keeps swearing angrily under his nose. The Pakistan neighbour gives Peter a complimentary smile. Peter looks around and spots an empty row of seats. He waits to make sure the stewards are not around and secretly crawls to those empty seats.

The plane takes off.

After about 2 hours flight the sun rises and its warm yellowish rays touch kindly Peter's sweating face. The stewards serve breakfast.

"SUNSHINE IN THE BALLROOM"

Samia opens a window of her apartment that leads to a small blossoming garden. Samia does her morning prayer.

In the ballroom of hotel Egeria a new employee Vietnamese waitress Sunshine Thuoc carries fresh cold water in huge pitchers on a steel tray. She can barely handle the enormous weight as she is of a rather subtle form…It seems that the balance can be lost at any given moment. The morning light entering the hotel's premises sparkles in the transparent liquid making the playful flashes on Sunshine's cute face. Suddenly someone behind her says, "Hey, Miss, let me take that…"

Someone grabs the tray from her tiny thin fingers.

She looks up and in her mind, 'What a big guy - hmm…black kimono, black belt, mustache, a big fat mother fucker…'

Sunshine, "Thank you so much!"

"No problem, will you be in the ballroom later?" Sensei walks away, but Sunshine follows him.

In front of the entrance to the hotel Egeria's ballroom there is a stand with the following notice,

INTERNATIONAL AIKIDO SEMINAR WITH SENSEI S.S.
"International Aikido Federation"
Welcome to the 16th
CONGRESS in KARLOVY VARY 2020
HOTEL EGERIA

The waitress stops to read more,

"CREATE EACH DAY A NEW"
"Morihei Ueshiba"

She then follows Sensei inside. The hotel Egeria ballroom is turned temporarily into a spacey Dojo. While the whole hotel Egeria sleeps, there are Sensei and his many disciples - participants of the session preparing for the training. They will spend a whole day in here. Sunshine Thuoc observes…There are rubber mats covering the entire floor. A balanced mixture of many disciples - men, women, girls, boys, old, young, kids - in white kimonos stretch & warm up their bodies, they wear belts of different colours. The flip-flops are lined up to the edge of the mat, the participants train barefoot. As the disciples enter the mats they bow towards the framed picture of Aikido originator Sensei Morihei Ueshiba.

All participants sit in seiza-style, kneeling on the floor - folding their legs underneath their thighs, while resting the buttocks on the heels. They do meditate.

Chaos devolves into order & stillness…

Sensei S.S, sits in "seiza" near the "SHOMEN", which is the front wall of the room; **sho** means "true" and **men** means "face". In traditional dojos, the "KAMIZA", a miniature Shinto shrine, HATA, the International Aikido Federation's flag, and DOJO KUN, the training hall rules are placed at SHOMEN, thus making it into a somewhat sacred area.)

Suddenly a bell gongs loudly through the ballroom.

All participants practice now kihon.

The disciples now train the techniques in couples or trios. Sunshine Thuoc - the waitress on duty wakes up sitting on the chair at the Dojo, respective hotel ballroom. She realises she fell asleep. Sunshine starts laughing to that awkward situation. Sensei observes her and starts laughing too, or at least his eyes laugh or smile.

"OVER THE OCEAN"

Peter Willington wakes up in darkness and only after a couple of seconds his eyes adjust to see the shadows first and then the sleeping people in their seats. They are covered by blankets supplied by VIRGIN ATLANTIC. Pillows, personal things, blankets are scattered all over the place. Peter crawls out of the blankets, his body seems to be broken and he stretches in the aisle and goes to the self-service spot to get some fresh squeezed orange juice to drive away the morning thirst. He grabs a sandwich too.

Peter opens a small window and almost immediately is struck by the unexpected revelation of our Earth's beauty. Down below the plane there is the vast Pacific Ocean space, its surface reflects refracted rays of the rising sun creating the feeling the sea is light emerald green, brown-red and yellow. It looks like in a vivid dream or lost paradise. The water is still, no waves visible from up here… Many small fishing boats sailing the sea in the morning hunt look as if they were painted and photoshopped down there.

Tears enter Peter's eyes. For the first time - after many months - he feels kind of relief - freedeom. A soft victorious smile enters his wrinkled old face, he escaped the hotel Egeria - the "Thucydides trap", even for a little time, but…who knows… Peter puts his hand into the deep pocket of his sweater and finds there something - as we can see in his facial expression. He pulls it out - it's the 8 faces shaped stone. He examines it once again and remembers the words, 'the signs are the numbers'…The numbers of his flight and time actually…Peter whispers, "This can't be a coincidence…"

Someone taps Peter's arm, which gives him a little shock. Peter turns quickly around. It's a woman, a Chinese older woman, perhaps in her mid 50's. "Can I please have a look as well, Mister?"

"Yeah, sure." and Peter makes space for her.

"Wonderful view." And her eyes glance.

"Yes."

"You know, I missed it very much."

"Really?"

"I'm returning back to China after living many years in Texas."

"What did you do there, if I may ask?" Peter interested.

"I was teaching at Rice University in Houston…it's close to what they call "The Medical Center". Many many hospitals. There's a small group of shops, restaurants, and pubs nearby in what they call "Rice Village". It's a nice place. Not as famous as Texas A & M maybe, but I preferred Houston as College Station…I also worked for NASA at Johnson Space Center."

"Wow, interesting! You mean…in the space program?"

"Something like that…"

"I see your English is excellent."

She laughs, "Oh stop flattering me."

The woman is of a subtle full body and makes an impression of heartily straight forward persona.

"My name is Peter, by the way…and…"

The Chinese womand with a soft, but confident smile, "Elen" and she stretches her hand.

They shake their hands.

"Nice to meet you, Elen."

"Likewise."

"You see, I don't speak any Chinese. In fact I only speak English, nothing else…"

"Well…The truth is, language is the door to…"

"Yeah. Perhaps you could teach me a few words? But not "NI HAO"…" Peter laughs.

Elen joins him laughing, "Yeah - not that… Hěn gāoxìng jiàn dào nǐ."

"What that means?"

"Nice to meet you. Mhgoi. Please. But this is Cantonese…"

"Mhgoi."

"Yes, MHGOI."

"They speak Cantonese in Hong Kong, right?"

"In fact, they do in the whole Guandong province, so also in the mainland China, but in general, people usually speak both Mandarin and Cantonese… there…"

"Interesting."

"Are you staying in Hong Kong or will you continue on to some other Chinese cities?"

"I don't have a plan…"

"That is the best! Elaborate plans finish in graves…"

"True. God decides."

"Do you believe in God?"

"Yes."

"I don't."

"Everyone has to make their own choice."

Elen with an apologetic smile, "I'm a scientist."

"That's the problem."

Elen serious but still smiling, "That's a fact."

"Even Albert Einstein said that God exists…"

"Even Albert Einstein might have been wrong…"

"You keep your science. I'll keep my faith."

Elen laughs, "Agreed."

Peter suddenly recalls one of his latest dreams, "Funny enough, you mentioned that you worked for NASA, in the space program…"

"Something like that…"

Peter continues, "Recently, I had a dream about a spaceship that exploded shortly after its lift-off…"

Elen is acting as if being scared, "I hope we land safely, Peter." Putting her hand in front of her face. "Anything else…?"

"…I saw the General killing the technician, responsible for that catastrophic failure."

"OMG! Scary."

"It was such a vivid dream, Elen, I have many vivid dreams, but this one felt like reality."

"That's normal, you are a sensitive person, good heart, generous, the brain follows."

"Hmm…Stop flattering me…"

"And you're sarcastic too…A man with a big EGO. A vengeful man."

Peter now serious, "Oh…"

"You don't think so? No one is just good or bad."

"You're very straight forward, Elen. I like it."

"I don't."

"Why? Does it cause you a lot of problems?"

"You use the word problem a lot, maybe too much… I prefer to use more positive terms, terms that invite solutions…"

"You're a dangerous opponent, Elen, I'll give you that!"

"I can swear too, you damn asshole!"

"Hěn gāoxìng jiàn dào nǐ."

"Good boy. Jiàn dào nǐ wǒ yě hěn gāoxìng! I'm very glad to meet you too."

Both, Elen and Peter, laugh heartily as if they knew each other for the whole eternity. They feel they are a perfect fit, instantly.

A moment of silence.

Then Peter starts, "You said you don't believe in God…what you believe in?"

"What if we live in a simulated world?" remarks Elen without any emotion.

"Sorry? I can't follow your thoughts, Elen."

"It's weird that we spend some much time trying to figure out the Universe…" and she continues, "I hate to break it to you, since you're a believer, but…You've played video games before…?"

"Yes…"

"Any game in particular comes to your mind…"

"Super Mario Brothers"

"Mario…runs around, jumps…"

"…yeah, 'cos you press buttons…"

"And he'll jump of a cliff…but he comes back somehow…he doesn't fall all the way down…"

"Hmm"

"If you were in that game, Peter and you were scientist, you'd start asking yourself, what are the laws of physics in my world …"

"Hmm"

"…and you'd come up with a catalog of how things move, how things jump, how things fall, and this would be canon…the things that matter…"

"Yeah, Ok"

"So, I'm scientist in Super Mario Brothers and I unravel the laws…There you are and that's your world. Why is this any different…from our world where I'm a scientist trying to figure out how this World works?"

"Hmm"

"As our computing power gets stronger and stronger, our storage capacity gets greater and greater, we can, in principle, program much more than "Mario", we can simulate characters that have free will."

"Yeah"

"And if you let them go, discover things…they'll create their own computers and use them to create simulations…and they'll give them free will…it's probably simulations all the way down…"

"But, we're in the real Universe, Elen…"

"…and that's the thing…there is a big chance, Peter, we live in a simulated World, programmed by some alien or entity…, because it doesn't just spiral all the way down…it can also spiral all the way up!"

"Oh!"

"We only think we're real, Peter…"

"It's just a theory…"

"It's a hypothesis…And it's difficult to shake this hypothesis."

"But this proves there's God after all! Someone must have had started all this…"

"Have you heard about the Nigerian boy who woke up from the coma speaking Spanish? Sounds like a programming glitch."

"God's work…"

"Or the programmer's…"

Peter wants to add something, but he is interrupted by the Stewardess, "Please fasten your seatbelt. We've begun our descent."

Elen smiling to Peter, "I hope she means a slower and easier descent than the one you mentioned…"

The pilot announces, "Ladies & Gentlemen, this is your captain speaking, please fasten your seat belts, we'll be landing in approximately 10 minutes… The weather in New Orleans is rather sunny & warm, 75 degrees of Fahrenheit"

Peter and Elen look at themselves in shock and say unisono in disbelief, "New Orleans?"

A moment later, the pilot again, "That was a joke…Hong Kong."

The laughter spreads among the sleepy passengers.

Elen and Peter are still talking, siting in the seats next to each other. The flight attendant serves them an orange juice and hot coffee. They enjoy it and heartily chat. The sun shines through the windows and as they look out…

Peter sees the hotel Egeria's mirage floating in the white clouds. There is the magician Atomus taking the hotel into his hands. He wears a black mask of a fox and black gloves with silver rings with sculls. The hotel now seems to be beautiful again to Peter.

Time to time shadows appear – the ones of Atomus and his hand moves showing the numbers

0-5-2-5-A-M-X-1-9-9-1

and hints of his obscure facial expressions:

"ARCANE ✈ CIPHER"

EPILOGUE

You think that this book has too many open stories? You are right!

Therefore we are writing Egeria – Turmoil.

What is going to happen to Peter Willington? Will he have a relation with Elen or will he intensify his relation with Layla.

Does Peter Willington return from his adventure?

James Willington & Jane, is there a future?

Does Raul Renderman find out the secret of James?

Will Juan Polpo survive the challenges with the Russian mafia?

Are Jonathan and Ronald getting hold of the hotel Egeria, or is their strategy going to be a failure? Is Juan really helping them?

Sebastian Hunter & Jane Willington, is their love going to be destroyed by Juan?

Is Thomas finally successful to get Yuki?

What are Sylvester's and Aida's intentions?

Will Mr. Tea be supportive to Peter all the time?

Has Bony Eins the guts to oppose Jonathan's ideas?

And of course there are many stories from the daily hotel operations at the Egeria, as the guests and their demands change on a daily basis... no business is as colourful and as challenging - by all means.

Egeria – Turmoil, is expected to be available in 2021.

9 788027 081462